NASTRAGULL

— BOOK FOUR —

SECTION TWENTY-ONE

ERIK MARTIN WILLÉN

ASC
PUBLISHING

NASTRAGULL: SECTION TWENTY-ONE
Copyright © 2022 Erik Martin Willén

This book is a work of fiction. The characters, incidents, and dialogue are drawn from the author's imagination and are not to be construed as real. Any resemblance to actual events or persons, living or dead, is entirely coincidental.

Published by ASC Publishing

ISBN: 978-91-988090-3-9

ALSO BY ERIK MARTIN WILLÉN

NASTRAGULL

PIRATES
BOOK 1

HUNTED
BOOK 2

DAWN SETS IN HELL
BOOK 3

THE BEAST
BOOK 5

OTHER NOVELS

THE LUMBERJACK

For my friends…
Thank you!

In memory of the best "host-mother" ever.

Patricia (Pat) Ann Strauss
October 19, 1952 – November 23, 2016

When all else fails, use the pen.
ERIK MARTIN WILLÉN

PROLOGUE

A sudden strong wind blew in from the north, sending an icy fog rolling across the landscape. Clouds merged in the center of the sky, and with them came a rolling thunder presaged by flickers of inter-cloud lighting. Torrents of rain poured down in an avalanche of water.

From atop a hill crowned with a thick mist, pierced by thick beams of light like the rays of a rising sun, a lone rider emerged into the rain. He wore dark body armor with strange inscriptions adorning it in a delicate silver filigree. The armor was something like that of a medieval knight's, but was made of a far more advanced material than mere steel; a composite with the best properties of both plastic and leather, it was lighter and stronger than any metal. On his head rose a helm resembling a nightmarish monster. Bat-like wings graced each side; a gnarled nose-guard covered half the rider's face. It was decorated with black leather that contrasted with its shiny metal surface, the skin of some omanoid monster's face that had been flayed off and tightly stretched across the helmet. The rider himself appeared Oman.

The creature he rode possessed only a passing resemblance to a horse; it was more of a cross between a black tiger and a Clydesdale-sized unicorn. Scales covered the muscular body, topped by thin, silky gray fur, and two small bat-like wings flapped nervously from its massive shoulders. The head belonged to some nightmare chimera of wolf, horse, and reptile, with a single horn jutting from its forehead. Fangs as long as a child's finger filled the jaws, and the light of intelligence filled its proud blue eyes.

The creature's legs were like those of a horse, but much thicker and muscular; the hooves were like a goat's, but bore some resemblance to a lion's paw as well. The forefeet could be used as hands; hidden fingers were curled beside the hooves, consisting of a large, strong thumb and two opposable fingers. The tail may have been its most striking feature: It was long and hairless, like a rat's, thick where it joined the rump but thinning out toward the end. At the tip was an exposed bone blade that the creature and rider kept honed to a preternatural sharpness. When the tail lashed at the air, there came a snapping sound from the bone end, as from a lashed whip.

The rider struggled with the creature's reins for control, as it was thirsty for blood. Vapor steamed from the beast's nostrils. As the wind grew stronger, the creature reared on its hind legs and let out an angry roar. The rider almost fell off, but caught himself, lifting a horn nearly identical to the animal's to his lips with his left hand. From the horn came a sound so puissant and horrible that it made the creature even madder; it answered with a deeper tone from its own horn.

For the briefest of moments, the wind stopped blowing, and the creature calmed down. The rider gained control over the beast...but then the sound of thousands of horns followed. The ground trembled as a horde of mounted cavalry appeared around a rocky crag with their weapons drawn and ready, battle flags blowing in the wind. Two large fighter craft flew up from behind the lead rider, hovering a tall man's height above the ground to either side of him.

From the hill, a large city was visible, covering the land to the horizon in all directions. The lead rider raised his hand, and a small orb the size of an orange formed in his palm before shooting off in the direction of the city, where it sped through a landscape of sedate suburbs and parks, beautiful organized. The orb reached the city and moved towards its center, finally stopping before an enormous palace.

From a breach in a hillside behind the lone rider swarmed thousands of soldiers: mostly infantry, mixed with scattered cavalry riding various strange beasts out of fairy tales and nightmares. From a second breach flew hundreds of hovertanks, airships, and personnel carriers. The fighters quickly lined up in ranks behind the lead rider, their general, while thousands of similar riders positioned themselves on the flanks of the formation. The infantry lined up behind the tanks and other support vehicles for protection and fire support. Behind them ground large artillery and missile carriers.

For a moment, after everything had settled in place, there was an eerie silence, as if the world was holding its breath. Many of the troops themselves were breathless, and had teary eyes behind their facemasks.

A rider emerged behind the first, carrying a large standard, something that had been customary thousands of years before but had long since fallen out of favor. It bore a round insignia, in the center of which was a large blue eye. On the left side of the eye were two vertical lines; on the right was one. The eye rested on the bottom side of a triangle. Under the logo was a long rectangle emblazoned with the words *XXI Sectorious,* and under the rectangle hung strips of red and black cloth, whipping in the wind. The new rider stopped to the right side of the first, and was followed by a third rider who took position to his left. He also carried a large standard, this one decorated with the holographic image of a young woman. The standard-bearers forced the pointed butts of the flagpoles into the ground, hard, leaving the flags to fly on their own; they then rode past their leader, exchanging silent salutes with him, and joined the troops below the hill.

The General on the hill savored the moment, and then said loudly, so that his voice boomed over the battlefield: "I am Death, Devourer of Worlds, and you are my tools. Spare no one."

His voice echoed through the entire army, amplified by the soldiers' ubiquitous wrist computers, from the ships above, and from the speakers on the tanks. His words were followed by a cheer from thousands of throats.

Alec von Hornet removed his winged helmet and nodded to Bull the Butcher, who raised his own standard high; and from Alec's lips sounded The First Horn, followed by thousands more, as the fighters took off toward Handover's capital at a slow but steady, ground-eating pace, attended by the hovertanks and personnel carriers.

There would be no quarter.

Alec's dark blue eyes radiated hate as he focused on the enemy far ahead. One might think such an obvious, slow approach would be suicide for the army, since a sensible enemy would have strafed and bombed them to ashes well before they reached the city; but Alec's plan depended on this show of force, and the enemy couldn't know, at least not yet, that his men were all but untouchable.

A second orb flew up next to him; attached to it was a basket. A flick of his hand sent it shooting through the landscape towards the palace.

Taking a deep breath, Alec reveled in the sensation of his long hair flowing in the wind. Ever since his rescue from the continuous, painful hell of Zorif af Sun's "art installment," where he was left literally half a man, hyped up on drugs that heightened his pain and never let it fade, he had enjoyed the pleasures of the simplest physical sensations. Sighing, he stared tiredly at the standard with the mysterious logo on it; and then his eyes moved to the left, where the second standard stood. A tear trickled down his cheek as he observed the holographic picture of Alexa, under which was printed a simple message: *In loving memory.*

ONE

BEHIND the starship lay an enormous shell, resembling a massive fluid tanker, of the type used to supply arid colonies with water hewn and purified from the comets of the local Oort cloud. It had served as a fine cover during the ship's last raid and was now discarded, its purpose served. The Drummel Class cruiser accelerated away through open space, bleeding ice crystals in its wake; the ruse had required a thick layer of real water between the hulls.

Here, on the outskirts of the Herica galaxy, there were no other ships in sensor range; the region was short of habitable planets and had few resources left worth exploiting. The *Red Dagger* was the new flagship of the once-mighty pirate clan that called itself *The Night-Hunters*. In the last few Galactic years, the Night-Hunters had suffered some...setbacks.

The clan leader, Ogstafa, stood on the bridge of the *Red Dagger*, her feet planted firmly on the deck a shoulder's width apart, regarding the viewscreen that covered most of the forward bulkhead. Behind her were almost one hundred people, working at various workstations and consoles; it took a huge bridge crew to run a ship this large. Ogstafa was furious, though her anger was tightly reined, waiting for the right target to feel its wrath. Her force had been reduced to less than fifty ships of various sizes, and the Night-Hunters no longer had a home base; it had been wrested from them by a rival clan. She knew she must find one soon, or her clan would eventually fragment and cease to exist.

Someone approached from behind and cleared her throat. "My lady, we have casualties."

Ogstafa turned quickly towards the young woman behind her. "It had better not be the cargo."

"It's not the cargo, my lady," the girl hastened to answer. "We have lost five of our own people, and Commander Tag wants permission to use some Tilters."

Ogstafa just nodded and snarled, "Want something done, do it yourself...it's been almost an entire day since we captured that ship, and...never mind, Commander Loccier. You have our permission, but keep this in mind: if any one of the cargo is harmed or injured, you will wish you were dead before I'm done with you."

The commander looked uneasy, and seemed just about to say something when Ogstafa interrupted her. "I thought the entire crew and all the guards had surrendered?"

"They have, ma'am. Apparently, it's Lady Hornet's chambermaids who are causing the havoc."

Ogstafa snorted. "Get me Tag."

"As you command."

A sweaty saurian female named Myra appeared on a large monitor, cursing like a demon while firing a slug-thrower at someone in the background. Smoke darkened the image, and there were several casualties visible on the deck. Myra looked at the screen and scowled.

"Where is Tag?" Ogstafa demanded.

"Injured," Myra snarled. "We need the damn Tilters, and now, or our crew will probably damage the cargo—like it or not."

Ogstafa nodded her consent and switched off the image. "I hate Tilters—hear me, commander? They stink."

The young commander nodded, agreeing as she looked in a different monitor at the beautiful pearl-white cruiser docked inside one of the *Dagger*'s larger bays. If not for some well-directed hits from laser and plasma cannons during its capture, the ship would be intact; as it was, most of it was there, and it was still spaceworthy and would be easy enough to repair.

Commander Loccier swallowed hard when she sensed Ogstafa leaning over. The clan leader smelled none too sweet herself.

"She's a beauty, isn't she, Ebeen?" Ogstafa whispered.

"She is that, my lady. We're repairing the engines now. There was some minor damage, and we're making a few modifications before sell it, so we can fetch a nice price."

"Ha! You think like a true pirate, Commander. But no, this one we keep. We'll probably return it along with the cargo once it's been paid for by the Hornets. Believe me, we'll get far more than the ship itself is worth."

The younger woman nodded, her cerulean hair shining in the overhead lights. She touched a hand to her ear and listened. "Ah. Myra is on her way now with the prisoner, and several of her chambermaids also."

"Good. Have the rest of the crew locked up in blocks inside their own ship, and double the guards. I'm planning to return everyone and the ship for ransom—after all, we don't want to upset the Elites any more than we have to. Make sure our shields are on maximum power, and that no ship leaves any of our docking ports. The prize ship's distress signals can't penetrate our shields, but if any of the main cargo doors open, then the signal will get through."

"We're doing everything we can to silence it, but it's difficult. Whenever we shut off one source, it seems two more are activated."

"Have your people do their best, Commander."

"Aye, Captain."

Ogstafa snapped her fingers, and a large command chair—more like a throne, really—rose from the deck. She purposely kept the back turned towards the bridge's entrance, because she liked to hear the prisoners coming; and just as they arrived, she would turn her seat towards them. It made for a powerful effect, and she did enjoy a prisoner's expression once they realized she was a woman. Most polity fleet command structures were dominated by women, but this was not the case when it came to pirate fleets. Those were traditionally male-dominated.

She could hear many feet entering the long metal gangway leading up to her throne. Just as they reached her chair, she turned it around and raised her head slowly; and then her eyes grew wide.

"Put them down right here," Myra ordered six other husky female pirates, who were struggling to carry three grayish packages that writhed and kicked, head-butting whenever they could. Muffled sounds came from inside the Tilter cocoons, and Ogstafa glanced at the bloody beasts in the background, which were each controlled by a dedicated handler. There were six Tilters "dogs', unusually many for only three prisoners. *Something is very wrong here*, Ogstafa thought; this was not the way she had imagined an Elite such as Lady Hornet to behave, nor her chambermaids. She frowned as a sudden suspicion struck her about the contents of the cocoons.

The three cocoons were laid in front of her, each still struggling like mad. Ogstafa nodded, and gestured for the head parts of the cocoons to be removed. Myra walked over to the "packages" and sprayed a thin mist on each; as the silk dissolved, the prisoners within coughed and spat, following it up with a storm of curses. Ogstafa spread her hands as if to say, "What's this?", and Myra just rolled her eyes and walked over to the cocoon to the far left, lifting it up and turning the face towards Ogstafa—whose eyes widened to the size of dinner plates.

She raised her right arm and choked, "Isn't that...?"

"Allow me to introduce you to Alexa, former daughter of Zuzack of Clan Wulsatures," Myra sneered, unable to hide the note of surprise in her own voice.

"But how...how can this be?"

"She fell in with good company, apparently."

"Rot in hell, you ragged old cow, you bitch of a whore and basta..."

Myra gagged Alexa, even as she struggled, holding her in a firm grip. An avalanche of additional cursing came from both

Tara and Nina, who gladly filled in the blanks where Alexa had been interrupted.

"Gags all around," Myra shouted.

Soon all three prisoners were silent. Two guards each took hold of Nina and Tara, and held them facing Ogstafa.

"Myra, is this *it*? Where is Lady Hornet?"

"She wasn't aboard," Myra said flatly. "These three were the only passengers. Apparently, the old battle-axe lent the ship to them for some reason. We're searching the ship and scanning it, but we did that before we boarded, and I doubt we'll find anyone else."

"Nevertheless, search it again—extremely carefully."

"And what about these lovelies?" Myra moved her head towards the girls in their cocoons.

Ogstafa stood and moved toward the three prisoners. "You will tell me everything: why you were on board, and not Lady Hornet. Where you were bound. Where have you been. The location of Zuzack and his clan. The one who speaks up first will live; the others will die or be sold. Which one is their leader?" she asked Myra.

"This one. Alexa's always led these two and a few more of the worst troublemakers."

Ogstafa reached to the side of Alexa's head and stripped off the gag. Alexa saw her opportunity, and bit down hard on the old woman's hand. Ogstafa tore her hand free, cursing fluently herself while dark purple blood dripped to the deck. "Feisty, I see. We'll see about that. Ebeen, how many males officer do we have in our crew?"

At first Commander Loccier looked puzzled; she knew very well that her leader knew the number of males in her crew, but she only shrugged and said, "Thirty-six, my Lady."

"Good. Take these little monsters to the Wall of Shame and inform the male officers they can do with them as they please. No permanent damage, though."

Loccier smirked and nodded.

"Leader…"

Ogstafa raised her hand, interrupting Myra, knowing full well that she would try and protect her former mates. Besides, the Wall was popular among the crew, and used regularly for entertainment or whenever someone lost a bet. But for these younglings, it would be a nightmare…or so Ogstafa thought.

Myra shot the girls a sad expression as they were dragged away.

Ogstafa said, "You don't care for my decision, Myra?"

"Just a little worried, my lady." Myra shouted to the guards as they left, "Make sure you get more security. Double their guard!"

The guards in charge only gave Myra a sarcastic glare, and their lieutenant hissed threateningly, "You mind your business, and we'll mind ours."

Myra ignored the officer's behavior. She and the guards only obeyed Ogstafa, their supreme leader, and whenever they could, they snarled at other higher ranking officers just to piss them off.

"Your funeral, Kerr. Don't underestimate these younglings." Myra then turned to Ogstafa, who had raised a shield around them to keep anyone from hearing their conversation. "You can't break them like that, my lady, especially not Alexa."

"She bit me. What kind of message do I send to our clan—what's left of it—if I allow anyone to draw my blood and not be punished for it?"

"Yes, I understand that, but having them raped…it's not like they haven't been there before. They were captured at a young age and initiated as soon as they matured. Why don't you just have her whipped?"

"And leave marks on my cargo?"

"They can be healed."

"A good slaver notices such things."

"Alexa probably has quite a few scars already, my lady. Besides, shouldn't all the cargo be returned?"

"Why add more scars? And besides, I'm not sure I want to return these lovelies. Alexa has a huge bounty on her head, does she not?"

"Bounty? The Hornets can match any bounty, easily. Please, no rape. Do as the slavers do, whip the soles of her feet—anything but gang-rape. I think many of our crew would agree, considering most of them are women."

Ogstafa said harshly, "Sometimes rape is a necessary evil. I'd rather do that than torture them."

Myra knew when to stop arguing. Once Ogstafa's mind was set on something, nothing could change it. Shrugging, she changed the subject. "So, what's the next step in your plan to get your hands on that map?"

"Didn't Alexa have a relationship with the Hornet heir?"

"Yes, they were a couple."

"Were? They must still be—else why was Alexa in a private yacht belonging to the House of Hornet?"

Myra nodded. "You're right, of course. And now you want to use her for leverage—and if that doesn't work, you can cash in the bounty."

"It might work with the heir, and if it doesn't, then the bounty will help us outfit the clan as we rebuild."

Myra let out a sigh. "Ogstafa, old friend, there is something you must…no, *need* to understand. I've fought alongside Alec von Hornet, and I have seen him in action on the command bridge, controlling hundreds of ships and *beating* the two largest and most feared clans in the universe—namely, ours and the Wulsatures."

"Your point?"

"I've never seen a more terrifyingly effective and determined warrior. Ever. After my betrayal and…whatever Zorif af Sun did to him, who knows how he'll react to us? He'll certainly hunt us, that's a fact; but he will *never* barter with us. He may kill us all to make example of us, but he will not make a deal."

"You're sure about that?"

Myra walked toward the forward viewscreen, and a railing appeared. She leaned on it, looking down and out over the *Red Dagger*'s prow in the distance. After a long moment, she said, "Yes. I'm absolutely sure, and so should you be. He can be a generous man —he bought me these legs—but he becomes a cold, cruel, unemotional monster when crossed. I know you were never close enough to him to watch him in action, as I did, but you were there at New Frontier and you saw the slaughter he caused—not to mention the Incident at the Gate, or before that, when he tricked us at the *Black Moon.*"

"So, you're saying he's a good officer, and he knows how to handle himself in battle. I gathered that much. But..."

Ogstafa stopped, scowling, when she saw Myra shaking her head.

"He's that, too, but what that young man really is...he's a conqueror. If he were of a mind to, he could take over all the pirate clans and unite them into an unstoppable army in less than a Galactic year." She turned and looked back at her old friend. "That's no reflection on your qualities as a leader; he's just that good. He'll always be hungry for more. He'll never stop. We'll never win against him."

Myra stared at her friend with teary eyes. "Look at us. We're reduced to kidnapping members or friends of the Elites for their ransoms...and we happened to pick the lover of the one man who almost exterminated us. We can't barter with him. If you try, old friend, you'll put an end to our clan."

"So, we should kill our new guests?"

"No! Then he'd hunt us to the ends of the universe!"

"We've been hunted before."

"Not like this."

"You want me to *return* them?" Ogstafa said in disbelief.

Myra looked up and dried her face. "Yes, and unharmed. Please."

"What's wrong with you, Myra? Standing there crying like a little bitch! Remember what you are!"

"I'm a pirate. I want to keep being a pirate. I have a very bad feeling about this, my lady."

Ogstafa stepped up to the railing and clutched it tight with both hands as she stared out at the Big Dark; the metal groaned in protest. In a gentler voice she said, "I'll *think* about returning them... possibly through a trader, so we can make a few million in claims. Sell the ship, make it look like an average kidnapping. But in the meantime, they *will* be on the Wall of Shame. At least the one that bit me will."

"You are making a terrible mistake." With that, Myra turned and left the bridge with a heavy heart. She had almost let Ogstafa in on her most private secret: that she was in love with Nina, and didn't want to see her hurt. As she walked down a passageway illuminated with the lights of a hundred different buttons and screens, she increased her pace. She didn't want anyone to see her displaying any emotions, especially any involving tears. She hurried to the docking bay that held her own ship, the *Titan*, a small sloop-class vessel with a crew of 35. She was proud of the ship, which she'd bought with funds stolen from Alec von Hornet after the mutiny on the *Predator*. It could carry 100 soldiers for long-term space missions; for shorter missions, it could carry almost double that number. It had begun life as a cargo ship, a kind of "tramp starmer" as they were called, but Myra had quickly put an end to that; she'd had it renovated into a fast, highly effective little battleship.

Half the ship's crew was comprised of old friends, some of whom had participated in the mutiny; the other half were new, freshly recruited from Ogstafa's much larger crew. Where their loyalties lay, she dared not gamble. She had no troops of her own, at least not yet. Most of Ogstafa's had been lost during the Zuzack campaign, and later during what she thought of as "the Alec campaign"—something she would soon look into. Well, at least she had about twenty people loyal to her; where the other fifteen's loyalty lay only time would tell.

She stalked along a balcony towards a gangway leading to a lifetube attached to her ship. She entered, and just as she was about to board the *Titan*, she stopped and stared at the deck. Free Alexa be damned; nothing could save her now. But Nina was not going to be hurt, no matter what. A plan began to form in her head. Ogstafa might be her only true friend, but after all, in the end she was a pirate; and even a pirate could fall in love.

The young officer on watch greeted Myra at the entrance of the ship, and her friendly smile morphed to a concerned and frightened expression when she saw her captain's face. Myra turned in her tracks and hurried away, ignoring the officer. She hurriedly made her way through the enormous space cruiser, running at times, taking many different elevators and small transport trams when she could; she didn't want to be tracked easily. When she finally reached the Wall of

Shame, located in a vast unused cargo bay, there was a huge crowd there before her; she couldn't even get through the entrance.

Desperate, she looked for another way in; and down one corridor, she saw several of Ogstafa's guards, apparently the same ones who had escorted the prisoners. She tried to see if the bitchy Lieutenant Kerr was one of them, but by then the squad had turned a corner. Growing more desperate, knowing what would or worse *was* happening to her beloved Nina, Myra used her big, muscular body to push herself through the cheering crowd, generating many angry shouts and looks. She ignored them. She couldn't think clearly; all she had in her mind was to save her love.

The Wall of Shame was made to look like an enormous square rock, with only the victims' heads sticking out on one side and their lower abdomens out the other. Any other time, she would have thought it humorous. The Wall itself was actually a small rectangular room, with two large walls and two smaller. On one of the smaller walls was a hidden door. The many men and women surrounding it now were screaming at the top of their lungs, and many bottles changed hands, as most of them were drinking. Myra headed towards the hidden door, but suddenly two large non-Oman guards grabbed her from behind. Both were dressed as security; Myra knew better than to try to fight them.

"Get in line like the rest. There'll be no more bullying from you," one of the guards warned Myra.

The guards pushed her outside to the end of the line. She struggled some, trying to get a closer look at the heads protruding from the Wall, but her vision was blocked by all the people. Her shoulders sagged, and she walked away from the hellish display.

She was just about to shed a tear when she heard something weird.

"Hah! *Finally* Ogstafa is letting us have some fun with her shitty security detail."

"I know—especially that hot Lieutenant Kerr. I've always wanted to fuck her, and boy, am I going to do her in all her openings!"

The two officers were laughing as they took their respective spots in line, waiting for their turns. Myra noticed a few female officers with enormous strap-ons trying to cinch them around each other's waists while scrambling to the line, encouraging each other on whom to fuck first—and not to stop until there was blood.

Myra had to think twice about what had been said as she walked down the long corridor outside the cargo bay. She was very puzzled, and had lost her bearings. Sighing, she stepped into an adjacent lounge and stared out the glassteel port. A security person caught her eye, and she turned to address him or her about what was going on, pretending not to know about the victims on the Wall. As she thought of Nina, she forgot what the two men had said, and was about to shout to the guards—when another guard whisked by her, making her lose her concentration. Then she felt the cold muzzle of a weapon again her back.

"Make a sudden move, you fat cow, and I'll keep my promise of turning your ugly hide into a pair of boots," Alexa hissed threating.

Myra looked around frantically and decided to attempt a break-through, but a faint whistle from the other side and then another from the front made her stop. "Triangular formation..." she said bitterly. "Only Elite units use them. Guess you girls picked up some bad habits this past year, eh?"

"If you only knew," Tara assured her, keeping her distance.

"Ladies, there's no way you're ever gonna make it out of here—"

Nina interrupted, "Yeah, yeah, we'll be tortured, captured, raped, and all that kinky shit...we know. Now shut the hell up, you old hag, and do as you're told."

The Vixens holstered their weapons just as several officers entered the lounge, laughing and joking about what they'd just done to Kerr's security detail. The girls began moving forward in a triangular formation around Myra. She knew she wouldn't stand a chance; these girls had nothing to lose...not to mention the strange stare all of them had now. It was a dead man's look, she decided. They were ready to die. She followed Alexa, who was dressed smartly in Kerr's uniform; the others wore uniforms taken from the other guards.

"You crazy bitch, you *had* to go back, didn't you," Tara muttered to Nina.

"So I was curious. I just wanted to check out the wall."

"Idiot, you're so bloody horny that you don't make any sense."

"Bite me, Tara. When I get a home of my own, I'll build me a bloody Wall of Shame, and have some fun with it—whaddya say?"

"You forget you're going to need a male or two, and if I know your sexual appetites, you'd probably want a few babes," Alexa intervened.

As Myra listened in, she was no longer concerned about where they were going; besides, she had Nina next to her, and her feelings were playing her. She couldn't help but smile towards Nina, and Alexa noticed it as they waited at a station for a monorail pod.

"You guys have definitely been hanging around the wrong crowd for too long," Myra noted as they boarded the pod.

"No shit. You used to be part of that crowd."

Myra glared at Tara, and then she realized where they were heading: towards their yacht, *Beala-One.* "Let me guess. You've become honorable types, and are going to rescue the crew from *Beala-One.*"

"See, she's a smart one," Nina said sarcastically.

"Wait...listen to me. I don't care if you believe me or not, but I was on my way to rescue you girls, and..."

"Shut the hell up!" Tara hissed as a couple of crewbies on the other side of the pod looked at them curiously.

They exited the train pod at a large platform at the lip of the bay where *Beala-One* was docked. Alexa and Nina moved over to a nearby holomonitor, while Tara kept a safe distance from Myra with her hand on her holster. With her back turned towards Myra, Alexa said, "Your clearance code, please."

"Then Ogstafa will know it was me."

Alexa turned her head and just stared at Myra, who was shocked to look into a pair of dark blue eyes. Omans didn't *have* blue eyes; the trait had been purged from their genome after the last Universal War. Even wearing blue contact lenses was a death sentence on many worlds. Goosebumps crawled across her flesh as Myra felt fear for the first time in many years. Without a word, she moved to a console next to Alexa and hit a few buttons. "She's all yours."

Nina and Alexa switched places, and again Alexa observed the expression on Myra's face as she looked at Nina. "How many?" Nina asked.

"Send away as many escape pods you can. We only need to break the shield," Alexa answered, still observing Myra.

"There we go…well, I only got one cluster away, all one hundred of them. Too bad we can't send the rest."

Alexa assured Nina, "Don't need to. It's only a matter of hours, if that, before help arrives."

"Hours, you say?" Tara grinned. "I doubt it."

"Let's find a place and hide out until then."

"Alexa, I know I don't stand high with you, but *please* listen to me," Myra begged. "Once security realizes what happened, they'll scan the ship and detect those uniforms. So unless you're planning on running around stark naked, I suggest you hide where the sensors can't pick them up, or find some civilian clothing. By now, Ogstafa probably knows about your stunt at the Wall of Shame. I can help. I want to help."

Alexa glared at the saurian woman, eyes narrowed. "Fine. I'm listening."

"Let's head over to my ship—you'll be safe there. But first, let's get you some new outfits."

Tara grimaced. "Wait, isn't that were they'll look first? After all, we just used Myra's security clearance to launch a bunch of escape pods so *Beala-One*'s rescue beacon can be heard."

"Eventually, Ogstafa will discover that, but for now it'll do. This is an enormous ship, with over 100,000 crew. Come on, let's go."

Alexa nodded, so they followed Myra. She led them down a long corridor studded on both sides with locked, numbered doors. Finally, she stopped in front of one of them, and was just about to open the lock when Tara motioned for her to step aside. Tara opened the door and quickly assessed that there were no threats inside. All of them moved quickly after Tara. Myra hurried over to a large crate and opened it; inside were maintenance outfits and spacesuits.

"Get out of the uniforms. Put on the maintenance overalls and grab a space kit each."

One at a time, the girls changed; and never did they lose track of Myra, who just stood aside, observing them. Alexa could have sworn that she looked almost proud.

Nina turned towards Myra and asked. "What about these?" She nodded at their old uniforms.

"We'll bring them and dump them on the way."

Myra couldn't help sweeping her eyes over Nina, who stood guard, and Alexa noticed it; and so did Nina, who nodded to Alexa.

They hurried down several corridors to reach a small landing platform, where they were able to get a good view over the main docking hangar. Inside were many ships of various sizes, attached to both the deck and the walls, with maintenance andies and crew swarming over the vast space. "There's my beauty," Myra pointed towards a huge pillar with several ships attached to it.

"Which one?" Alexa demanded.

Myra leaned closer to Alexa so she could point it out, and automatically Alexa stepped aside. Myra frowned at Alexa and shook her head. "There—there she is, my little *Titan*."

"Looks like a piece of shit," Tara sneered at a frustrated Myra.

"Yeah, well, maybe she's supposed to, in order to confuse people. Anyway, she's mine and she's a very fast little ship. She also has a Grasshopper routine programmed into the system—in an emergency, she can make one quick, long jump. She's too big to make more, because it drains most of the power and it takes time to recharge. But one long jump is all it takes to get away from most pursuers. Even if they can figure out where we jump to, it takes too long to follow."

"Unless they use scout ships...like Grasshoppers?" Tara teased.

"Those ships are scouts, built for stealth, and are very small. Don't carry many weapons on them."

Tara was just about to say something sarcastic when Alexa stepped between them, shaking her head at Tara. "It will do for now."

"What about her crew?" Nina wanted to know.

"I'll tell you on the way. It's a very small crew. I could use you girls..."

The Vixens ignored the last remark, and hurried after Myra to the *Titan*.

A completely unexpected explosion interrupted them; more followed, shaking the vast *Red Dagger* like a planetquake. The braying of an alarm followed, calling the crew to General Quarters in a great stampede. Warnings and shouts intermingled into an unintelligible cacophony, although most of the crew behaved relatively calmly; this was nothing new to the experienced people.

After a few moments, the alarm altered into a more intense pulse, followed by a voice message: "Attention all hands! The *Dagger* is under attack by Omega class Nastasturian battle cruisers, approaching on vectors Red 2, 3, 5, and 9, and Blue 166. All hands to battle stations. All hands to battle stations. All non-combatants to your cabins and strap in. This is not a drill. Repeat, this is not a drill. Prepare to launch all available battle support vessels. All destroyers and frigates, launch immediately."

TWO

CAPTAIN Eerized Mi, a dark-skinned Oman with intelligent dark eyes—and a very young woman indeed for her position—sat in her command chair aboard the Nastasturian capital ship *Crusher-12,* calmly observing the images resolving in the holotank before here. After assessing them for a moment, she turned her attention to the forward viewscreen, which showed the pirate vessel *Red Dagger* surrounded by its retinue of support ships, all in considerable distress. Flashes from its hull indicated hits from the missile batteries of *Crusher-12* and her fellow battlecruisers.

"Commander T'taim, make sure you don't destroy the pirate cruiser," she ordered. "We only have to contain it for now."

"Aye, Captain. Messages from the other Captains; shall I patch them through?"

Captain Mi nodded, and suddenly five miniature holographic faces appeared before her. She increased the size of the only female, a non-Omanoid with three eyes and very pale skin. "Admiral Hannak, my scout was right: we have identified the signal coming from the ship we're incapacitating right now as the distress beacon of the *Beala-One*."

Hannak moved her double lips; there was a brief silence and delay while the translator did its work, converting her ultrasonic voice into the audible range. "How did you verify this? I hope for your sake that you did, because you are currently firing on what appears to be a civilian vessel in the Fourth Neutral Sector."

Used to Hannak's crustiness, Mi looked calmly at her superior, whom she hated—knowing full well that the old bag had similar feelings towards her, since Mi was barely thirty years old. "Escape pods were launched from the *Beala-One* several hours ago, and my scouts managed to pick up the distress signal from inside the cruiser's hull in the larger docking bay about an hour past."

"You had better be right."

"Admiral, I *am* right. Transmitting a copy of the distress signal." Mi tapped a few keys on a holographic keyboard; the admiral looked down briefly and nodded.

"Good; everything seems to be in order. Hold your fire and remain on station while I have my Elites board this ship. Name?"

"Transponder has it as *Green Blade* out of Tonionas. I have already launched my own guard, Admiral, and they should be on the ship momentarily."

Admiral Hannak's head increased in size, not that Mi had anything to do with it. The admiral stared furiously at the young captain, who returned the stare evenly. "Why?

"Admiral, my ship was the first to engage, and the rules of engagement clearly state..."

"Spare me your lesson." The grizzled woman knew full well the rules of engagement, but now saw her chance to take credit for the rescue operation slipping through her fingers...or did she? "Captain Mi, you will report to my bridge once this operation is over," she stated, her voice quivering with barely contained rage.

"Protocol states that I must report to my own fleet Admiral, milady—Admiral Darram."

"Young lady, I'm the highest-ranking officer here, and you will do as ordered!"

Mi bit her tongue and nodded.

"What was that?"

"Aye aye, Admiral Hannak, as you have ordered."

"Now order your Elites to position themselves in reserve, as my own are already on their way."

Captain Mi stared at the old bitch in disbelief, and then her anger got the better of her as she said in a very bitter tone, "Admiral, that will put my people in extreme danger." She looked at a battle map displayed in the center of the bridge, and saw the small blips indicating the battle in front of her, noting that the admiral's crew shuttles were still very far away. She returned her attention to the holographic image of Admiral Hannak, and with a quick gesture decreased the size of the image. "Your orders are contra-indicated, Madam Admiral. Your troops will take another two minutes before they reach our target, while mine will be in position in less than half a minute."

"Do as you're ordered. The rest of you captains maintain your positions, and make sure the target is contained."

Certain that it would mean the end of her career one way or another, Mi stated stiffly, "Madam Admiral, I must request written and timestamped versions of the orders just issued, and all henceforth," making sure the other captains were witnesses.

Glaring in disbelief, Hannak transmitted them to her. All the other captains responded, and then one by one, the images vanished. The last image to vanish was Hannak's.

Mi bit her tongue as she hissed her order: "Colonel Ocsyrb. Order Major Bree to withdraw."

An infantry Colonel in his sixties, a youngster by his species' standards, waved a blue six-fingered hand and said calmly, "If I do that, my captain, the stealth shield will be broken, and the other ship will be able to lock onto our six shuttles."

"Only six shuttles?" Mi regretted her comment immediately, as she should have known how many shuttles were on their way with the boarding party; after all, it was displayed on the holograph facing her.

The colonel swung around his seat and, with raised eyebrows, continued, "One shuttle had engine malfunctions; a second's stealth program was inoperable, my captain."

"Thank you, Colonel. Just order them back, after launching our drone fighters to protect them."

"As you wish, oh captain."

"Too late," a younger officer said in the background, "Major Bree has already begun his attack."

"But it's another minute before he reaches the ship, is it not?" Captain Mi questioned.

"My boy does what he does," a proud Colonel explained.

That's when Mi noticed the colonel's hand leaving the keyboard next to him as he laid the hand calmly on the other. Mi smiled and said, "Thank you, Colonel."

"Of course, my captain. How was the admiral to know that it was too late to countermand your orders, due to the time lag in communications?"

They exchanged the grins of predators.

"Rest assure I will put exactly that in my report to Admiral Darram, oh captain my captain, should you have any problems."

"Thank you again, Colonel."

From one of the stealth battle shuttles, fifty battle androids and fifty live troops launched into space. The andies took up cover positions, fanning out ahead of their living counterparts on jetpods. The troopers carried the tools necessary to board the ship. From three other shuttles, more andies and troops were ejected into space; the other two remained to the rear, still cloaked, acting as a reserve. In the distance, on the opposite side of the enemy cruiser, eight uncloaked shuttles approached, still too far away to make a difference.

As Eerized Mi watched, a particle beam licked out from the so-called *Green Blade* and turned one of the uncloaked shuttles into a cloud of plasma and free molecules. She winced; the Admiral was an idiot, no doubt yet another political appointment. If they were lucky, the destroyed shuttle carried only andies, but she doubted that was the case; Hannak was a gloryhound of the highest order. The other seven shuttles shimmered into stealth mode in the wake of the other shuttle's destruction, but it was too late; any decent battle computer would be able to calculate their positions, and any possibility of surprise had been thrown away.

Meanwhile, *Crusher-12*'s boarding party zipped through the sudden cloud of heatlances, missiles, and magma blasts, zig-zagging through the minefield of point defense with consummate skill. Some of the andies leading the charge were hit and more or less vaporized; some were luckier, receiving only minor damage. The troops and the androids engaged their own automatic point defense, taking out or diverting the approaching shots when they could.

The Major reiterated the order he'd already given his troops before they even left the *Crusher-12*: "Remember who you are, and remember your orders. Avoid killing when you can, and focus on the hostages. All squad leaders report." Then he focused on the target looming ahead.

They darted all around the large ship, doing their best to avoid getting hit. When they were close enough to the hull, they fired lines with magnetic disks at the ship, securing themselves and letting the attached motors reel in the cords, dragging them to the hull. Once there, the troopers attached spin-cutters to the hull that whizzed through the plating, while the battle andies used their heavy-duty arms to peel apart other plates; meanwhile, the biological troops took shelter, and methodically began to destroy the smaller weapon turrets nearby. Some of the boarders rigged a few antigrav mortars and started to fire on the cruiser's drone fighters.

"Something is definitely odd here," a young lieutenant reported to the Major. "This ship has far too many different weapon systems to be a true civilian ship, even a converted battle cruiser."

Major Bree studied the melee and nodded; she was right. That's when heretofore undetected hatches slip open, disgorging a horde of enemy battle androids that immediately began firing at the Nastasturian troops, ignoring the other andies. The fighting was fierce, both sides suffering heavy casualties.

Several missiles were launched from the "civilian ship," detonating in near space. The charges did no damage, but they did reveal the entire stealthed fleet approaching in the opposite direction, as well as the two shuttles remaining in reserve from *Crusher-12*. A hail of missiles and magma blasts followed; one of the reserve shuttles was vaporized in a huge explosion. The Major cursed in furious horror, then caught a few faraway explosions from the corner of his eye; he whipped around, and that's when he realized that more boarding shuttles were on their way. Some of them had already been destroyed; this operation was fast becoming a fiasco. But he had no time to worry about it; he had to think about his troops. He ordered harshly, "Anyone who's not working on getting inside, just dig in and fight off any enemies appearing in your sector."

He turned to the young lieutenant and was just about to give her an order when an enemy battle andy bisected her at the waist. Bree raised his left arm, and one of his attachments blasted the andy into shrapnel. "12-Actual from Stalker-One: we need support ASAP. We have heavy casualties. Our intended target is responding very aggressively. I'm aware of the other boarding fleet, but it's being chewed up by the point defense."

"12-Actual. Roger that, Stalker-One, we're sending in reinforcements stat. Do not harm or allow the hostages to be harmed."

The major took cover behind the shattered remains of some sort of weapons turret, and observed as his androids hacked away at the hull and as the spin-cutters lased their way into several personnel hatches. Suddenly, one hatch was ejected or exploded outward; a trooper who had been working on it was cut in several pieces as the pieces of hull-metal were hurled into space. Several people in brightly-painted pressure suits emerged, and a fierce melee broke out between his troops and theirs. The Major left his cover and shouted out orders to his troops while firing at the attackers with the magma blaster built into his right gauntlet. A battle android flew past him and landed in the middle of the attackers, slaughtering them in a whirl of blades and precision shots; then, having sensed the opening in the hull, it launched several small grenades into it, waited for the explosions to clear the way, and dove inside.

"Double-time, people, we have a breach!" someone shouted on the platoon comline.

Seconds later, three more breaches had been completed. Major Bree glanced at the heads-up display inside his helmet, checking on casualties among his troops and androids, then ordered First and Second platoons to advance and engage the enemy. "Third Platoon, remain on the hull and take care on the threat in space," he barked. "There are still plenty of those bastards on or near the hull, and I don't want them to fall on our backs."

A large, soundless explosion forced him against the hull as his faceplate darkened to compensate for the flash. The ship shuddered violently. As his vision cleared, he saw that a shuttle from another Omega cruiser had crashed into the *Green Blade* a few dozen meters away; that was one way to breach the damn thing. Fortunately, it seemed mostly intact, so he was fortunate he hadn't been scraped away by shrapnel. He wasn't confident that many of the troops inside had survived the sudden deceleration, though.

Meanwhile, Nastasturian soldiers and battle andies launched from a pair of shuttles stationed 100 meters away—just as another shuttle exploded after absorbing one too many magma blasts. The soldiers and andies in space instantly flipped over feet-first to the blast, to present as little surface area as possible to the debris as it sleeted through their formation; the major dove through an open breach, and flinched as a couple of pieces of Nastasturian steel punched through the *Blade*'s hull next to him. He popped his head out of the hatch, just in time to sense something behind him; he dropped instantly as the last reserve shuttle from his outfit accelerated over him, followed by a swarm of unmanned drone fighters. After it clawed back out into open space, he watched, his pulse pounding, as the shuttle made a wide left turn, trying the shake off the drones. So he was perfectly placed to witness the large bay doors open in the side of the *Green Blade* and vomit ships out into the ether, including several destroyer and frigate class vessels, amid a cloud of smaller ships. He clicked over to the command line and snapped, "12-Actual from Stalker-One: we've got company."

"We see it, my major," the colonel's voice answered, calm as a breeze. "Sending countermeasures. Get all your people inside;

you're just above *Beala-One*'s signal, and with a little luck, the crew is still aboard."

"Aye sir." Major Bree relayed the orders to Third Platoon and was just about to follow his troops inside when he saw his last reserve shuttle, the one that had moments before nearly decapitated him, fly straight inside the docking bay that had released the other ships and open up with missiles and magma blasts. He cursed, hoping they had avoided the *Beala-One*. If not, heads would roll—literally. Not knowing what would happen to his reserve, he focused on the mission: rescue the hostages. The last thing he saw before withdrawing into the ship was a stream of dozens of destroyers and frigates heading towards the melee, all launched from the other Nastasturian Omega cruisers.

MYRA couldn't help but admire how the three young girls moved in sync as they escorted her to the *Titan*, always in triangular formation. And even though their blasters were holstered, she knew that if she tried anything, they would kill her in an instant. It took them almost ten minutes to get to the other side of the enormous hangar, but finally they reached the pillar to which the *Titan* was attached. Nearby was the *Beala-One*. Alexa looked thoughtfully at the yacht, and Myra stepped up next to her as the other Vixens watched warily. "You can't save the crew from here, and whoever happens to be attacking us, I think we have to try to leave."

"It's our friends attacking," the head Vixen snapped. "They've come for us, as I knew they would. I figure we just hang around for now, until we're rescued."

Myra knew there was no point in arguing. The *Dagger* trembled from time to time, and many of the ships inside the hangar bay rose and started to head for the main exit in the far distance. A strange metallic rasping and grinding sound came from a nearby wall, and suddenly the wall exploded inward, followed by an enormous battle android. It quickly surveyed the region, returning fire at the few pirates who fired at it, taking them out with ease. The girls and Myra hit the deck; Alexa, Nina and Tara also dropped their weapons, not wanting to be taken for hostiles. If the andy sensed a threat, it would fire against them. Its gun was probably set for stun, given the nature of the rescue mission, but why take any chances? Besides, one always woke up from a stunning with a hangover from hell.

They heard the clatter of many feet approaching. "There they are!" Ogstafa bellowed; they looked up and saw her pointing her finger at them. A holographic face of Ogstafa formed atop the battle android beside her, and the two machines leaped upon each other to fight to the death as a dozen security guards charged toward Myra and the girls.

The Vixens grabbed their weapons from the deck and begun firing while crawling backwards into a side corridor, while Myra hurled herself inside. Three of the pirates charging them went down, hit messily in the chests and head, causing the other pirates to hold back. Pirates never fought an enemy they thought they couldn't beat; to hell with orders if it endangered their lives.

"Tara, here, fix the door." Alexa tossed Tara her holster, along with some spare charge batteries; Tara snatched it out of the air and then hastened to break open the panel next to the door before she did something with the batteries and the wires. Myra looked on curiously. They hurried down the corridor to a T-junction, and just after they ducked to the right, an explosion followed from the door they had just left.

"You booby-trapped the door with only a few magma batteries?" Myra sounded baffled.

"Shut your hole, or I'll booby trap your ass, bitch," Tara threatened.

Myra gave her a quick, hateful stare and suddenly felt the muzzle of a gun on her neck—again. "Move, my love," Nina hissed.

She knew Nina was mocking her, but the only thing Myra could think of was the words "my love" as she took the girls to her beloved little ship. When they reached the *Titan,* Myra realized that something was very wrong. The fact that there was no one there to greet her was expected, given the circumstances; the fact that there was no one there at all, no service or maintenance crew, or any of her bridge crew, was not.

Something large suddenly fell from above: the huge battle android with Ogstafa's face, stationed in front of the ship's main hatch. "Going somewhere?" it snarled with Ogstafa's voice.

Myra had nothing to say. What *could* she say?

"Traitor!" Ogstafa screamed. The andy reached for Myra; obviously she was controlling it from elsewhere. Unfortunately, the girls' blasters could do little to harm the giant robot, though they held it at bay.

"Ogstafa, listen to me, please." Myra held her muscular arms in front of her in a stopping motion. The large android actually stopped, and Ogstafa gave Myra a puzzled expression. "They've taken me hostage, Ogstafa, and if you kill us, you'll have nothing to bargain with."

"Why don't I just kill you and stun them, then?" The android raised one of its four arms, one with a large weapon attached to it, and Myra's eyes widened.

"Wait, wait, didn't you listen to me? I'm a bloody hostage!"

"You know the saying, dear; one doesn't make an omelet without breaking a few eggs."

Myra snarled, "You bloody old bitch! Wait'll I get my hands around your neck...!"

She stepped toward the android just as its Nastasturian counterpart, battered and bleeding hydraulic fluid, falling on top of Ogstafa's and started pounding and pulling at it, tearing at the pirate andy's arms; it actually managed to break one with a resounding *crack* that echoed through the docking bay. They bashed each other and rolled all over the landing platform, destroying anything in their path. The girls hurled themselves toward cover; Myra was struck in the face by one windmilling robotic arm, sending her crashing to the cold steel deck.

As quickly as the melee had begun, it was over. The Nastasturian android, or what was left of it, lay on the deck in pieces; Ogstafa's slowly stood, now with only one arm and two legs left, having lost two legs and three arms.

"Now, little angels," it said in Ogstafa's voice, "you will surrender and let my security troops bring you back to me. I think you'll like these particular security officers." Ogstafa let out a hoarse laughter as half a dozen security officers came crashing down the gangway.

"Crap, it's the bitches we locked into that wall," Nina said.

They were quickly surrounded, and a much-battered Lieutenant Kerr reported to the large android, "Prisoners secured." She then gave the three girls a hateful smile.

"Bring them all back to me. Do not harm them; that's an order."

"Yes ma'am."

Ogstafa's android took the lead, followed by the prisoners and security officers; and just as they were about to leave the platform, an explosion shattered the main hangar doors. If not for the emergency force screen that hummed into place over the gap, the atmosphere would have howled out of the gap, taking everything loose—including people—with it. The screen was not, however, enough to hold back the battle shuttle that followed the shrapnel that scythed through the docking bay, launching more troops and battle androids.

But the shuttle commander must have misjudged his or her speed, because the shuttle slammed straight into a large destroyer that was about to clear the entrance. Neither had their shields up, since a ship can't have its shield on within the shield of another ship—and so there occurred what always occurs when two objects try to occupy the same space: a shattering crash, causing an explosion that engulfed both ships. The shuttle was completely destroyed; the much larger destroyer was crippled, and diverted from its course as secondary explosions shattered its hull.

Lieutenant Kerr let out a shout of anger and looked around desperately. Myra, being dragged along by her shoulders by two similar saurians, gasped, "My ship is...our only chance...for us," before she passed out.

"Crap, she's right," the lieutenant snapped. "Let's get into the sloop, get out of the *Dagger,* and raise its shields before this place turns into a supernova!"

"You will do no such thing!" The Ogstafa android raged. "You get your asses back here to the command bridge!"

"With all due respect, ma'am, we..."

An EMP beam struck the Ogstafa android, and the entire unit went dead, toppling to the deck. The security officers—or rather, the pirates—were suddenly aware that about twenty soldiers wearing Nastasturus spacesuits surrounded them.

"Disarm this scum and get everyone aboard the sloop," Major Bree ordered. He brought up a scanner to check the girls, but Nina misunderstood the gesture and kicked it out of his hands. The scanner fell over a railing into the void of the space dock. A soldier quickly subdued Nina and the other girls, her blaster set for stun. A medic brought up another scanner and scanned the girls.

"It's them, Major. We've found the hostages."

"Good; report back to base. and let's take cover inside the sloop—" Bree ordered, and was interrupted by an enormous explosion.

"**CAPTAIN** Mi, Major Bree has the targets secured," a proud Colonel reported to Mi.

"Good. Make sure they return ASAP, and get me the Marshal of War." Mi was ready to implode from pride; she was about to make direct contact with the universe's most powerful man, not something someone in her position would ever do normally. But the order was clear: the first captain to make contact and rescue the targets must contact the Marshal ASAP.

"Will do, but I doubt a certain Admiral will like that."

"She most certainly will not; and you, Colonel, will order your troops to report to *my* ship, despite what she might tell you."

Suddenly, Admiral Hannak's holographic image popped up. Mi cursed herself, guessing the old cow had spied on her bridge activities; then again, an Admiral could legitimately do that. No matter her frustration, she had no choice for now. The officers on her command bridge gave the holographic picture more than one unseen obscene gesture; irritated, Mi motioned with her hand for them to stop. She appreciated their allegiance, but enough was enough; she would have no insubordination whatsoever.

"As ordered, Admiral." She hit a few buttons and then turned to the hologram. "It's done."

A happy expression beamed from Admiral Hannak's face as she looked down at her computer and then sent out a message on an open channel so anyone could see and hear: "Success! All key hostages saved and rescued. Officer in charge; Fourth Rank Admiral Hadra Hannak, Nastasturus Federation, 71st Galactic fleet."

Soon after, an image of an Admiral wearing the old guard's uniform from HQ appeared on many screens around the ship, with a dead stare on its face. "Stand by, Admiral Hannak. I'm patching you through."

Just as Guss Af Hornet appeared on the screen, the pirate ship *Red Dagger* exploded, whiting out the forward viewscreen.

THREE

ORBITING Alún, the second moon of Tallas—the Nastas-turus capital—was one of many large space stations, simply designated Near Space 10. Among the many Omega-class cruisers perched along its outer docking ring was Captain Copola's *Crusher-5*. Shuttles and support crews flew in an intricate *pas de deux* among the docked ships, making repairs, performing routine maintenance, and delivering newly transferred crew members. In the distance was stationed an entire Galactic fleet: or at least, what was left of the proud 11th Galactic fleet, which had been decommissioned a year earlier.

"Scavengers," Admiral Cook muttered as he glared out a plastisteel viewport on the command bridge of *Crusher-5*. He preferred the port to even the best of viewscreens, because the Mark-One eyeball couldn't as easily be spoofed as anything electronic. Many civilian and military ships were warping towards the former fleet, some already darting among the darkened, quiescent vessels.

"Vultures would be a more appropriate word."

Cook ignored the remark from Captain Copola, who stood next to him. In the past, he would have disciplined the man, friend or not, for correcting his wording.

"It's hard for me to understand the politics behind the decommissioning of our fleet, Admiral." Copola looked questioningly at his commanding officer, who would remain in charge of the remains of the 11th until the fleet no longer existed. It was a form of punishment.

"Politics are never comprehensible, Captain; nor are they ever right. The Battle of New Frontier-16 was considered a loss; and because back then we were under civilian rule, the Senate could and did vote for decommissioning. I think it was more an act against my brother than it was against me or anyone else working in the fleet. Had it happened now, while we are at war, then the decision would be at the War Office, and I doubt this would have happened."

"So now other fleets are allowed to steal our ships?"

"Yes, or break them for parts. And when they're done, civilians will be allowed to help themselves to the leftovers."

"For independent fleets?"

"Yes, Captain; because of the war, we'll see many independent fleets forming."

"Like vultures, I tell you. So now we'll fight alongside civilians?"

"Those are the orders from our civilian government, yes. First President Alexander and his Republican Guard, and now this. In the past, ages ago, independent fleets did exist, but only for support and escort. I've heard that these will actually be allowed into battle."

"Will any of them be Galactic fleets?"

"No telling. Then again, why would a civilian fleet bother? Intergalactic is where all the money is. Imagine being in charge of the invasion of individual planets. Can you imagine the riches that will be looted? Sad, very sad, this entire affair. Seems this war is only about credits."

"Aren't all wars, when you get right down to it?" declared a new voice.

Cook raised his eyebrows, looking at Copola, who did the same to him. They turned to face the young man who had interrupted them—and worse, had had the audacity to sneak up on them without indicating his presence.

Alec von Hornet stepped up between the two older men, grabbed the railing with both hands, and ignored their reaction as he stared out into the Big Dark. He wore civilian clothes, something Cook frowned upon, and his hair reached his shoulders. Looked like a bloody rug, the older officer thought, and had mentioned many times to Alec...not to mentioned that barbaric beard he had started to grow.

"So, Captain Copola, are you ready to begin your last mission as the last commissioned officer from the proud old 11th?" Alec asked now.

"As soon as my Number One reports that we're ready, sir. Should be in a day or two."

Alec only nodded, still staring into space. The two older men decided to leave him alone and started to walk away. "Say, Uncle?"

Cook and Copola stopped in their tracks, and Cook turned red from the civilian address. Alec had turned down his father's offer of an officer's commission as a Lieutenant on a fleet of his own choosing, but he did know protocol. Angrily, Cook turned, facing Alec, who still stared out into space. "What?" he snapped.

"Will you be joining us on this rescue mission?"

"No, Alec, I will not. I must remain here and watch my fleet being devoured by vultures." He turned and walked a few paces, then stopped and turned back to Alec. "I do hope that you find your Alexa," he said, his voice softer, "and may the two of you have a wonderful life."

There was no reaction from Alec, aside from the young man suddenly looking down and shaking his head slowly. Due to his long hair, Cook could not make out his facial expression.

MARSHAL Guss von Hornet sat behind the large wooden desk in his office at the military HQ in the capital, thinking. The desk, facing a window opening onto a large city square, provided a beautiful view of the Presidential Palace in the distance. The room was crowded with visitors, an enormous amount of tension vibrating among them. Several Admirals and Generals from the House of Hornet intermingled with some from the Old Guard, as well as officers dressed in modern Nastasturian uniforms. No one had ordered attention, but almost everyone stood at attention anyway, ramrod stiff and blank-faced. Guss was reading a report on a tablet, with the help of old-fashioned eyeglasses. When he finished, he pressed a button on his table, and the glasses, attached to a mechanical arm, folded into the tabletop; Guss refused any unnecessary implants. He handed the tablet to his right, where it was taken by an older, handsome woman wearing an Old Guard Admiral's uniform.

Standing at attention in front of his desk stood two officers: Admiral Hannak and Captain Mi, both looking ill at ease. Guss leaned his head towards the Admiral to his right and whispered something. The Admiral then walked over to Captain Mi and carefully removed the captain's insignia from her shoulders. Mi swallowed hard, and couldn't help but tear up; and despite her best efforts, a tear trickled down her cheek. To top off her humiliation, she sobbed out loud, unable to control her emotion. When she heard a quiet chuckle at her side from Admiral Hannak, she strengthened herself; and despite more tears coming, she swallowed hard and stared straight ahead, determined to accept her punishment.

The admiral who had removed her captain's patches then nodded to a General standing nearby. Handing him the insignia, she then moved in front of a smirking Admiral Hannak and raised her eyebrows. Hannak immediately stopped smiling. The other, higher-ranked admiral then proceeded to remove the insignia from Hannak's uniform; and suddenly, Hannak didn't understand what was going on.

Surely they're going to promote me, she thought, and with that she straightened her back even further; unable to prevent it, she smirked again. The Admiral facing Hannak only moved her left arm toward the waiting General, who put Mi's captain's insignia in her extended hand; and then, to everyone's surprise, she attached the captain's insignia to Hannak's uniform, before quickly moving over to Mi and placing the admiral's insignia on the young woman. The Elite Admiral, known for never smiling, gave Mi a wink before moving back to her place next to her supreme commander.

Both Mi and Hannak sagged, something neither should have done in the presence of the Marshal; one did not lose one's posture under any circumstances, at least not while one could still stand. The Admiral next to the Marshal cleared her throat angrily. Mi immediately returned to attention, while Hannak stood there with her mouth gaping, her back arched, her three eyes wide, absolutely unable to fathom what had just happened.

The Marshal spoke, his voice as harsh as a trump of doom. "Captain Hannak. Were we not in a state of war, you would be facing a court martial. Had it not been for your somewhat satisfying track record as a captain years ago, I would have dismissed you from the fleet, war or no. Your actions during the *Red Dagger* incident were execrable and entirely at odds with the traditions of this service. If you want your rank back, you'll have to earn it; and if I ever discover you trying to steal someone else's glory, especially in ways that endanger the members or ships of this fleet, you *will* be facing a court martial."

Guss then turned his head to stare at the youngest Admiral in the entire Nastasturian Fleet. "Admiral Mi. Your actions, on the other hand, were in the finest traditions of this service, and I personally extend my thanks to you. Don't make me regret my decision. Admiral Borgun, show our new Admiral to her new fleet, and stand by her side for the first year."

"Aye aye, Marshal." An elderly Admiral moved up swiftly from behind Mi, and standing at attention, the old saurian saluting the Marshal cheerfully.

While Captain Hannak was escorted out by her new fleet admiral—an older man neither knew—she stopped next to Mi and gave her a hateful stare. Mi calmly looked back and said, "Yes, captain? Anything I can do for you?"

Hannak was just about to say something when her new Admiral threw her a questioning glare. Quickly, Hannak stood at attention and then, expressionless, said loudly, "Admiral, I wish to congratulate you on your new commission. Please wear it well."

Guss stood by the window, looking out at the Presidential Palace; suddenly, he nodded his head angrily towards a guard, who immediately said something in his helmet microphone, and Hannak and her new Admiral were quickly removed from the office. "Admiral of the Guard, prepare my shuttle," Guss ordered. "Admirals Mi and Borgun, you will accompany me on a short trip."

The shuttle, with a dozen fighters flying escort, dipped and zigged through near-planetary space with impunity, ignoring the standard traffic lanes. Several police corvettes took up flanking positions and escorted the shuttle with the current war leader of the Nastasturus Federation to its destination. Inside the shuttle sat a very nervous Admiral Eerized Mi, facing Marshal Guss von Hornet. "I will be brief and to the point," he told her.

Mi just nodded wordlessly; she was prepared to hurl herself into a sun for the man in front of her if he asked it of her.

"No one knows about what happened during the *Beala-One* rescue yesterday," he began, "but soon the media will have their filthy hands all over it. My son made a formal request to the board of the House of Hornet—not to me, bear in mind, but to our board—for a briefing." Guss waited, making sure his words sank in for the young Admiral, who only stared at him. "My son is a civilian now, and I would be grateful if you would tell him exactly what happened. I would not normally ask you to report to any civilian, you understand, but I would be grateful if you spoke to him. He's been through a great deal, more than you will ever know, and Captain Copola of the *Crusher-5* was about to take off on a rescue mission of his own."

There was a brief silence, until Mi realized that it was her turn to speak. "I'll do anything you ask, Marshal. My pleasure, sir."

Guss just nodded and turned his seat away from Mi.

The shuttle and its escorts entered the main hangar bay of *Crusher-5,* touching down with surprising delicacy on the deck. As might be expected, the pilot was a virtuoso of his profession. Once the craft was settled in the bay, the fighters peeled off and headed back to patrol the region around the cruiser, waiting for the Marshal's return.

Guss, surrounded by several guards and his admirals, exited and faced thousands of troops lined up in perfect squares; in the center stood Captain Copola and Admiral Cook, with their staff of over two hundred officers. The sound of thousands of boots hitting the deck simultaneously as the troops stood at attention echoed throughout the ship. Guss marched dead ahead, and with no formality at all, he said, "You no longer have a mission, Captain, thanks to Admiral Mi here."

Captain Copola half-smiled, then spoke quietly into his wrist-comp. There was an eerie silence in the docking bay as everyone remained at attention. Guss, meanwhile, looked down at the deck; with his mind busy on a million and one things, he'd forgotten to order "At Ease." After a few tense minutes, Cook leaned over and whispered in Copola's ear. Copola gave him an irritated glance, and called out, "Troops! At ease!"

There was a shuffling as they assumed the parade rest position.

Guss waved his hand, and Admiral Mi, standing at attention herself, presented a brief summary of the mission, leaving nothing out, including Hannak's perfidy. When she finished, another eerie silence followed. Mi looked at the Marshal, who nodded in consent; she tapped a button on her wrist comp, and images appeared in the air above her.

The space battle around the *Red Dagger*—they had since determined its true name from captured pirates—was blurry and difficult to observe because of the speed at which events occurred. At first, it seemed that the Nastasturian cruisers were attacking an elite civilian cruise liner; but that façade was quickly dropped as point defense lasers, magma blasts, and missiles reached out from the "liner" to take down drone fighters, missiles, and other munitions. When the scene shifted to the boarding action of the Nastasturian troops and battle androids—all of whom had been wearing cameras attached on their helmets—some of the sailors of the *Crusher-5* began to mutter among themselves, impressed by the actions of their fellow troops as they fought their way into and through the defenses and into the pirate ship. Suddenly, there appeared some hasty, jumpy scenes including Alexa, Nina and Tara; Alec reacted to those when he entered the room late. A Major Bree reported in, and then there was a long burst of static as the young women and several others hurried into a small ship or shuttle in the docking bay. As the ship rose and arrowed toward the open bay door, there was another burst of static, laced with indecipherable speech—followed by a series of explosions of increasing strength.

The screens went black; the next scene, taken from *Crusher-12*, zoomed in on a series of shuttles and fighters milling around the *Red Dagger*. Suddenly, small explosions blossomed on the large ship's hull, spreading and brightening until the entire cruiser itself detonated with nova-brightness. Most of the smaller ships around it were swallowed by the explosion, but some clearly escaped. The scene made many of the watchers jump, because it came so suddenly.

Many of the soldiers watching the battle holo had recorded the images as they appeared, and now reran the recordings, watching the events from various angles and vantage points, looking perhaps to see if they recognized a friend in the melee. Their comments rose to a buzz and soon became deafening. As suddenly as the images had appeared, they vanished; after several long moments, the docking bay fell quiet. The Marshal repeated into the silence: "Captain Copola, I regret to say you no longer have a mission."

Guss stepped back and nodded to his brother Cook, who knew instantly what he must do as his final act as a Galactic Fleet Admiral. He bellowed, "The last active remnant of the 11th Galactic fleet of the Nastasturus Federation: Attention!"

His words were followed by the sound of thousands of pairs and triplets of boots snapping to, echoing as one sound.

"Troops: Dismissed!"

Not a single sentient moved; everyone remained standing at attention.

Cook frowned and shouted again, "11th Galactic Fleet: dismissed!"

Still, no one moved. Cook looked around, flabbergasted, at the thousands of crewmates who refused to obey his order—something that had never happened before. Not knowing what to do, anger suddenly caught up with him; and the admiral was just about to dismiss everyone for a third and definitely final time when Alec saved him from any embarrassment.

He drawled, in a voice that somehow carried throughout the hangar deck: "The 11th Galactic Fleet is no more, ladies and gentlemen and gentleherms, and all its ships have a new owner—who needs loyal crew members."

"What the hell—" Cook began.

Alec said in a low voice, "That's why I was late, uncle; I just bought up what was left of your fleet before the vultures could get their hands on it. Mind you, our federation has already taken the best ships...however, I still got about half of what remained."

Guss, who had been listening, brightened up for the first time. "Let me guess, son: you wouldn't take a commission from the War Office because we would give you a lesser rank than you already have. And now you're going to create an independent fleet group; is that correct?"

"Yes, Father. It will be a long road, a road that will be a challenge, but I'm willing to give it a go."

"The few independent fleet groups that President Alexander is commissioning through his ridiculous Federation Guard Force will only be limited to escort and support," Guss reminded him.

"Why, of course, Father. Do I have your blessings?"

Guss stared at Alec, and after a brief moment he nodded in consent.

"And what about what just happened...with Alexa? She's gone, son. No one could have survived that blast."

Alec lowered his head and closed his eyes; and then, when he slowly looked up, his eyes shone that deep, illicit blue. "I shall cross oceans of time and space to slake my thirst for vengeance, Father. If there can be no love for me, then let there be *blood*."

Guss was taken aback by the vehemence of his son's words, and was just about to respond—how, he didn't quite know—when Alec turned to the crowd, which still stood at attention, waiting for something.

"Sailors of the 11th Galactic Fleet," he said in a deep voice that, again, managed to reach every member of the crew. "Once again, you are being punished by incompetent politicians for doing your jobs well. Bad policy enacted by weak politicians has led to this war we'll soon be involved in, and if we let it continue, this war against evil will be lost. The sentients we've allowed to take charge of our great Federation are themselves evil, or blinded by ambition and stupidity. President Alexander should have left office long since; instead, at the worst possible time, he's splitting the Nastasturus Federation in two, breaking the law in the process. You have three choices: you can join other fleet groups, retire and become civilians—or join me."

No one moved; there was complete silence. Admiral Cook saw his opportunity, and stepped forward at attention in front of Alec. "Sir, allow me to be the first volunteer in your quest to create an independent fleet."

Suddenly someone shouted something from the back of the room, and everyone took one step forward in unison and then, section by section, reported in as volunteers. Alec nodded to his uncle, who had saved him from any embarrassment; they might not follow Alec—at least, not yet—but they would certainly follow their respected Admiral. Someone cheered, and soon everyone was cheering for the resurrected 11th.

Word spread through the fleet like wildfire, and soon captains on all the remaining ships were pledging their allegiance and reporting for duty.

Hundreds of people surrounded Cook and congratulated him, while Alec and his father moved through the crowd with their many bodyguards, away from the commotion and into an adjacent hangar. Guss clasped his hands behind his back and cocked his head. "I suspected you would do something like this, boy. I'll give you as much support as my position allows me. There's much that you need to do, and I hope you will listen to your old man during all this...or at least to your uncle."

"Of course, Father. You didn't raise an idiot."

"Normally, one gets his commission *before* building a fleet... well, in your case, purchasing half of one."

"Alexander be damned, commission from him or not."

"You can always get one from the War Office..."

Alec tucked his long hair behind one ear. "But Father, I thought you and your staff were against private fleets."

"We are. It was tried three centuries ago, and it didn't work. The fleets were only interested in looting back then, like commissioned pirates. Thought of themselves as privateers. But I think that can be controlled; and why should Alexander and his politicians get all the glory...not to mention our best officers? Now we can keep those beings, and give them a chance to make these private fleets as professional as possible. We've already lost too many good officers, and that's why we've forbidden any others from leaving their current posts. Drives Alexander nuts. Why do you think he decommissioned the 11th? Well, now it's yours, and you can have all the crew—and welcome to them."

They stopped by a large port looking out towards the remnant of the 11th fleet in the far distance; the ships hovered there like large grey meteors, waiting in lethal silence. The both stared out at the fleet, and Alec felt a small thrill in knowing that it was now his.

A small thrill was all that could get through the numbness around his heart.

Someone cleared their throat, and both Alec and Guss turned around. The bodyguards made a path for a young officer reporting to Alec. She did not stand at attention, since he wasn't, officially, military; however, she bowed low, and said, "My Lord, our admiral is requesting your presence in the hangar bay." She then saluted Guss and said, "With respect, Marshal."

They marched back into the adjacent hangar, where the troops were still gathered, standing at ease this time and observing Alec with curious expressions. Alec and his father, with the young lieutenant and their coterie of guards, stopped in front of Cook. The Marshal snapped, "Well?"

"My Lord, the former 11th Galactic fleet reports for duty," Cook said to Alec. "The fleet will stand at attention!" he bellowed. Looking straight ahead as they snapped to, he murmured calmly to Alec, "It's customary that you name the fleet, and give it a slogan."

Alec turned to his father and whispered something, who nodded; then Alec cleared his throat and said calmly into his wrist comp for everyone to hear, "Because we are independent and not yet commissioned, we are allowed only to have a section name. Henceforth, we shall be known as Section Twenty-One." He then stood silent for a while as his words sank in before continuing, "Much has been lost and little gained—yet we must move forward. For if we do not, then we will all become slaves, and that I will not abide. To all of you, I say: follow your hearts, and let's forge a universal carpet of blood," and he whispered so that only his father could hear him, *"just like our ancestors did."* He then raised his voice again: "Let's make the universe tremble with the sound of war. Let's make our enemies tremble with fear; for we shall *sack* them. *Hack* them. And PACK them!"

His words were followed by a roar from the crowd, and soon everyone was chanting the slogan: "*Sack* them. *Hack* them. PACK them!"

Cook and all the officers rushed Alec, embracing and patting him on his back while cheering out loud. Everyone joined in the celebration—all but one, who moved away from the commotion towards a waiting shuttle. Guss von Hornet was disturbed because Alec had barely displayed any emotions in regards to Alexa's death; instead of being saddened, he seemed almost relieved. To top it off, chills went down Guss's spine as he heard his son's whispered words over and over again in his head: *"Just like our ancestors did."*

FOUR

IT was a nice breeze, bringing with it the scent of thousands of bright flowers blooming like miniature suns. The sound of happy, chirping birds brought some joy to the somber atmosphere.

The Civilian Memorial Park in the capital contained many different sculptures and statues, all with names indicating whom they represented or honored. Some were simple, and the most popular memorial lately was one from a system where innocent lives had been taken far too soon. Several hundred people had gathered beside a newly erected asteroid collection, formed into the shape of a large wet navy ship from the old days, when people still sailed the seas of the motherworld. Each stone represented a life lost. Relatives and friends walked among the asteroids in silence. No words were needed. On the larger stone at the end of the ship formation, names were inscribed; the crew and passengers of *Beala-One*. Small holographic faces above each stone glowed whenever someone touched the rock, and a brief text about that person could be read. Three tall rocks, standing together at the end of the formation, bore the images of Tara, Nina and Alexa. Weeping silently, the surviving Vixens—Kirra, Mohama, Miska, and Zicci—laid flowers on the ground, then embraced each other. Next to them, on each side of Alexa's asteroid, stood two First Knights af Grisamm, Lord Asturius and Baron Bentor. Grimm, the head of the order, was not there; his position did not allow him to display individual grief for anyone, so he could not attend funerals or memorial services. Waiting for his or her turn, however, stood many Grisamm, from high ranking officers to recruits, all of whom had some type of connection with the lost girls. The line of military kept growing, making many of the civilians nearby seem uneasy.

One by one, the many Grisamm visiting the stone made the images appear, and swore various oaths in front of the rocks—but with a focus on Alexa's asteroid. Most whispered, as in prayer; while others shouted out in anger, with each oath seemingly bloodier than the last.

On a hill nearby stood one man, wearing a black cloak that flapped in the wind as he regarded the scenario below. Another man joined him. "I thought it was against tradition for you to part take in any form of funeral," he said quietly.

Grimm glanced at Alec, nodding reluctantly. "No remains or DNA from any of the three were recovered," he noted. "Officially, they are still alive."

"Ten years, and they will be officially declared dead."

Grimm nodded again. "Then I will deal with that in ten years, if it comes to it." He cast his visitor a sharp glance. "You must understand that losing Alexa has come as a blow to the Grisamm; many thought that she was one of the incarnations of the ancestors to the universe...just as they do you."

This time, Alec just stared dead ahead. "You want me to lead your order into battle, don't you, old man?"

"The universe is burning for war, and it's only getting worse. You have tamed the beast at Samari; you have purchased half a Galactic fleet. You'll be needing troops and crew."

"More ships, Grimm. I need more ships and better ones. However..."

"What?" Grimm turned towards Alec, who still stared straight ahead—whether at the ceremony or infinity, the old warrior could not tell.

"I'm not suitable for leadership, at least not for now. Besides, why would your people want me to lead them? I lack the experience; I have some, but not enough."

"But that's not why you're hesitating, is it, Alec? That's only your excuse."

"What do *you* know, *old man*?" Alec snarled, making an insult of the last two words.

"Fool your parents and the rest of the universe, Alec von Hornet, but you cannot fool me. I know what you desire most; and even if Alexa were here, you would treat her as secondary, subordinate to your main avidity."

Grimm turned and looked down on the people in the distance; some cried openly, while others helped each other by supporting and embracing. "This fleet you're creating is a façade," he continued. "A front. What you really want is revenge on the people who hurt and humiliated you."

Alec smirked. "And what of it?"

"I do not judge you, Alec of the House of Hornet."

"Oh, but you do—silently. How selfish of me, you're thinking; but yes, Grimm Master af Grisamm, that's what I want, and have wanted for a long time now. The very thought of not hunting these monsters down makes me sick, and I will do you and the others no good on a battlefield, whether in space or on-world, as long as my focus is purely on revenge."

"It will take us at least a year to prepare the new fleet group, and there's not much you can do right now. You could spar with one of our knights, and the two of you could learn much from each other, while Cook and I get your new toys ready."

"Asturius?"

"No, he's too emotionally involved with the loss of Alexa."

"And I'm not?"

Grimm ignored Alec's comment and said calmly, "I need him here, but Bentor has told me that he'll happily join you on a—a safari, I think he called it."

"Father," Alec said suddenly.

Grimm turned, and was immediately embarrassed when he realized that Guss von Hornet was approaching them, having left his contingent of guards and officers some dozens of meters back. He should have noticed. "One day I'll be able to sneak up on you, son," the Marshal said gruffly.

"Not today, though."

Guss walked up next to his son, looking over the memorial park as he handed Alec a data stick. "I think you want this."

Alec, still staring dead ahead, just placed the stick in a pocket without even looking at it.

"The list of names you requested, of scientists and engineers that our laws prohibit from working for our Federation...and before you ask why that is, let me just say that politics sometimes does not work in our favor. I've also included dossiers on each."

Grimm cast them a puzzled look just as Guss turned and acknowledged him.

"You'll find names of various inventions, and the inventors as well," he said to Alec, his eyes still on Grimm. "These are inventions, some new and some old, that we could use for our military, but a lot of red tape stands in the way of their acceptance." He turned back to Alec abruptly. "Should you create and train your fleet in neutral space, of course, then you'll have no restrictions as far as technology goes; just be careful whom you recruit. Everyone must be approved by our High Command. Be especially careful when it comes to Marengo and any of its citizens who volunteer—Oman, Crested, or otherwise."

"Are they still neutral?"

"Yes Grimm, they are neutral. Officially. It seems our ambassador at Marengo failed in her quest."

For a moment, the only sound heard was the chirping of the birds.

"So: when *are* you going on your safari?"

This time, Alec and Grimm both turned their heads, facing a smiling father and Marshal. Alec's mouth moved at the same time as Grimm's did, but no audible words left either mouth. Guss only waved his hand in the air.

"It's a normal emotion, Alec; however, I can't support it. That said, I'm sure you'll use your own judgment while training with Grisamm intelligence to better your skills as a fleet commander. I do hope you will pass all our tests when you're ready."

Guss reached for his peaked officer's cap, and touched the brim while nodding his head towards Grimm. He then walked away, and after a short distance, he turned to his side and said, "Stay with your fleet, Alec. In time, you can find the monsters who have done you and so many others harm. Let them wait; let them tremble while awaiting for your vengeance. Why rush the inevitable?"

He then continued his slow walk to his waiting entourage and shuttle.

"Will you heed his advice, Alec?" Grimm asked after the shuttle was away.

There was a long silence as Alec looked at the ground, and finally said, "For now."

"And what about the safari?"

"I'll have Bentor join me on a treasure hunt. We'll need more funds."

"You're going to use the map again?"

Alec nodded.

"Then I strongly suggest you use Bentor's flagship."

Alec, still staring towards the memorial, remained silent for a moment before he said, "I do not wish to treat you as a servant, Grimm."

"What do you need?"

"Need? No, not that. I'm going to show you something, a place no one else knows of, and I want you to help me get all our people and material there."

Grimm nodded. "Whenever you're ready."

"It will be a major challenge, in terms of establishing Singularity Gates and making sure no one can locate our headquarters."

"We'll make it."

"There's more, Grimm; I need you to acquire several things for us. I'd rather have you do it, or your order. I don't want anything to come back to my name. The madman is keeping his eyes on me."

"Madman?"

"Yes. President Alexander."

Grimm smiled at the morbid joke. "Oh, that madman." Grimm was about to crack a joke himself when he saw the tear sliding down Alec's cheek. He stepped closer to Alec, and placed his right hand on the younger man's shoulder.

"Friend," he said quietly, "mourn your loss, and never forget her. Honor her name in all that you do from this day forth, and her loss will not have been in vain. Do what you must to turn anything negative into something positive. Take your father's advice—and please promise me that you will. Losing Alexa is terrible blow for us all, especially after finding out that she was of the Old Blood, just like you. We can't afford to lose you too."

Alec smiled grimly. "You won't lose me, at least not yet. I have promises to keep, and I will find no rest nor sleep until they *are* kept. Make me an army and a fleet, Grimm, and I will give you and the universe exactly what you want."

Alec gestured with his head towards the memorial. A sudden silence had crept over the park; and next to the *Beala-One* memorial stood thousands of people, all staring up towards the hilltop where Alec and Grimm stood. Suddenly, little Zicci stepped forward and raised her right arm straight towards Alec, fist clenched, honoring him with the forbidden salute—the one representing a dictator. Still, to many, the salute represented loyalty to the death, especially among the pirate clans. Stepping up next to Zicci were Mohama, Miska, and Kirra, all of them saluting identically; soon they were joined by Asturias, Bentor, and shortly after that everyone else in the crowd. A police officer monitoring the crowed reported this horrific act to her headquarters, but that was all she could do.

Slowly, Alec begun raising his arm, but was stopped by Grimm. "For Gull's sake, think of what you're doing! This is neither the time nor the place."

Alec whispered, "Wrong, Master Grimm; this is the perfect time and place."

So he raised his arm towards the sky, saluting the crowd below who remained standing there in silence. No words needed to be said; he had accepted his part in history, as the one and only leader of Section 21.

THE very excited Lieutenant waited nervously outside the Marshal's office. She had broken protocol by not reporting to her superiors, but Glare was a young woman with ambition. It had been difficult to get to the main office, and she had another nine steps to go before she could meet the most powerful man in the Nastasturus Federation—or so she thought. Suddenly the large old-fashioned double doors swung open, and in charged a group of bodyguards, followed by The Man himself. Glare saw her opportunity and took it before one of the secretaries could stop her.

She rushed forward, only to be stopped by four guards—all dressed in antique ceremonial uniforms, but aiming deadly modern weapons at her. She said loudly, "Marshal, Lieutenant Aldis Glare of Galactic Intelligence reporting with urgent and important news!"

Guss knew right away that the young Lieutenant had broken protocol, and decided to ignore her. He had too many urgent things to attend to as it was, and so he marched straight ahead towards another doorway, where two modern doors slid into the walls. Glare saw her opportunity slip through her fingers, and knew that if she didn't come out of top on this one, she would surely be reprimanded, if not broken, for ignoring the chain of command.

"It's about *Beala-One*, sir! It's very important!" Glare shouted.

Guss stopped in his tracks, turned, and glared at the brown-nosing shit. For a moment, he thought of the many different ways he could punish the young officer. Finally, he nodded his head for her to follow. "Better be good," he growled.

"It is sir, if you'll allow me—"

"NOT here. In my office."

They quickly hurried into the Marshal's main office; and while he took a seat behind his massive desk, Lieutenant Glare snapped to attention. Guss motioned with his hand for her to start her report.

Glare tapped her wrist-comp, and a holographic clip on the battle in which Ogstafa's flagship had been destroyed was began running while the young officer, sounding very excited, started her debriefing.

"I have seen this already Lieutenant," Guss said sharply. "Too many times."

"Yes, Marshal, but have you seen *this*?" She tried to hand a tablet to him; it was intercepted by an admiral standing beside her, who scanned it for safety before handing it to her commander, while casting the young brownnoser a not-so-friendly smile. For some time, Guss stared at the display, drumming one index finger on his lips. In time, he raised his eyes towards the waiting Lieutenant, without moving his head; and suddenly Glare fell a cold chill down her spine. Perhaps she had gone a bit too far this time.

"Who else knows about this?" the Marshal asked.

"Marshal, you are the only one I have shown this to."

"For once, being insubordinate pays off. You did well, Lieutenant; however, you will still be reprimanded for your actions."

"Sir?" she said, feeling the swelling pride in her chest die a bitter death.

"We have rules in the military—and for good reason. There is a chain of command to be followed; you have broken it rather thoroughly."

A general motioned towards Guss, who nodded; and then the general moved swiftly to him and whispered something in his ear. Guss nodded again, and the general waved towards two guards by the doors. The doors opened, and in charged an elderly man wearing the rank tabs of a commander.

"There you are, you little..."

He stopped speaking when Guss waved his hand for him to be silent, snapping to attention so abruptly he practically vibrated. "So, this is one of yours, Commander Regla?" Guss mused, and turned to his aide. "Get me Admiral Mi."

The Admiral standing next to the very pissed-off Commander and an extremely nervous Lieutenant passed on the order, and shortly thereafter a holographic mage of the newly-fledged Admiral Mi popped up near Guss's desk.

"Admiral Mi. You will take your flagship and go to the coordinates I'll send you by courier. Three *Crusher*-class ships will meet you there. Take command of the squadron and execute my orders. You will report back only to me personally, and no one else. I'll have my people inform your new fleet admiral that you will be on a mission for HQ for a while."

Without a word, Admiral Mi saluted the Marshal, and then the image vanished. Guss turned back to the two officers waiting before his desk. "Lieutenant Glare, you will report to your commander here, and then you will report to Admiral Mi. You are no longer on staff duty, but on active battle duty."

"But...but sir, I'm a staff officer, I haven't trained—"

The stares from both the Marshal and her commander told her to be silent, so she shut up, looking down at her spit-shined boots. "My punishment, sir?" she ventured after a long moment."

"We have protocols, Lieutenant, and if you ever want to advance further, I suggest you follow them."

Lieutenant Glare saw her future as a politician vanish right before her eyes...or did she? Perhaps she could turn this to her advantage; after all, it was she who had found and picked up the very secret signal that no one else had noticed, amongst the mélange of scrambled battlefield communications.

FIVE

THOUSANDS of Florencian capital ships hung in space at the designated rendezvous point, clustered in various formations, surrounded by clouds of support vessels and more agile warships, all of their captains waiting for the next order. Among them lurked four enormous battle stations of the new *Titan* Class, like orcas in school of barracudas. More fleet groups arrived every other moment, an indiscriminate mixture of Galactic and Intergalactic fleets. In the center of the melee lay the gigantic *Gull*, the Marquessa de la Hoff's flagship, the only ship in the galaxy that could create its own Singularity Gate at short notice. The rest of the fleet had to make do with superluminal drives and natural gates.

While the *Gull* was a giant among spaceships, compared to one of the Titan stations, it was like a tiny fly.

From a distance, all the activity made the accumulating force resemble a kicked beehive embedded in the starry expanse of the Big Dark. Hoff took in the view from a large diamond-glass port in her personal quarters, one of the few extravagances she allowed herself; it provided for a grand panoramic view of the multitude of vessels surrounding her. She thought of the millions of souls crewing those ships, and felt nothing; but then she thought of one man in particular, and her heart ached as the connection she still felt with him seemed to tighten around it.

Someone cleared his throat behind her, and she motioned with her head for him report. The grand admiral again cleared his throat before he spoke: "Beloved Marquessa, there have been no major changes among the enemy fleets—not even after news got out about the last system we conquered."

Strange, she thought, *Why won't you make your move, brother?* She turned towards the admiral, a white-haired Oman stooped with age but still of superlative mental capacity, and said, "Display the battle map."

A large holographic image displaying the galaxies in which Florencia and Nastasturus operated appeared in the center of the room, decorated by brilliant colored dots representing the fleets spread throughout the known universe. Hoff touched a holographic display, zooming in towards the center of the cluster, where most of the fleets were stationed in two separate but adjacent galaxies. After a while, she grew bored; she snapped her arm in the air, and the holographic map vanished. "Admiral, report to me immediately when one of Nastasturus's smaller fleets begins to behave...differently, almost irrationally."

The admiral looked uneasy and said, "Differently in what way, milady?"

"It will move quickly, penetrating our territory and conquering major Florencian systems one-by-one, as inevitable and as unstoppable as death," she hissed.

"A single fleet conquering an entire system?" He sounded surprised, even a bit amused. "But as far as we know, they have nothing like milady's flagship, or stations large enough to carry Intergalactic cruisers as fast as ours."

Hoff turned towards the old admiral, not remembering his name at the moment. But she knew this officer; despite his being male, she happened to like him...but she also knew that the monster in her hated him because of it. Her memory sometimes played mind tricks on her, especially lately, and she feared that her second self—the monster—had begun to try to gain control of her mind. When she had been awakened, the monster side of her had been in charge; but after the disastrous Incident at the Gate, she had fallen into a temporary coma and her true self had been able to retake her mind. She knew it was the potent mixture of other beings in her DNA that had kept her alive for long these many centuries—and she hated it. She welcomed death, but would never dare tell anyone. She had promised herself that this was the last time she would serve her God. If she were to be frozen down again, the beast would control her when she eventually wakened; and if that happened, she feared that her real self, her original mind, would remain alive but helpless, trapped in a horror of her own making; and she would never die and move on. Before and during battle, the beast in her was always in control; but lately her true self had begun to win over the monster.

"Do not under estimate this warrior," she informed the grand admiral. She again snapped her arm, and a holographic image of Alec von Hornet appeared. "That's the young man who led our and other fleets against the pirates during the Battle of New Frontier 16."

"The media reported that it was the leader of our 9th fleet from Handover who won. Don't you believe that?"

Suddenly the old Admiral looked frightened, and cleared his throat in a desperate attempt to distract her for his injudicious words. Hoff just smiled at him and shook his her head. "Don't concern yourself with trivial politics. Of course you're right, and I suspect most of our senior staff knows the truth. I read Admiral Nass's report, and I will soon discuss the future of Mr. Rimez with my civilian equal, Marquessa De La Peck. Unfortunately, it is a civilian, and therefore *we* can't easily remove it from its position."

The grand admiral said, "This young man you've shown me is a Hornet, is he not? I believe it's the son of Marshal Guss von Hornet."

"Yes, our Alec is a Hornet...for now. You must report to me personally any time you learn of developments concerning this young man; I also want you to locate and surveil him if possible, but you must not harm him in any way. Is that clear?"

The admiral nodded mutely.

"Also, there is one more person your intelligence section must locate, and bring to me alive." Seven more images appeared, all young women: The Vixens. The images weren't especially clear, and there had been some touch-up work done to them. "I fear this is the best your intelligent section has been able to procure for now. It's of the outmost importance that *none* of these young girls are to be harmed in any way."

The admiral looked on, and for an instant felt a bit bored, thinking that these new assignments were below his position, more suited for a sub-admiral. Hoff observed the old man, amused. Tilting her head, she purred, "Not liking your orders, Admiral?" She raised what was left of her eyebrows, and before the Admiral could say anything, she let out a very strange laugh. "One of these women is the love of young Hornet's life. We believe it's this one."

The image of Alexa increased in size, and the Admiral nodded, knowing full well what his military supreme commander was after. "A means of leverage, I take it; but what about the other girls, milady? Leverage too, perhaps?"

"Perhaps."

"May I?"

He gestured towards the images, and Hoff nodded in consent. Written information appeared in the air around the holograms and he quickly looked it over. "There are many bounties on this Alexa," he said at length.

"Yes. You must make them vanish, and find the girls before they are harmed."

Hoff stopped speaking, noticing that the Admiral seemed uncertain, as if he didn't agree.

"You have a better plan?"

"Not better, but different, my lady," the grand admiral said cautiously. He was experienced enough to know that no superior officer liked to be corrected, and he also knew that if you pissed off this one, you could die. He took a deep breath and continued, "What if we took advantage of these bounties? We could send operatives to follow up on the progress from the sources...it looks like most are traders...instead of us sending operatives looking for a few particular grains of sand. That's all, ma'am."

Hoff herself took a deep breath. During his explanation, the monster in her had tried to take over and punish the man for his perceived insubordination; but with some effort she forced the monster back into its cage, where it belonged. She wouldn't have been able to do that half a year ago.

"Do what you must; just find all of them and bring them to me unharmed," she snarled. "Should anyone harm them in any way, then use whatever force necessary to stop them and punish them. Terminally."

She then gestured for him to leave, as she could sense that another migraine was about erupt like an avalanche.

PHILOXENIA-105 sped on a collision course for Florencian territory. Not too long ago, this sector of space had been neutral; but once the war started, Florencia had annexed the territory. It was open space, and with its newly upgraded engines, *Philoxenia-105* could quickly disappear into a neutral territory before any hostile ship could come near. The new captain was a proud Grisamm; Nadia was also a former mentor to the infamous Vixens. Her commission had gone through, and now she was master of a new Grisamm research vessel, recently acquired by her new Knight-in-Charge, Bentor—alias Bull the Butcher.

The crew onboard included five officers, one of whom was in charge of the infirmary. Dr. Rues was a purplish non-Omanoid with very large, friendly eyes. There were fifteen enlisted who also acted as a security force, with everyone undergoing Grisamm military training along with science and engineering schooling. All of them were women. There were also three scientists and three engineers, two women and four men in all. Had the ship's captain had anything to say about it, there would have been no men onboard her ship at all. Bentor had said nothing when he signed her commission and orders and approved her crew, but his expression had told her well enough that he didn't like her favoring women.

But she was finally in charge of her own ship and crew, and it was up to her. Her dream was to become a Knight, one of the very few women who had made it that far, in charge of her own Ambassador-class cruisers with supplemental ships—and only allow women onboard. Even though Nadia knew that such segregation and discrimination among the Grisamm was frowned upon, she didn't care.

She would miss her Vixens, but her new assignment made her forget about them. She looked over her small bridge while sitting comfortably in the command seat. To her right her best friend Mikka, and to her left a young cadet, Sondra. Nadia mentally licked her lips when she looked at the beautiful cadet, who was focused on the computer display.

Nadia's current assignment was a research mission that she had little or no interest in. They were supposed to launch several probes in the region: Nastasturian Sector 23, Coordinates 4.67.552-3. That Florencia also claimed the space was typical; but according to both the Nastasturus Public Intelligence Office and the Grisamm not-so-public intelligent office, the entire region remained effectively neutral, since there was nothing of significant strategic value in this region of space.

The only warning she had received from Bentor was that there might be scavengers looting what was left of the destroyed vessels after the Incident at the Gate, and that had been one of the main reason why her ship had been refitted with better engines and a formidable defense system.

The compartment nearest the first cargo/docking bay was the largest; it was the supply section, containing all the necessary consumables, recycling tanks, tools, clothing, and pressure suits. Adjacent to that area was a service station where repairs could be made. This was also the place where fifty various-sized androids were attached to the walls, unless of course they were busy on some task. They could also be launched into space from their positions. In the center of the ship lay the engine compartment, in a circular room on the second and third levels. The old engine had required fuel that had been located on the forth level, but the new engine ran on *Anti-Materia*, so the fourth compartment, which once had been filled with pale-blue crystals, had been converted into an infirmary.

Currently the scientists and engineers were gathered in the second section, which once had been used for hauling liquids. The entire section had been re-built for their needs purpose. The third section had also been rebuilt for carrying extra supplies. The remaining seven sections were filled with water and gel-fluid; these sections were the ship's decoy, as the mission was a classified one.

Nadia glanced at a monitor tracking what the scientists and engineers were up to, and decided to go down and check on their progress. She could have called them on the com, of course, but she believed in spending as much time with each person onboard as possible."Mikka, take the conn," she said. "I'm going down to Science for a while."

Mikka took Nadia's seat immediately after Nadia left it. A Grisamm cadet stepped aside at the doorway when Nadia exited the small bridge, then took Mikka's seat. Nadia gave the cadet a friendly smile as her eyes undressed her. Nadia had selected her new crew for looks rather than brains; after all, she and Mikka had brains enough for all of them. She walked calmly through the ship towards the Science Division. She was in no hurry, and whenever she ran into anyone, she stopped and exchanged friendly words. As she entered the labs, she found herself facing a large table where Professor Ocla and his daughter, Pirits, were animatedly discussing something with Dr. Ratla, a Nastasturian citizen and member of the Grisamm Order's Science Division. Whatever it was went completely over her head; she wasn't even sure they were speaking Standard.

There were also two engineers present: Becklaw and Pinto, both men, both Grisamm. They were working in a smaller lab with transparent walls, poking at a large probe with its guts exposed. Several other probes were stacked along one of the walls. She looked on with some displeasure at the mess around the engineers, but before anyone noticed it, she forced a smile while clearing her throat. When no one turned to face her, her displeased expression reappeared without her realizing it.

She stepped forward to interrupt the wild discussion between Ocla and Ratla, who was insisting at the moment, "With all due respect Dr. Ocla, I'm telling you that my way will work better than yours. Milac's technology is not as advanced as ours, and…"

Ocla thrust his face toward the ursinoid's snout. "And I'm telling you that we must use *my* program because nothing else works, and…"

Not really listening, Nadia shouted "Hey!" To her annoyance, she had to repeat herself a couple of times before they shut up. Glaring at the three scientists, she snapped, "I came to tell you that we'll soon be arriving, and—"

A buzz on her wristcomp interrupted her. "Yes, Mikka?" she said, not bothering to hide her annoyance.

Without preamble, Mikka stated, voice tight, "You need to come to the bridge immediately. Company."

"Who? What happened to our long-range sensors? We should have detected them half a light away."

"You need to see this for yourself."

Nadia turned to the others, who now listened with interest. Before she could say anything, the room lights flashed red in an alarm sequence, and several science cadets hurried into the labs. "We'll continue this later," Nadia told the scientist.

Nadia stopped after having walked only a few paces; turning, she said, "I suggest you all find a way of working with each other instead against each other; use both your programs to see which works best, even if Becklaw and Pinto have to build a few more probes. We can afford the resources. Now, please follow standard safety and security protocols to the letter, since we're about to make contact with someone or something unexpected. Have your vacsuits ready." She then turned and hurried to the bridge.

Mikka left her seat as she arrived, displacing the cadet to the nearby weapons station. "Online and armed," she said simply.

"On screen," Nadia ordered.

Nothing was visible, except for deep space with its thousands of stars. "Well, Mikka?"

"Check the reading on your comp, Captain."

After a quick glance at the sensor readings, Nadia ordered, "Lower blast shields and increase hull integrity shields." Puzzled, she continued, "Emit an omnidirectional tachyon ping." The tachyon ping, a brief burst of faster-than-light particles, was no secret, but few realized what the Grisamm had quietly learned centuries before: it could disrupt most cloaking technology, including their own.

Another ship, very stealthy looking and bearing no exterior markings, appeared a hundred kilometers off the port bow. Nadia and Mikka leaned forward, both concerned.

"Try hailing it."

"No response."

"Try it again. Run the ship's profile through Jorrin's." Jorrin's Starship Recognition Registry was a standard reference guide used throughout the known universe. It included files for all the known polities, as well as most of the pirate clans.

Mikka watched the computer scan through the thousands of hull configurations on file. "It's not in Jorrin's database," she reported after a long moment.

"No way in hell this is a first contact."

"I think I know what it is," Sondra spoke up hesitantly. "To me it looks like a new stealth scout the Nastasturus Federation has been working on, or at least what I'd expect it to look like. There are a lot of rumors about this ship. I think the science and engineering community refers to this ship as a 'Grasshopper.'"

"A what?"

"A grasshopper, Captain Nadia, is a type of motherworld insect that moves by jumping around. A 'Grasshopper' ship is one that can make long single FTL jumps rather than the usual series of smaller ones. And if this is one, then it's the most advanced stealth scout ever developed by the Nastasturus regime. They've never denied or confirmed its existence, though."

"What so secret about this Grasshooper?"

"Er, Grass*hopper*, actually…it's supposed to be able to make hyperspace jumps just like we do whenever we use a singularity gate."

"No black hole gate…?" Mikka mused, looking impressed by dark little spacecraft. The hull seemed to alter its surface as it eased trough space, star trails flowing across it like pouring water. "Let me guess: it leaves no wake to detect, and can jump in and out of a system before anyone can get a lock on it—if they ever see it coming in the first place."

"…Something like that," Sondra answered.

"But why reveal itself to us now?" Nadia wondered. "Surely they knew we'd detect it."

And in a blink of an eye, the strange ship was gone.

"It scanned us," Mikka report.

"Sondra. Now that it's scanned us, can you locate it? Did it leave any trail at all?"

Sondra was busy for a moment before she reported, "All I can detect out there now is normal space, captain. Nadia?"

The second officer, who'd been furiously running her own scans, shook her head. "No, nothing."

"Well then, let's use my latest scanning protocol," Dr. Ratla insisted as he entered the bridge. Nadia glared angrily at the rolypoly bearish Nastasturian, and doubled down when she saw that Ocla had also appeared uninvited.

"Next time, ask for permission before entering the bridge," she said icily. "Consider it an order."

"Aye, captain," Ratla said contritely, while Ocla echoed him.

"Transfer whatever information you have from your latest scans to the science section, Ensign Sondra, Mikka." Turning toward the scientists, she said, "Dr. Ratla, Dr. Ocla, should either of you come up with anything, let me know right away."

They failed to respond; they were too busy staring wide-eyed past her, and Ocla raised a trembling arm to point at the viewscreen. Nadia whirled back toward it and spat a curse. "Where the hell did that one come from?" she demanded.

A large stealthed frigate lay dead ahead.

"It's definitely Nastasturian!" Sondra exclaimed, no doubt louder than intended, as she tapped keys on her workstation.

"Calm down, Ensign, let's see what they want."

"They're hailing us," Mikka said.

"On screen."

A young man in a Nastasturus commander's uniform appeared. Expressionless, he said, "Unidentified Grisamm vessel. Stand by to be boarded."

The screen went black, then reverted to its exterior view as a battle shuttle exited from the frigate and headed towards *Philoxenia-105*. Not five minutes later, a subtle *thump* heralded its docking at the *Philoxenia*'s primary airlock. By then, Nadia had a welcoming party in place, she and Mikka at its head, all armed to the teeth.

When the airlock finished cycling, a Nastasturian sergeant entered with a pair of security soldiers. "Flight plans," he barked, without any formalities.

Nadia handed him an e-tablet, and the sergeant eyed the content before handing the tablet back to her. "Captain Nadia, I'm Sergeant Bexxor of the Nastasturian Federal Space Service. Have you had any contact with any other ship in this region, ma'am?"

Nadia was already angry, and she *really* wanted to slap the bastard for calling her ma'am, as if she were some old cow; but she calmed down and relaxed after a deep breath. "We just had contact with an unknown stealth vessel," she replied evenly. "It did not answer hails, and simply disappeared from our sensors. We have never seen a ship like it before—there were no readings at all from its engines—but we assumed it was Nastasturian."

"Nothing else?"

"No," Nadia snapped. "Now, could you please explain what's going on, and..."

The sergeant held up his hands for Nadia to be quiet, then tapped something into his wrist-comp. The tablet lit up as it received a transmission. "Report on this frequency if you see anyone in this region. I saw that you're going to be here for a while, so you will act our eyes and report to us about anything you discover."

Mikka chimed in, "Why don't you just leave some bloody scanning probes? And what about the ship we saw?"

The sergeant only smiled pleasantly as he turned away and entered the airlock, followed by his troops. He allowed them to pass and exit first, then turned at the entrance and said, "What ship? Check your computer. Now: You have your orders, and we expect that the Grisamm will aid us in this matter. As I said before, report on that frequency whenever you have any encounters."

He then left, and a few moments later, the ships shuddered as the shuttle detached to go back to its nameless mother ship.

Ensign Sondra's voice came over the intercom: "Captain! Somehow, that bastard just wiped everything on our mainframe about the bogie!"

"Only reason why they docked with us," Mikka muttered.

"Lucky thing we copied everything over to Ratla's and Ocla's personal comps, then," Nadia said, then smiled wickedly. "Now: let's find out what this big secret is they're hiding. Sondra, continue on our present course; Mika and I will be there soon."

They headed down to the science section, and when they arrived, the two professors were still arguing over whose software to use. Rolling her eyes, Nadia walked over to Becklaw and Pinto. She eyed the man-high probe they were working on with a curious expression; the two engineers were simply leaning on their work tables, waiting for the arguing scientists to make up their minds.

"Build one for each program," Mikka ordered the engineers. A strange silence followed, as the scientists stared at her as if she were an idiot for a moment before turning their heads and continuing with the argument.

Mikka snapped, "Did you hear me?"

Pirits laid her hand on Mikka's arm and gave her a friendly smile as the two professors kept arguing. "The signals from each transponder are too strong, and would interfere with each other. That's why they're arguing."

"Then launch one at a time, and compare the results," Nadia suggested, while still eyeing the first probe.

"My father's software needs six or more weeks to gather all the information needed, we think; Professor Ratla's software supposedly only takes a week."

"Then we launch the faster one first, and then... "

An angry Ocla turned to Nadia's back and practically shouted, "Oh, so I'm the one who discovered this new phenomenon, but my esteemed college here gets to be the first to prove MY theory?"

"Ah, if that's the problem, then it's easy to solve. I have no authority over the work of either one of you, but as this ship's captain, I say that Dr. Ocla's probe goes first." Noticing a potential objection from Ratla, she raised her eyebrows and said, "That's final, Dr. Ratla. You may be a scientist, but you're also a Grisamm; and a Grisamm never steals, ever, from anyone in any way."

Ratla only gave her a long stare, and she knew he was thinking about the delay Ocla's probe going first would cause. Nadia was beyond caring; she had to get this started. She motioned to Mikka, and the two of them left the science section in favor of the more peaceful bridge.

LATER that day, after having traveled at a leisurely half-light speed, they arrived at their destination—whereupon they immediately picked up the impacts of a swarm of small debris on their forward shields. It was fully expected, given what had occurred here during the Incident at the gate.

"Ensign, start scanning for other ships," Nadia ordered, "and take us to Ocla's coordinates."

The *Philoxenia* zigzagged slowly through the debris field; most was smaller than a clenched fist, but some fragments were as large as a frigate. There was quite a bit of organic debris out there as well, Nadia was unsurprised to note: sentients whose remains would never be recovered and returned to their loved ones.

"I can't believe that Florencia's propaganda machine got away with blaming this on an accident," Mikka said sourly. "Anyone in their right mind can see that this debris is from warships. There's a magma gun turret. There's most of a plasma injector. And look at the thickness of that shielding."

"Politics, Mikka; just the standard lies. Probably didn't sit well with the Nastasturian politicians, though."

Two hour later, Ocla's probe was launched. "So, what do we do now?" Ensign Sondra asked.

Nadia looked suspiciously at the screen in front of her, where millions of debris fragments still spun and tumbled with the energy imparted by the quaintly titled Incident at the Gate and subsequent impacts, and would forever, or until something stopped it.

"We wait," she said at last.

SIX

THE once-peaceful, isolated world of Omar was facing the fourth stage of invasion by Handover, a member world of the Florencian Federation. A beautiful world, which some swore was more suitable to Oman habitation than the half-mythical motherworld, it would soon turn into a hell for its inhabitants.

The first stage of the invasion had been simple research, which included abduction of the locals for study as well as climatology and a thorough geographical and geological survey undertaken by cloaked satellites, accompanied by a cataloguing of all indigenous plant and animal species, whether unique or introduced. Microbial surveys had pinpointed any potentially dangerous viruses, bacteria, prions, or other microbes that might harm Florencian citizens. That process had taken several years; the Florencians were very meticulous in their conquests.

The second stage, infiltration, had been performed over the course of a century. Normally, the infiltration of a new world would take five or ten centuries, in order to keep the planetary culture intact, while simultaneously making sure the locals were feuding among themselves. Religion had always been a major player in that process, more so than politics could ever be. The Florencians were in a hurry this time, so they whipped both to a fever pitch—then stepped in and took control of everything.

That was the third phase of the invasion: physical occupation of the planet. That had been accomplished smoothly and efficiently, cutting the Omar system off from the rest of the known universe. The stage was set for the fourth and final stage of the standard Florencian invasion process: planetary rape.

The cottony white clouds half-filling the lapis sky suddenly separated as yet another enormous ship began its landing sequence. This one was a hauler, carrying in its "claw" beneath it what looked to be a misshapen monster of a vessel. But it wasn't an actual spacecraft: it was a ready-to-go factory, built to forage for local materials, living or otherwise, and convert them into whatever the invaders needed. It would also begin mining operations. The hauler descended towards the planet's surface, stirring up strong winds in all directions, almost like a reverse hurricane; ancient trees, some of them centuries old and strong as stone, were blown down. People and structures in or near its path never stood a chance. Soil was scoured down to the bedrock by the wind and the gravimetric forces manipulated to lower the factory into place. It didn't matter. The collateral damage was expected, and all the raw materials destroyed during the initiation of this phase would soon be transmuted into useful items by the factory. They would have been anyway.

City-sized braking blasts scorching the ground, carbonizing anything left alive, right down to the microbial level. The factory, already active, drew in the ash and gasses and spat out unneeded water vapor as a by-product. Soon rain started to fall.

Colonel Effron Ronza stood at minimum safe distance from the factory installation, on the foothills of a local mountain range. Even here, the wind stirred the sparse tendrils that served him for hair, and he could sense the distant heat in the infrared detection pits above his eyes. Behind him was a midsize shuttle, flanked by the staff officers who had been allowed to observe the landing. Some had tears of joy and happiness in their optics; some, like Effron, were not capable of such. Their homeworld, Handover, was soon to be but a memory; it was more or less lost to pollution. But now, finally, the beloved, religious, and peaceful citizens of Handover had a new home.

Their President had initially promised his people that this world would be wisely cared for, and that maintaining and protecting the natural environment would be everyone's first priority. But then someone from the geological survey had found not one, but *five* veins of rare and precious Tritonium silver ore, which formed only on planets condensed from the supernova residue of the largest and hottest-burning stars. Once the Cabinet had found out about the Tritonium silver, it was immediately voted that at least one factory for each vein must be in place before the Handoverian citizens arrived. The politicians would then blame the factories and their blight on the locals, and of course promise that all of them would eventually be disassembled. Meanwhile, mining for Tritonium silver was very dangerous, poisoning the environment severely and destroying the ozone layer.

The exploitation of just two veins of Tritonium silver ore had ruined Handover. Mining out five would render Omar uninhabitable for a century at least, Effron thought cynically. So much for a new homeworld. Colonel Effron's secret mission was to make sure that all of the precious metal had been extracted before any of the factories had been disassembled. Once the factories were in place, any of the troops and engineers involved, of course, would be sent on another mission where their services were sorely needed; their chances of returning to their new homeworld were equal to zero, assuming any even survived. In any case, the factories had all received a redesign makeover, and all looked very different from each other, not resembling at all any factory on old Handover. Those who saw the factories would believe they were native.

With a sound as loud as the explosion of a nuclear weapon, the factory finally settled down on the landscape, sending shock waves in all directions, causing the people on the plateau to brace themselves. The ground trembled for quite a while afterward, the clouds scattered and recondensed, and there soon followed a heavy rain.

Three down, two to go, Colonel Effron thought, smiling at the devastation before him. Nearest was the latest factory; in the far distance, at the horizon, lay another two. To his irritation, only one of them had started working, spewing a rich black from its many chimneys to blanket the ground to a depth of a hundred meters, choking off all life; above, the black was slowly staining the white clouds.

Colonel Effron understood why this must be done; the Tritonium silver brought with it a more favorable and luxurious lifestyle for all citizens, and more importantly, funds to continue the war effort against the decadent Nastasturian regime—and, of course, the campaigns and pogroms against the loathsome non-believers in Florencian peace.

While daydreaming in the rain, enjoying the success that he knew one day Gull would award him with, he never noticed the second shuttle landing well behind him on feather-quiet antigrav thrusters. Colonel Effron's staff tried to warn him, but too late. General Tross marched toward the man he considered his subordinate, ignoring many salutes, his body language and determined footsteps a language clear enough for anyone with a lower rank to more or less duck and cover. Behind him followed more officers and a few civilians, all of whom bore the same upset expression as the General.

"Idiot!" Tross roared into Effron's ear. "*Why in the flames of Gull did you not let me know about the third landing?*"

Suddenly, all Colonel Effron's beautiful thoughts about the future vanished in an avalanche of obscenities. He turned stiffly, facing the General, and then relaxed. The Oman facing him did outrank him, but in a completely different chain of command. This *k'ling'l'da* had no authority over Effron or his people. "Why, General T'Trahss," he drawled, deliberately corrupting the officer's name into that of particularly loathsome worm native to his people's original homeworld, "to what do I owe the honor?"

"Stand at attention, Colonel!"

Effron did not; instead, he dusted some dried mud off his coat sleeve, displaying his unit patch. The General's glaring eyes turned to at the patch, and went wide with horror. He actually stepped back. "M-my apologies, Lord Colonel, I, I was not aware that the Intelligence Division had made landfall on Omar already. I thought... "

With a wave of his hand, Effron ended the General's disgraceful attempts to save face. "What can I do for you, General? It must be something supremely important, since you've so flagrantly disobeyed the High Command's orders to avoid this region until I've cleared it for entry."

The Oman swallowed hard. "You... you know my work, Colonel. I only have so much time to get the factories up and running, and I need another hundred men at least to keep up with my schedule." He took a deep breath and raised his chin. "Please. Next time you land another factory, let me know in advance so we can place a few thousands of them in the area. Or who knows," he made a grand gesture with both arms, "perhaps even a million."

"Thousands or millions of what?" Effron snapped.

"Locals, Colonel. If you let me place some of the locals in the landing region, it will surely speed up my work and get us up and running faster...that's all."

"What about the selection process? We'll need many workers on the lunar and asteroid mines, not to mention the Federal facilities planned for the other system's worlds."

"Oh come now, Colonel, you know how it is. Besides, I have billions of lives I must end before our citizens arrive. There will be plenty of workers for us."

"So you want me to have them just stand there and wait for the next two factories land?"

"No, no, I and my people will take care of that. We'll rig some laser fences so that they won't escape. Besides—even if they did take off, the landing blast would kill them anyway."

Effron clashed his claws together. "Do what you must, General, but do not impede or delay my progress."

"Not a problem, Colonel. Also, would it be acceptable if I placed some of my camps near your..."

"No, it would not! Find your own territories; these are taken. We must have full control of the factory territories, and I don't want any locals near here, even if they *will* be ended when the factories land. They might attract the rebels still fighting us, or get intelligence to them. These savages are not above suicide missions in their misguided attempt to subvert Gull's will!"

A strained silence fell between the two officers, and their respective staffs waited breathlessly, hands moving surreptitiously toward hidden weapons. Then the General smiled broadly, and as if telepathically connected, the General and the Colonel said simultaneously, "For Handover and the War Effort!"

The two officers saluted each other respectfully.

On a small cliff far above them, well hidden in chameleon suits, lay two omanoids, observing both the officers below and the events taking place towards the horizon. Next to them, clinging easily to the rock, were two strange beings who needed no chameleon suits; they were naturally camouflaged, their contours barely visible to the naked eye.

THE Marquessa de la Hoff stood in the center of *Gall*'s Command Bridge on an elevated platform, staring at a huge holographic display consisting of thousands of tiny colored dots, some representing individual ships, others entire fleets; the system's natural worlds and other celestial bodies were grayed out and transparent, allowing un unimpeded view of the entire effort. Normally, Hoff could read the information it presented at a glance, something impossible for most individuals, no matter how well-trained or experienced. But today she wasn't paying it much attention at all; instead she was daydreaming, not that anyone nearby could tell the difference. Even if they could, no one would have dared to say anything. For the longest time, she had been in control of her own mind, and the monster she had long since become had more or less vanished.

"The Handover XO is reporting to us, my lady. Should we send them reinforcements?"

Hoff turned towards the voice, facing an Admiral she never seen before, or at least couldn't remember, flashing him a friendly smile. It actually frightened the Admiral, who automatically backed off a few steps, making Hoff squint eyes that had recently begun turning bluish, and more Oman than they'd been in centuries.

"Are they in need of any reinforcements?" she asked pleasantly. "Shouldn't Handover have sufficient forces unto itself already?"

"Well, my lady, my staff and I are concerned, since our main battle plan involves the Omar system. If our enemy discovers that it can serve as a universal hub, with all those well-hidden Gates…well, Your Grace, we thought that we should strengthen its defenses—"

"No, we should not, Admiral. If we do that, it will instantly attract the attention of Nastasturus. Guss von Hornet and his cadre are no fools. Ignore the Handoverians and inform me when their battle station has entered the system. Only then do I want our third reserve at Pakka deployed."

"Yes, my lady." The Admiral was hesitant for a moment, and Hoff immediately picked up on it.

"What, Admiral?"

"Well, my lady…actually, there are no reserves at Pakka… ma'am."

"Indeed? Get me the officer in charge of the Third Reserve, Admiral. We shall have a…chat."

The Admiral swallowed hard and saluted Hoff. He tilted to his left and whispered something to another Admiral, who tapped a few buttons on his wristcomp. After a long, tense pause, an older Oman woman's head popped up on a holographic display, a puzzled expression on her face.

"Why have you left your post, Admiral?" Hoff sounded curious.

Now the holographic face looked even more confused. "Milady, I received orders from Marquessa Nosassa de la Peck…milady, she ordered me to immediately advance and engage…"

"Why would you do that, Admiral…Nilssen, yes? Has Peck been promoted over me without my knowledge?" Hoff demanded. When the woman just shook her head mutely, Hoff asked, "Since when do you take orders from a *civilian*, Admiral Nilssen?"

The woman's mouth worked like a fish's before she managed to croak, "But, but... she said that it was fine with you...she showed me signed orders from you saying so. I had no reason to disbelieve her. She said she wanted to help you, since there are so many of our fleets, and..."

"*Help* me?"

"Well...given the enormous expense of this endeavor and the lack of much progress thus far, she, she thought she would do you a favor by taking some of the burden off your shoulders, and—"

Hoff motioned for silence. She looked down at the deck, shaking her head. When would these civvies ever learn? She looked up and asked in a friendly tone, "So, Admiral Nilssen, what are your new orders from my esteemed colleague?"

There was a brief silence before Admiral Nilssen took a deep breath and replied, "To invade and conquer the Empire of Marengo's capital world, so that with all the resources available on their planet, we can..."

The Admiral stopped speaking, quailing despite the fact that her Fleet Commander was light years away; for now, she found herself staring into a pair of red eyes flaring with the radiation of a thousand exploding suns.

The beast inside Hoff was back.

SEVEN

THE little ship exited the singularity gate and headed deeper into the system, passing several modest battle stations. In the far distance lay two massive Omega Class cruisers, attended by a school of destroyers and frigates, which resembled sleek sharks protecting killer whales, ready to pick off any ships attempting the secret passage into this system. Admiral Hadrian Cook af Hornet leaned back in his comfortable seat, observing several monitors facing him; and now and then he looked at the large screen on the forward bulkhead, which presented an image of what lay before them in several spectra. Once his ship cleared the secured sector, it hove to starboard, arrowing toward the system's only inhabited world.

Cook thought back to all those months ago, almost a year now, since his nephew Alec had brought them to this heretofore uncharted system—the new Section 21 HQ. It had remained a jealously guarded secret ever since; he wasn't even sure his brother, the leader of the armed forces of the Nastasturus Federation, knew about it. How Alec himself had learned about this system no one knew, and Alec refused to discuss the matter. There were twenty major planets in the system along with hundreds of moons, and millions of asteroids in two belts. Several of the planets and moons boasted enormous resources of gases and precious metals, including Tritonium silver ore. Mines were being worked and agridomes installed across hundreds of worlds and worldlets, ensuring the system would eventually become self-sufficient and that many of the natural resources could be exported to fund this new and very secret fleet.

The Grisamm Order had accumulated a great deal of very advanced technology from many different worlds over the millennia, but had never had enough money to fund all the research needed to exploit it properly. Alec's incredible wealth had changed that, and even Cook was flabbergasted by the many new weapon systems developed since by his R&D facilities, along with the many inventions that were expected to help people in general.

The Fantaka system actually had two worlds in the Goldilocks zone, but one required oxygen masks for survival. The other, Fantaka Prime, was a standard water world, almost three-quarters water, and to everyone's surprise lacked sentient occupants despite hosting a rich and varied biosphere. Alec believed it was a fallow nursery world, forgotten by one of the ancient empires that had once raised whole crops of sentients on various planets, like farmers raised grain. Domestic animals from other worlds were easily introduced to this new environment. The biology section had only needed a week to prove that the planet was free of hazardous illnesses, and that it was livable for most known races. This process alone normally took several years of research.

When Alec was asked if knew of more such worlds, he had refused to answer. Many had argued that if there were other unexplored, unoccupied worlds like this one for Nastasturus and Florencia to expand into, then perhaps the war could end. Cook thought that was naïve, and was one of the few who had taken Alec's side in the arguments; any such hidden treasures would soon be ruined by the greed of the two large Federations and other powerful polities, no matter how many there might be; and once they'd run through those resources, a new war would erupt.

No, sentients just had to learn to stop wasting resources and think of the environment first, using common sense to conserve what they were given. But because that was impossible to maintain from generation to generation, they instead applied a simpler solution to their problems: they conquered. In the process, they gained more resources while, temporarily, decreasing their out-of-control populations.

Nature was a real bitch.

"Captain, take us by the shipyards," Cook ordered, and the ship altered course, piling on velocity until it was moving at half the speed of light. Ten minutes later, the inertial dampeners groaned as the ship slowed to a stop near the shipyards in high-Fantaka orbit.

Ahead were dozens of ships of as many classes in various stages of completion, alive with hordes of andies and living workers. Nearby lay a mid-sized station that could house a quarter-million people; its docking ring was also being used as a shipyard. Hundreds of smaller ships, shuttles, and worker pods filled near-space, like honeybugs swarming a hive.

In the far distance, in their own spacedocks, lay two strange-looking ships, each four times the size of an Omega cruiser. Cook had never heard of them before his brother Guss had revealed that they had been a major pain in the ass and a mistake implemented by his predecessor. The ships were old and had never been used; but vacuum was an excellent preservative, and now the monsters were being refitted and updated, based on designs provided by his nephew Alec, a certifiable military genius of a type that Cook had never before encountered. He suspected, actually, that no one had encountered anyone like Alec for centuries, if not millennia. Guss had been more than happy to give Alec the two ships, so that he could close the books on the costly mistake.

Battle carriers hadn't been used for over a century, and seemed outdated to Cook; whereas most modern capital ships fielded drones, the carriers required piloted fighters. But Alec had access to plenty of loyal personnel. When Alec had explained to his father what he was looking for, the Marshal had been quick to hand them over, and Alec to take them. They remained a well-guarded secret from Nastasturan politicians. Once there had been plans to modify them to carry only drone fighters, but that would have brought their existence to light, so the decision was made at the highest levels to keep them hidden away.

After having inspected the shipyards to his satisfaction, Cook ordered the captain, "Take us to Mother."

The ship veered across the elliptical plane towards the other side of the star. Again accelerating to a high percentage of c, it arrived 20 minutes later at Fantaka's innermost gas giant, a Super-Jovian with wispy rings, over thirty moons, and twice as many enormous asteroids orbiting it. Mining facilities were at work on nearly all those worldlets, with several others siphoning gases, metallic hydrogen, and Ice-7 from the giant's interior. The ship vectored in towards one of the asteroids; and as it closed, two odd-looking fighters arrived to scan Cook's ship and escort it into the asteroid, where Cook undertook a quick inspection of the behemoth of a ship being built inside the asteroid. When he was satisfied, he directed the captain to return to Fantaka orbit.

The planetologists were still researching the new world, so as of yet there were only a few small settlements sprinkled along the seaboards of the major continents; most of the system's new inhabitants lived aboard the high orbitals and weapons platforms that formed a growing ring around Fantaka. Cook's ship docked at one of the smaller habitats in high orbit, whereupon Cook hurried to his office; he had million and one things to do. But there was one special problem that egged him on, as he wanted to have it solved as soon as possible: keeping all the people working throughout the system entertained.

This was essential, because the system was so isolated and, as of a few months before, deliberately cut off from the rest of the universe, due to the expense and difficulty of traveling to and from Fantaka. It was also a security risk. On more than one occasion, someone had tried to ferret them out; but because of the current state of war, the founder of a new colony—in this case, Alec—was allowed to keep the system hidden until it was otherwise discovered or the war ended. Only then would the new colony be made official Nastasturan territory. In any case, Section 21 was an independent fleet, not officially affiliated with the Nastasturus Federation. Meanwhile, Fantaka's political status was yet to be determined. Nastasturus would, of course, demand that Fantaka became a new colonial member of the federation if and when it was discovered.

Admiral Cook had no idea whether or not Alec's father knew Fantaka's location, and they had never discussed it. Perhaps his brother knew, and might consider this world to be a new start for Nastasturus and Tallas if things didn't go as planned.

Entertaining his people had proved to be a pain in the ass, but Cook knew how important it was to keep up the morale, not only among the officers and troops but also among the civilian workers. There were a few amusements on the planet below, but the lack of full clearance kept most of the new Fantakans in space. Alec had promised to solve this problem by the time Cook returned from the capital; and now Cook was eager to find out if he had, and if so, what he had done.

He hoped the solution hadn't been too radical. Alec could be an odd one at times, especially since his time as that depraved bitch Zorif af Sun's art installation.

Cook entered his office in an ambivalent mood, barely noticing the panoramic view of the beautiful ocean world below. He was greeted by several high-ranking staff members, half of them military, the rest civilians, all with their tablets ready for him to view. He maintained a casual atmosphere in his private office, and some of the officers even wore civilian clothes; anything went, for now, in the grand effort to keep up morale. He half listened as he moved towards his main office, his staff following, one-by-one reporting to him the latest updates and any new problems that had emerged. After the final staff member had poured out a few more problems that needed his attention, Cook let out a sigh and asked, "Have any of the existing problems been solved since I left, or do we only have more problems?"

His staff gave each other puzzled expressions and then General Frey, an omanoid woman in early middle age, tapped on her wrist-comp, sending him a file. "Here's a list, sir. We've been busy."

Frey wore her uniform, Cook noticed happily. He eyed the file display for a moment; then, with a satisfied expression, he nodded. "Now, did the Key Administrator take care of the entertainment situation?"

All the staff turned towards Frey, who cleared her throat. "I was going to mention that. You have a particular visitor—one among many clamoring to see you, sir—whom I allowed to skip the line by direct order of Mr. Hornet, and because I know the urgency of this dilemma."

"And where is this visitor now?"

General Frey motioned her head towards a commander, whom left the room and shortly returned with a small, strange-looking being escorted by two guards. Cook gave the little fat man a puzzled look, recognizing its face, but couldn't place it; and just as he remembered who he was looking at, the little fellow—to everyone's surprise and horror—made a long dash, jumping up and embracing Admiral Cook after landing on his chest. Two guards quickly pulled their weapons.

"Get the hell off me, Tota," Cook snapped loudly, a bit more angrily then intended.

"Ahhh, Admiral Cook! Alec's uncle is my favorite uncle too, and soon all your problems will be gone, for the one and only Tota is here!" Tota blurted, while his long nose mashed into the side of Cook's face, which turned a dangerous red. After his enthusiastic greeting, the little elephantoid slipped out of poor Cook's embrace and landed on the floor gracefully.

"We must immediately increase the size of the black hole gate, my lovely admiral, or I can't move my new casino and hotel station to this wherever-we-are-system!" Tota trilled, shielding one side of his face with his hand while winking towards Cook, who only raised his eyebrows.

"We'll have it done shortly. Now tell me, Master Tota, since you're apparently the last person in this room who's seen my nephew, did he by any chance inform you where he was heading?" Cook was frustrated, because he thought Alec's constant, careless gallivanting through space aboard *Crusher-5* wasn't a fit activity for a future field commander and definitely not for the Key Administrator of a new colonial system. Everyone in the room turned towards Tota with stern expressions, anticipating his answer.

Tota rested his right elbow in his left hand while smacking his nose back and forth in his typical thinking posture."As a matter of fact he did say something..."

"Well, what?"

"He said, 'Tell my uncle that I'm taking care of the next major problem with our pilots'."

"Why, thank you. Now, did he mention any specifics, or perhaps where he was going or when he'd be back?"

Again Tota took up his thinking posture, and after only a few annoying seconds, he shook his head. "Nope!"

"Very well. I'll see the rest of you in a little while. Mister Tota, please come into my office."

The other people in the room moved away silently, most of them looking frustrated. Cook closed his office door and locked it as Tota seated himself on a large, comfortable chair facing Cook. It was sized for Cook's Grisamm colleague Bull, so he looked like a child sitting in an adult's seat. Cook sat down behind his desk.

"So, Tota, how was Alec doing when you met?" Cook didn't bother to hide his concerned expression.

For a moment Tota was silent, and his normally merry face turned sad. "Considering what I know he's been through—and that's not much, except that he has lost the love of his life—he seemed fine...yet very distant, and very, very cold. This is not how I remember him; but then again who can blame him, after such a horrendous loss?"

"Indeed." Cook leaned back in his seat and looked down at his desk, nodding his head in agreement. "Sad business, very sad business, this whole thing," he murmured.

"Is it true..."

Cook turned his eyes toward Tota's without moving his body, raising his eyebrows.

Tota continued, "Is it true that young Alec was half eaten alive by the Gormé?"

Cook leaned further back in his chair, lifting his head and fixing his eyes on Tota, but he said nothing; but he didn't have to, because his eyes told Tota everything he needed to know.

Tota clapped a hand over his mouth while his eyes teared, and he said, "Oh my, oh my... Oh no, oh no..."

Cook just looked at the silly little creature facing him with ice-cold eyes.

"But, but...his father, the honorable Marshal of the Nastasturus Federation, must surely understand that his son is not fit for any sort of command after such a horrific experience, especially not something like a powerful galactic fleet, independent or not..." His voice seemed to deepen as his face settled into an expression that made him seem far older and more serious.

Cook maintained his stare, while Tota sat back in his own seat, his eyes moving rapidly from side to side as he thought. Gone was the ridiculous "thinking pose." After a long, uncomfortable moment, Tota lifted his head to meet Cook's eyes, a suspicious expression on his face.

"You're going to unleash Alec on the enemy, aren't you."

Cook failed to respond, and Tota spat with a disgusted expression, "Cook! For the sake of all that's good and right in this universe, you and your brother can't do this! Are you deliberately trying to recreate the Silver Guard? Alec will end up as a..."

The little man's voice trailed off as Cook lowered his arms and let his hands rest on his chair's arms, still transfixing Tota with that icy expression.

"As what, Mister Tota? What will Alec end up as?"

A tense silence followed, as Tota stared expressionlessly at Cook.

"Say it, Tota. Say it out loud," Cook ordered sternly.

Tota looked down for a moment before raising his head, giving Cook an equally cold stare. "A monster. If you unleash Alec in the fragile state his mind is in now, then he'll become a monster that no one can control...but then, that was the plan all along, wasn't it?"

Cook suddenly lowered his eyes and said in a friendly voice, "I'll see to it that one of my senior officers gets you everything you need."

Tota's expression changed also, and he said slowly, "I certainly hope I don't find out that you or Marshal von Hornet orchestrated any of the things that have happened to our poor Alec. I don't know what I'd do. I don't want to make an enemy of you, Admiral Hadrian Cook af Hornet of Tallas."

Cook just lifted an eyebrow as Mr. Tota hopped off the chair and moved toward the exit. He stopped in the middle of the room and turned back toward Cook, who had already lowered his head, studying a computer tablet. Cook realized that Tota was still in the room and raised his head just as Tota began to transform.

The little man seemed to stretch, his bones and ligaments crackling unpleasantly as he altered his physical appearance. Cook's first reaction was to raise the alarm to the two guards standing outside, but something in the back of his mind told him not to. After a fascinating moment, the formerly comical little being raised itself from a kneeling position, to stand facing Cook. He had become tall and slender, as tall as Cook, with a greyish-silver tegument and large, wide black eyes.

"I thought the Planetary Ringmakers were extinct, or perhaps a myth," Cook said slowly. "I take it that's what you really are, aren't you, Mr. Tota?"

"If you know of us, then you should know something of the history of my species," Tota replied in a smooth baritone, "and as you can see for yourself, no, we are not extinct. And no, I am far from the last of my kind."

Cook gave Tota a puzzled look.

"Nowadays my people live a peaceful existence at the fringes of the universe, keeping ourselves secret from the affairs of the younger races. We mostly do research on this universe and universes past, in hopes of understanding what we will face in the future. A few of us act as...Monitors, if you will. War almost ended my species, and we don't want what happened to my people to happen to those of you now living in this part of the universe. What you call 'the known universe' is but a small fraction of the whole, but it is significant...and we originated here, so it holds a special place in our oversoul."

Cook leaned back in his seat, and his fingers drummed against each other as he thought. He suddenly hit a button on his desk. "Commander, cancel all my meetings for today."

Cook then turned towards Tota and said in a neutral tone, "Guess we have a few things to discuss...Ambassador, I take it?"

EIGHT

THE log cabin sat beside a small lake, surrounded by a dense forest with high trees that concealed the area from prying eyes. The air was fresh and clean, scented with the fragrances of wildflowers and conifer trees. A small river ran through the woodland towards the lake, cascading over a rocky lip in twin waterfalls a dozen meters high, setting up a permanent turbulence that rippled across the water. A small, hand-build wooden dock extended into the lake from a flagstone path leading up to the cabin.

A large storage shed, more like a garage, had been erected a bit away from the house, shielded by the forest. A good eye might spot an old flitter parked inside, covered by a soiled oilcloth. Extending from the back of the house was a small porch, and on it a man sat on an old wooden chair, sleeping, a couple of broken clay bottles on the deck next to him. He was unshaven and unwashed, the stink rolling off him ruining the serenity of the tableau. He was very thin, and one look would tell anyone that food wasn't this man's first choice when it came time to fill his stomach.

A pair of strong hands grabbed the slumbering man, lifting him up like he was a rag. He suddenly woke due to the rough treatment and began protesting, slurring out one curse word followed by another while flapping his arms and kicking his legs. His accoster just laid him over a shoulder and headed towards the dock. The wooden planks creaked from their combined weight; the old man started to puke his guts out, seeing happily that the mess had landed on his abductor's back. He looked up and noticed, vaguely, a couple of people standing by his house, observing the events. Unfortunately, his vision was far too blurry for him to recognize anyone.

He did think he recognized one of them...but that thought fled his mind as he realized he was flying through the air, just in time to be shocked to alertness as he hit the water, still protesting. His award was a mouthful of pond water as he fell into the murky depths.

The old man sobered up instantly, and pushed up towards the surface, ready to fight for his life. But no sooner had he raised his head above the surface than he had to cough up all the water that had invaded his body. That leached all his fighting strength from him, and he decided that drowning wasn't so bad after all, maybe, his mind still hazed by all the booze. The only problem was, the pond wasn't deep enough to drown in without some serious effort. When he finally managed to stand up, the water only came to his waist. He dried his eyes and looked up at the bastard who had tossed him into the freezing water—and his eyes widened as he recognized the man hunkered down on the pier, looking at him with pity.

"Good morning, Captain."

"You, you, you...!"

"Nikko Behl. You were drunk the last time I saw you, and you still haven't sobered up. Sad business. Very sad, old man. I expected better things of you."

There was a very awkward, silent moment, and then Nikko squinted towards his house and the two other men, both of whom he recognized. Frances and Bax, wearing their typical Grisamm cloaks. He huffed angrily and started to breathe deeply, trying to relax. "I guess it's that time I've been waiting for?" he asked, after a long moment. The other man just nodded.

Nikko took a few paces towards the shore, and knelt in the water with his upper body exposed. He lowered his head and closed his eyes. "Do it quickly, son. I deserve it, and I understand. You have my blessing...just do it now."

Alec rolled his eyes, ignoring the little drama, then walked out to the beach and into the water, extending his hand to his old friend and mentor. "I'm not here to kill you, old man," he said firmly.

"But, but...then why *are* you here? After all, it was my fault—everything was my fault. We lost you. I was the reason why you were left behind, and—"

"Nikko, friends don't apologize to friends. We learn from each other, and we're always there when one of us needs help. Right now you could use my help, if you want it—and perhaps I might need your help, too."

Nikko, still on his knees, moved quickly towards the shoreline, splashing up water as he rushed forward. Kneeling again, he took Alec's left hand between both his own and held it tight. "Anything. I'll do anything. Name it and let me regain my honor, I beg of you."

Alec raised his eyebrows questioning. "Not if you're begging. Besides, the Nikko Behl I once knew never begged to anyone."

Nikko got to his feet and straightened up. He placed his right hand on Alec's left shoulder, and nodded, smiling.

"Breakfast, anyone?" Frances bellowed, motioning with his arms.

Several people emerged seemingly from nowhere, hurriedly erecting a large table and loading it up with various dishes. Some of the new arrivals rushed down to the shore, and suddenly four young women hovered around Nikko —Mohama, Miska, Zicci, and Kirra—embracing and kissing the old man while all talking at the same time about old and new adventures. Alec approached Frances and Bull.

"Still haven't taught them anything about communication discipline, have we now?" Alec joked.

"Oh, we have, haven't we, Bax?"

"Sure. Didn't take, though." The big saurian said, scratching the back of his head.

Nikko was, of course, the "guest of honor" at the newly erected breakfast table; after all, it was his property. He hadn't been this happy in a very long time, it seemed; his eyes teared up more than once, and the whole time, the girls hovered around him like busy little flies, annoyingly making sure he had everything he wanted. His appetite wasn't the best, despite all the nice dishes some gourmet chef was whipping up at a mobile kitchen in the shade of a large tree, with the help of several andies.

Suddenly someone placed a large clay bottle in front of him. Nikko looked up, seeing only the back of Alec's cape as he moved back towards his side of the table. Nikko looked at the bottle, and reached for it...but then he hesitated. He grabbed the bottle and stood up, walked to the shoreline, and without looking at the bottle or hesitating, he tossed it away. By the time it hit the water, he had already turned his back and returned to his seat to continue eating. No one mentioned the incident with the bottle; instead, he had to listen to four very excited young ladies as each one of them shared all their secrets, some of which were a bit too intimate even for Nikko. However, two things he did remember about these wild girls was that they never held back, and never got embarrassed, unlike old starship captains.

When breakfast was over, everyone sat in silence, their eyes turned towards Alec. He nodded, and suddenly everyone left in different directions. The girls pulled poor Bax towards the wooden dock, despite his protests; and even though he was three times their size and could easily shrug them off, he allowed them to tug and groan while forcing him onward.

Nikko beckoned to Alec to follow him down by the shoreline, and the two of them started to walk slowly away from the house. The sky was blue, with just a few clouds to mar it, and near-birds flew and shrieked through the trees on their grand quests for mates or food.

"Where are the rest?" Nikko asked after a time.

Alec walked on, silent.

Nikko stopped and placed his hand on Alec's shoulder. "The other Vixens? Where are they?"

"Didn't return from their last mission, I'm afraid," Alec replied dully.

Nikko stopped in his tracks. "Nina? Tara? What about Alexa? What...what happened?"

Alec continued a few paces onward, then turned to face the old man. "They're dead, Captain Behl."

Nikko wanted to ask more, but Alec's eyes told him not to. He decided to change the subject, but come hell and high water, he wasn't going to forget about it. Maybe the other girls were more willing to talk about this new tragedy. He cleared his throat.

"So what brings you here, then? You're the second set of visitors I've had since I returned home. First your father's agents came. I thought they were going to kill me, but instead they gave me money...a lot of it. I was able to pay off my property and retire."

"So that's it? You're retired?"

"I'm old, Alec, and with war springing up all over the universe, it's hard to find a place one can retire to in peace and solitude like this... well, at least until one of the powers decides to invade this sector."

"I'm here for two reasons," Alec said. "One, I'm visiting an old friend. Even though our adventures didn't last long, you saved my life, and I still consider you my friend. I hope you feel the same?"

"Of course I do," Nikko said gruffly. "And second?" "When we were escaping from Zuzack, you trained me to become a very good pilot. Later, I watched as you took seven wild women in hand and trained them up to become master pilots. I've never seen better."

Nikko, beginning to suspect what was coming, nodded, and they continued their walk. Suddenly they were interrupted by loud shrieks and laughter from the young women, followed by a splash; apparently, having being able to lure Bax onto the dock, the little Vixens had been able to do the impossible and make him fall in. He learned later that little Zicci had turned herself into a small ball behind Bax while the rest had pushed him into the wet. With a loud roar, the big saurian broke the surface and jumped back onto the dock, making what would have been an impossible feat for most look like it was the easiest thing he had ever done. With a loud roar, he ran after the Vixens, who all shrieked loudly as they were being chased.

"I guess you want me to train a few more like them, then?"

"Yes," Alec admitted. "Keep in mind that you would never have to see any action, or take part in any. The only thing I want you to do, if *you* want, is to train pilots. Almost all the good pilots end up in the standard Nastasturus space fleets. I need you to train raw recruits from scratch, most of whom have never seen the inside of a cockpit."

"Best way to do it. That way they don't have any vices to unlearn." Nikko Behl didn't have to think about it long. He turned towards Alec and said, "So, how many are we talking about—a few dozen or so?"

"Well, you trained seven of them at once," Alec motioned towards the dock, where the girls were now running back out towards the end with Bax following in their wake, all of them screaming like mad. "So, say, about seventy thousand of them this time?"

"Seventy *what*?"

"You always said you liked a challenge…Admiral Behl. Well?"

Nikko scratched his forehead, looking over at the commotion while staring flabbergasted. Then it hit him what Alec had just called him, and suddenly a smile lit up his face. He turned towards Alec and embraced him—and suddenly two guards appeared from nowhere in cloaked battle gear. Nikko froze while Alec gestured to the guards that everything was okay.

"Like I said, you only have to train them," Alec continued, "and then you can more or less return here whenever you want."

"More or less?" Nikko shot Alec a dubious expression.

"Well, we do have a few security glitches to work out regarding our new HQ location, but fear not, you'll be one of the few with direct access to me."

Alec motioned with his hand, and suddenly the region was again filled with servants and guards, cleaning everything up, making it look like nothing out of the ordinary had taken place. Alec turned and walked away, as Nikko watched him thoughtfully. Suddenly he shouted, "Hey, Alec! I won't let you down this time, sir. I promise."

Alec stopped and turned back, smiling at Nikko—but his smile never reached his eyes, and suddenly Nikko could feel goosebumps all over his skin. Something was amiss, he thought, but what?

"I know you won't," Alec said quietly, before going on his way.

NINE

"IT'S true, it's true! They—" The young civilian clerk blurted as he charged into the conference room. He stopped in the middle of his sentence as he realized fifty unfriendly faces were staring at him, telling him silently what they thought of the interruption. The clerk was at a loss for words for a moment, but the news overwhelmed his good sense and he shouted out loud, "Florencia has attacked Marengo! The empire has declared war on Florencia! It's all over the news."

The faces turned away as the exited clerk realized that he was no longer needed and quietly left the room, wondering if he still had a job after having seen the expression on the face of his Key Administrator.

As one, the people in the room turned towards the man who sat with his back towards a large panoramic glassteel window. The table at which they sat was circular in shape, made of the darkest nightwood from Sinrest and banded with silver, which led toward the center of the table to coalesce into a stylized sun. After a moment without a response from the man, who sat with his chin propped on his joined hands, many of the delegates began conversing about the news, some surreptitiously checking the news channels on their wrist-comps. What would this mean for Section 21?

Soon, the discussion devolved into an argument between the civilian administrators and the military personnel present. Suddenly Alec stood up, and after a few tense moments and some shouts to be quiet, silence reigned.

A civilian Key Administrator saw her chance and took it, making sure everyone could hear her words: "Whatever happens at the front line is of little or no concern to those of us here. The fleet isn't ready, and we have more urgent issues to deal with in regards to the civilian statutes of this new homeworld. Eventually, our location will become known, and millions of refugees will be transferred here."

Alec gestured with his right arm for her to be quiet. When he noticed that Cook was about to respond to Elaania, the Key Administrator of the future civil society of Fantaka, he cleared his throat and gave his uncle a quick glance, followed by a friendly smile and a nod. Cook settled backed into his seat.

"Admiral Cook, what is the fleet's current capacity?"

"Sir, we are at thirty-four percent readiness."

"How many infantry?"

"Only half a legion...less than fifty thousand."

"More than enough for the coming parade," Elaania blurted, apparently deciding that she should be in on this conversation so that she could make sure it would end soon, allowing the more urgent civilian matters to be addressed.

"We only need a few thousand troops representing us at the next induction ceremony at Tallas, along with a few escort craft," someone in the room noted.

"The next celebration for the new fleets is in a few weeks, but we're not really ready for that one."

"Perhaps we should wait until all our ships, crew, and troops are ready," someone suggested.

"Certainly not! What would be the point of having a celebration march if we already have all the people we need?" someone shouted out. "Those parades draw in recruits like sugarbats to honey!"

The newly appointed brevet-General Vito, who was in charge of security and police, interrupted angrily, "It's an inaugural parade for the new fleets that are going to the front, not a bloody celebration, even if a bunch of ignorant civilians might think so! It's a nice way to say goodbye to all of those who may not return."

Someone shouted, "We must be part of the parade! We need to be at our best!"

Another voice joined in: "It's of outmost important that we have our best troops and our most attractive ships on hand, making sure that the popularity of our fleet group will attract more recruits." Many voices contested this advice, and suddenly the orchestra was playing its tune again, mostly among the civilians present but also among a certain segment of military officers who seemed to enjoy arguing.

"SILENCE!" Cook pounded on the table as his voice thundered through the room, drowning out the petty bickering all around him. In that moment, he cursed himself for having fallen victim to his own carelessness, not wanting to display any emotion in front of the senior staff. But how else could he get through to them?

Everyone turned towards Cook, whose face had turned red. He leaned back again and turned towards Alec, whose back was facing them now as he enjoyed the view of the space around the fragile blue-and-white ball that was Fantaka. The region was busy with ships heading in all directions, lifting from the planet below and descending, all of it a nightmare for local traffic control. For a short time, he seemed lost as he stood there mumbling to himself. He then faced the crowd, nodding towards Bax, who tapped a few pressure plates on an android standing nearby.

All the windows in the conference room polarized, and thick metallic shields slid over them. An orange screen blinked to life where the panoramic window had been. Everyone knew that from this point on, nothing that was said could leave the room. All doors were locked, so no reckless clerks would be bursting in.

With a devious smile, Alec said, "I have a plan…"

For the next few hours, Alec outlined the details of his plan—or at least of the plan he wanted everyone in the room to believe in. When the meeting was over, everyone left satisfied and happy that their military Key Administrator had outdone himself once more. The shields lifted from the windows, revealing the peaceful (if busy) view of Fantaka. When Elaania approached Alec, Cook angrily waved her off; she nodded and quietly left the room with the others. Once the room was shut and secure, Alec turned towards his uncle and General Vito, who were the only ones who had remained.

"That was the foulest pile of dungo-crap I've heard from you in a while," Cook said, crossing his arms.

"Did you expect me to actually tell these…dungos the truth?" Alec smiled, then continued, "Let's go for a ride."

They moved toward a part of the wall that immediately opened up to an adjacent corridor leading to a small docking station. They entered the small, sporty runabout docked there, and it wasn't long before Alec hit the accelerator, heading towards the first of their temporary spacedocks in orbit about Fantaka. Fighters took up escort positions to either side of the runabout. While Alec was flying a bit too fast and wild for Cook's taste, Vito seemed to enjoy it.

After a while, they entered the hollow asteroid where their mother ship was under construction; Alec's runabout lit gently on a landing pad, and they exited the ship, bouncing along a long stone corridor that gleaned with iron and nickel ore. Lamps were flashing in some areas, and a vast buzzing sound echoed in the background wherever they went. Every section they went by was studded with large windows, displaying parts of the monster being built on the opposite side, in the asteroid's hollow interior.

"Impressive, I must say," Vito said, "but will all the new technology you've integrated with it work with ours?""I hope the darn thing will," Cook agreed.

"Some of the technology is actually ancient, preserved from before the last Universal War," Alec said, "and we're lucky to have it. We still haven't equaled the ancients in the biosciences yet, but our technology seems perfectly compatible. The technology the Grisamm have preserved and developed on their own is very advanced—and I'm glad to see that my money is doing something good."

"You think creating death machines is good," Vito asked, smiling.

"Death machines that will lead to peace," Alec admonished gently. "Besides I'm also funding a lot of research in pretty much anything that can be researched. Technology, medicine, engineering, space sciences, you name it."

"You do know all hell will break loose once Nastasturus finds out about all these new secret weapons," Cook noted, a concerned expression.

"He's right, Alec. Any new weapon system must first be introduced to the Military Board and eventually to the politicians for approval."

Alec shook his head. "Not in this sector of space. We're very far away from commercial space."

"About that…" Cook began, but Alec's expression told him not to continue.

"We've been over it again and again, and I *will* disclose the coordinates of Fantaka in time. But for now, the Singularity Gate is all you need to focus on when it comes to accessing this system."

They took a few lifts and escalators, and eventually they entered a temporary war-room that was empty except for a few androids busily at work. The place was currently a huge mess; from parts of the wall hung plastic wrappings, while wires and cables littered the floor. It was very dusty inside, and several vents were working overtime to clear the air. The cave-like chamber had a dry and confined fragrance. They moved towards a large octagonal table, from which Alec and Vito removed some tools.

Vito tapped a few buttons on his wrist-comp, and several battle andies marched out into the room from hidden compartments. Another tap, and the andies dispersed, locking and blocking all openings to the chamber; meanwhile, a holopic coalesced above the table, depicting the major systems in the local galaxy, and the positions of the various known military fleets and battles currently occurring: Marengan, Nastasturan, Florencian, and their various allies. The image was flanked by windows displaying troop and ship losses and other statistics. Alec's fingers flew across holo-keys, and he zoomed in on the Omar system.

"I'll take the forces we have available, and engage our enemy here," he declared. "We'll take Omar, or rather liberate it, since the planet hasn't reached the proper stage of evolution for space travel or First Contact. This will reveal the extent and seriousness of Florencia's crimes, and show how they've flouted Universal law."

"Well, Florencia's politicians have laid the blame on Handover," Vito said.

"We all know Handover is one of their capitals," Cook intervened.

"Their planet is dying, and they are desperate."

"Their planet is dying because they've fouled their home nest and are looking to foul another," Alec snapped.

"So…if you're able to take Omar—and how you'll do that I have no idea, but for argument's sake let's say you do—wouldn't that make them even more desperate?" challenged Vito.

"That's my plan, old friend. I want them desperate enough to listen to an alternative."

"And what is that?" Cook asked.

"I'll get to that soon enough." Alec paused briefly before continuing, "No, gentlemen, this is what we're going to do." He launched into his plan.

After Alec had revealed the first part of his plan, there was an eerie silence in the room, except for the faint electronic buzzing in the background. He allowed the older man and younger man listening to digest everything he had said before he continued.

"And these so-called Sephtha creatures and other scouts on Omar are *sure* that there's no Intergalactic fleet securing the system?" Admiral Cook said at last.

"Like I said, sir, less than half a Galactic fleet secures the outer rim of the system, and only a small military station orbits the world of Omar itself."

"And the space station—you're sure it's meant for Omar, and not the Rangyyr system, as it looks to be on the travel plans?"

Vito murmured, "Rangyyr could be a decoy. We know Florencia has established at least two artificial singularity gates there, and it's possible one of them leads directly to Omar."

"Did you take that into consideration, Alec?" Cook asked. "There are at least three Intergalactic fleets at Rangyyr, and a number of mid-sized stations, some of which are probably disguised Omega battle stations." Cook zoomed in on the Rangyyr system. "It's one of their reserve gatherings."

"Indeed, I *have* taken it into consideration," Alec replied, "and the situation is well in hand. We'll sabotage both gates if necessary. However, once they discover that they're about to lose one of their precious Omega stations, then where do you think they'll send reinforcements? Omar or the Omega?" Alec said with a mocking smile. "Florencia will want to use most of those reserves against Marengo, I suspect. I could be wrong, but it doesn't matter. Trust me on this one."

"It's doable," Cook murmured.

"So you like this plan?"

"What is there to like? We're at war, and with your father and the military being held back by a mad dictator and a bunch of greedy civilians, *something* significant must happen, and very soon at that. Look!" cook gestured towards the holoimage. "Except for a few bloody battles, nothing has changed the front line—not to mention that many of our fleets are being directed to that one-way system of Milac."

"It's a trap or a front, that entire campaign, to lure many of our fleets there to engage Florencia, only to be stranded there for months before they can reach normal space again."

"Smart move by the enemy," Alec responded to Vito.

"Doesn't your father understand this?" Vito said, sounding upset.

Instead of answering, Alec zoomed in on Milac, and tightened in on one of the many fleets fighting in the system. The Nastasturian fleets were marked NFF, for Nastasturus Federation Forces. "Does that answer your comment about my father? He sent two fleets there, one galactic, and one InterGalactic, while President Alexander sent ten times as many from his new Federation Force."

"Why doesn't your father stop him?"

Cook intervened, "Vito, please. You know better than that. Our Marshal is doing what he can, but unfortunately the politicians are far too powerful, and they're afraid that Guss is going to become a dictator."

"Yeah, well, they've got their own now. Boy, I'm I glad you made me this offer, Alec."

Alec said, "The 'front war' must end and those regions must be taken, or all we're doing is sending good people into a black hole to die."

"Simply said, but you're right, Alec. Your plan...well, normally I wouldn't give it a day, but what the hell. What do we have to lose?"

"Wonder what Father might say?"

"Leave him to me. Just make sure that if you think or sense that anything is amiss, then withdraw immediately. You definitely don't have the numbers when it comes to ship, crew, or troops. Whatever it is you decide to do, do *not* divide your forces—not that there will be much to divide."

Cook turned towards Alec with a very stern expression, and kept staring until Alec finally nodded in consent. "Promise me," Cook demanded. "Say it."

"I promise."

"I'll do what I can to speed things up from here, and will send you reinforcements as soon as we have any."

"And I'll go to Samari and gather what troops are available there from the Samarians and the Grisamm, as you have ordered," Vito added, sounding a bit more enthusiastic that his older colleague.

"At least Grimm and Bentor will be happy that something is finally happening," Cook said, shaking his head.

"Can you imagine? Bentor finally gets to use that hammer of his," Alec joked, but the others failed to understand his reference.

They went back to their ship, and just as they were about to board, Vito stopped and stood there, staring thoughtfully at the overhead while tapping his fingers on his lips. Cook had already entered the cramped craft, and leaned out, asking, "Something troubling you, son?"

"I was just thinking…what about the inaugural parade?"

Alec and Cook looked at each other and laughed.

"Well, you young Turks have a few weeks before the parade to do some conquering," Cook chuckled, and as he thought about what he'd said, he laughed again.

Five minutes later, the little ship headed back into space, escorted by the two fighters.

TEN

ONE of the first temporary military bases erected on Fantaka was the Pilot School. Every pilot, new and old, had to train or retrain from scratch, because Alec demanded that they be able to fly in-atmosphere as well as space, and that they be able to handle different types of atmospheres. Since the atmospheric flight simulators were only so good, it helped to learn within an actual planetary atmosphere. They used one Omega cruiser, *Crusher-11*, as a mother ship, and its main docking bay had been remodified for the new fighters that were still in the early stages of development. The training fighters looked very different from the actual fighters, and as soon as the pilots and instructors noticed something amiss or something that could be improved, they informed the engineers who had taken up half the space in the cargo region and turned it into a factory and science dorms for research. Normally, the Nastasturian military had special facilities for this kind of R&D, but Section 21 had none, and had to make do with what they had.

Former Captain Behl—now Master Instructor and Wing-Admiral, head of pilot training—leaned back in his comfortable chair and looked out the window of his office as *Crusher-11* finally reached its home port of Fantaka. Something was definitely amiss; ships in their hundreds, perhaps thousands—from small fighters to shuttles, supply ships, scout ships, frigates, and even destroyers—were docking with their respective Omega class ships, all of which were acting as motherships. Larger ships had been covered with camouflage shells, making them look like ugly, clumsy transport ships. *Decoys*, Nikko thought. He suspected that the fleet, or rather part of it, was heading away for a major training run; at least, that was what he and he knew many others hoped for.

Over the past few months, he had trained and drilled the best of the pilots in the forces; the selection progress had been rigorous for the fighter school, so those pilots were very good indeed. Any pilot that didn't make the cut was sent back to the fleet and given an assignment piloting some other craft; still important work, but it didn't have the cachet of the fighter accreditation. Today he would report proudly to Alec that he had almost 600 new fighter pilots so far—far from the 70,000 Alec had requested, but still good progress. Then there were the reserves, as Nikko called them: about 2,000 fighter pilots, good enough but not as good as the ones he had trained personally. They hadn't quite made the cut, but they were still good pilots, and would soon have their own fighters as well. Nikko would advise Alec not to use these pilots against drones, as they were definitely not ready for that; but then again, perhaps in time some of them would improve.

Behl wasn't surprised that most of the 600 pilots he'd taught came from worlds that were far less advanced than Nastasturus in general. Their technology was limited, but their pilots made up for that being some of the best he had ever trained—just like those crazy little Vixens.

Thinking about the Vixens brought a smile to his face, as he thought back to when they had met their first class and helped Nikko to train them. Nikko had left the Research and Development HQ regretting having gone there in the first place. One thing was for sure: there were definitely too many bloody chefs in that kitchen. No matter what the many different arguments were about, two things were certain; one, they were building and improving all different types of fighters, scout ships, and battle shuttles in various sizes, and a few new types of bombers and missile craft. Second, they were rushing everything, and that was never a good thing. But still, somehow, they had been able to prepare many new goodies and inventions, upgrading some of the old craft and grafting their best aspects onto the new ones.

The problem was that the oldest fighters were almost a century old, and needed a lot of modifications. Behl had always thought that when the modern worlds had start using unmanned drones for fighters, the people in power had lost several generations of good pilots. Many of the colonial worlds and polities that weren't as technologically advanced as the larger federations still used manned fighters, though, and Behl knew that Alec had purchased many fighters from the worlds that remained neutral. All of them needed upgrading, and that was done back at the Fantaka system, to his and everyone else's relief.

Sighing, he rose and headed to one of the many hangar bays, where his best pilots had gathered. He had handpicked them himself after rigorous testing, and his plan was to turn them into a cadre of instructors. The original instructors back at Fantaka had proven themselves to be excellent at training pilots in the basics, and therefore Behl didn't want any of them here; they were needed where they were. This was the place where the best pilots were sent, and only the best of those would pass his tests; those that didn't would be sent back for normal pilot duty. For battle, only the best would do.

All one hundred pilots were present, hovering around and climbing over the latest test fighter like the curious monkeys they were, sharing what in Nikko Behl's opinion was their somewhat limited expertise. They barely noticed his arrival. For a while he stood there observing them, and was just about to clear his throat when someone must have noticed him, for there was a sudden shout of "Admiral on deck!"

A moment later, the pilots were lined up in a perfect ten by ten square. There were at least a dozen different species present, with roughly equal numbers of males and females, and those who were both or neither. When the room was completely silent, Nikko cleared his throat and gestured for everyone to turn around and look out a large port into the main docking bay of the ship. There were many ships docked there, from frigates to destroyers, shuttles and other service vessels carrying people and payloads between them. Suddenly, seemingly out of nowhere, four single-being fighters shimmered into view that looked like no others any of the pilots had ever seen before.

At first, they flew in a tight diamond formation through the enormous open docking bay, then split up in four directions and darted around the enormous space in all directions, nearly causing accidents and barely scraping by the occasional shuttle with a hairsbreadth of space. It wasn't long before an alarm sounded, followed by many blinking lights and warning shouts from hidden speakers. The onlookers observed in awe.

Behl muttered something into his communicator, and suddenly the four fighters formed up and carefully descended onto the platform where their audience stood, landing in a perfect row within microseconds of each other. The cockpits opened up, and out jumped four small-framed pilots, all wearing the latest piloting gear, including their most advanced comp-linked helmets yet. Each bore sidearms, and as they scurried up to the waiting admiral, they affixed small machine blasters on their backs, then lined up facing the admiral at attention.

"As you were," Nikko bellowed, and everyone stood at ease. He walked a few paces towards the onlookers, who quickly dressed their lines; and as he did, the four new pilots, still helmeted, took up positions next to him, two on each side.

"Allow me to introduce to you some of best pilots who've ever flown. These are the infamous Vixens, whom I know all of you have heard about, and probably none of you believed really existed. Be very aware of them, for all the rumors you have hear about them are true. They were stolen from their families as children, and raised to serve under one of the most feared pirate leaders in history. Though they are former pirates, they have been pardoned by the highest levels of our governments and are now recognized as Nastasturian citizens of the Second Elite Class, in gratitude for their service to our Federation."

A murmur swept the pilots; most were twice the age of the girls, but some were just as young as the Vixens, or even younger. All of them stared in awe, because the flying the Vixens had demonstrated had been exceptional.

"Lassies?" Behl said expectantly.

One by one, the helmets were removed and there stood Kirra, Zicci, Mohama, and Miska, all of them sweaty and their hair a mess. They looked mischievous, though, and little Zicci eyed the male pilots with an obvious appetite, blowing hair from her face, while Miska wet her lips and whipped her tail around like a cat's. Mohama released a lady-like burp, while Kirra spit on the floor, saying something about how the humidifier in her crappy helmet worked about as well a lame dick. Otherwise, they completely ignored their new fans, focusing on their Admiral and mentor.

Nikko observed each and every one of the recruits in-depth for anyone showing any animosity or dislike in general towards the young aces, but he could make out none—at least for now. He knew that many people hated pirates, while others didn't even know of their existence, or dismissed them as legend. Slowly the pilots approached the girls, and in moments they were surrounded and bombarded with questions.

All the pilots present were first rate, and now Admiral Behl had to turn them into aces like the girls, and eventually into instructors; and he knew time was of the essence, as Alec's last communication had indicated they would soon see action. There had been no reason to argue with the young man, because Nikko Behl knew Alec better than most. He turned his attention to the little crowd.

"Vixens," he said loudly, heading in their direction. There was some shuffling of feet and commotion as a path was made for him. "Ladies, pick a squad of 25 recruits each, and initiate the program I have discussed with you. Their fighters are down in Bay 17. These are top-notch pilots, you'll find, and we need them for the war effort—so don't break them, please."

There was a rustle of nervous laughter among the recruits, but little did they know he hadn't been joking. Oh, they'd learn. "Otherwise," he continued, "Do what you must, and don't hold back. Just make them ready, and then report back later on tonight after supper. Questions?"

There was a brief silence, and then Zicci cleared her throat while the other pilots lined up again in a perfect square. "So, we can do anything we want with them, you say?"

There were some strange expressions amongst the pilots at the cheeky question; they looked on curiously, waiting for their Admiral's outburst. However, Nikko knew better than getting upset with the Vixens' lack of discipline. They had trained with the Grisamm for over a year, and if the Grisamm Order hadn't been able to teach these little troublemakers discipline, then why even bother? However, this laxness was extended to the Vixens alone, and no one else.

Not realizing that it was a trick question, Behl just repeated, "Don't break them," and nodded; but in his defense, he did look a bit suspicious. He then turned away, heading back towards his office many levels up, and far away in the bowels of the moon-sized ship. The last thing he heard was the girls arguing.

Zicci: "He's mine."

Miska: "No, bitch, he's mine."

Zicci: "I'm going to blow them all!"

Mohama: "By Gull, you two were around Nina too bloody much."

Kirra: "Why argue? We'll eventually fuck all of them anyway."

Mohama: "Zicci, don't you have a boyfriend? Dack or something?"

"Dropped his dumb ass. Caught him with some dude."

"Didn't knew you were such a prude, bitch."

"I'm not, you twin whore from hell, that bastard lied to me about it, and…"

Admiral Behl stopped in his tracks and squinted his eyes hard; then he just shook his head and left the poor newbies to their fate.

He smiled, thinking back to those first training days; he hadn't felt this alive in a long time. But then, his mind and expression grew dark when he thought of the time ahead; after all, there was a war raging, already murdering people in the millions and causing billions of people to flee for their lives, becoming refugees. He started when he realized he had lost himself in thought; now he was running late. All senior staff had been ordered to report to the Key Administrator for War, Alec von Hornet.

He hurried to his waiting shuttle and scrambled into his seat. He didn't like being pampered by a bunch of snot-noses, but he'd started to become accustomed to it. Several young officers made sure he was all right, and anything he needed was provided. He waved, irritated, when a young officer asked him if he wanted some refreshments. Shortly thereafter, the shuttle docked to one of the larger space stations orbiting Fantaka. He hurried towards the assembly hall, and when he reached it, he noticed that he wasn't the last person at least, and that the meeting hadn't actually started. He let out a sigh as he calmed himself. He had no idea who most of the people in the room were. Ornately dressed civilians and many different military uniforms; *what a mishmash*, he thought. *Alec should do something about it; there must be more unity among everyone here.*

Suddenly Alec himself entered, followed by Grimm and Cook. The Lord Chamberlain was just about to announce them when Alec waved with his arm for him not to do so. All of them quickly took their seats around a large table that rose out of the floor, causing some people to scuffle out of the way. The room was circular, like the table, and one bulkhead was lined with large windows offering a clear view of near-space.

"I hope everyone is doing well, and that everything is going according to plan," Alec announced, his voice amplified by nano-speakers floating in the air around the room. "It's time to take out some of the available crew and fleet for a few test runs. I will leave Lord Asturius of the Grisamm Order in charge until I return."

Alec raised his hand as he noticed interruptions from several civilians. "Gentlebeings, please. At the beginning of this endeavor I was liberal with the code of conduct around here, but that has to end, because I'm tired of the endless squabbling. So all of you are temporarily hired by me for the formal establishment of this colony world, and the rest of the worlds in this system, including the moons and larger asteroids and Kuiper Belt objects. I and I alone will determine what's going to happen to this world and system, and no one else. You can answer to me as a single, unified force, or you can leave the project."

He stopped speaking, looking one person after another dead in their eyes, making sure they understood the seriousness of his words. Then he continued. "I am not a despot, and I will not become one. I am a loyal Nastasturian citizen, and a citizen of the universe. I have their best interests in mind. In time, I will reveal my plans for this system; and again, if you don't like it, then you may leave. For now, follow my newly-posted procedures for fleet departure, and then keep up the good work. Lord Asturius will arrive later today to assume command. He is your acting Key Administrator for War until I return, and his words and will should be treated as my own. Should something go wrong, then official guidelines will be addressed by House Hornet."

After a few questions and answers, Alec dismissed the entire assembly but for some of his senior officers, and he gestured for Nikko to follow him.

"Old friend, you will remain here and continue the pilot training. *Crusher-11* is still at your disposal, but I'm asking you to keep to this and adjacent star systems. Now, I haven't had time to read your report completely, so how many elite pilots vs. standard pilots do we have for our fighters?"

Nikko gave Alec a suspicious look. "About 600 elite and about 2,000 regulars, but they need more training. I need the Vixens and at least one hundred of the new elite pilots to form a training cadre and continue the training, and at least half of the standard pilots. That'll let us start turning out decent pilots *en masse*."

There was a brief silence, and then Alec turned to Grimm and Cook, who were whispering to one another.

"I need two of the Vixens," he stated, "more because of political reasons than anything else, as well as 400 of the elites and 1,600 of the regulars. Their new ships are at Shipyard 37. Have them report in and follow the instructions on their respective log computers."

"Alec, enough!" Behl snapped. "I wasn't born yesterday, son. You're going to war, aren't you? That's why Vito isn't here. Let me guess: he's at Samari, and that's where you just came from, Grimm."

"How very perceptive of you, Nikko," Grimm said cheerfully. "I told you that you should have let him in on everything, Alec. You have to start trusting more senior officers."

Alec snorted. "Enough lecturing. And before you ask, Nikko—no, you can't come. I need you here."

Behl was about to object, but when he saw Alec raising his eyebrows, he held back and said instead, "Why two of the Vixens? Why risk any of those who are left?"

"When word gets out about what we've done, we'll need them as front runners for our new fighter fleet. Their reputation alone will scare the crap of our enemy. That's the idea, anyway," Cook intervened.

Behl thought about everything he'd just learned and then said, concerned, "But we don't have a proper battle commission, or any fleet attachments to one for the main fleets from Nastasturus, do we?"

"You might as well let him know," Cook told Alec.

"We aren't engaging Florencia as a bunch of marauders or a group of scavengers, Nikko. But we *are* liberating a certain system that Handover has invaded illegally, something few people know or care about. We won't conquer, but we *will* liberate."

Behl wasn't happy with the answer, and his body language didn't hide his emotions.

"After all, in a few weeks, we must look our best for that very important inaugural fleet celebration, before receiving our official marching orders." Alec walked up to his friend and placed a hand on Nikko's shoulder, then fixed him with a calm stare. "Trust me on this one, old friend."

Nikko nodded, then looked Alec dead in the eyes; and, giving no regard to Alec's currently civilian rank, declared, "If you're expecting me to stay here once you have your fleet at 100% and only train pilots, then you have another think coming, boy—unless you want a bloody revolution on your hands. If there's going to be action, then I'll be there. I'll let it go this time, but..." He stopped in the middle of his sentence, because he noticed that Cook and Grimm didn't like the way he had addressed Alec, but Alec only smiled.

"I promise you that in time, you'll see more than enough action, Nikko. But don't make me beg as a civilian for you to remain here. We both know that we *must* have many more Elite pilots, and you're the man for the job."

Nikko nodded, then grabbed Alec in a trembling embrace and whispered, "Give them hell for me...and Alexa. Give them hell, boy."

Alec pulled back, both men still locked by the forearms. Nikko looked into a friendly smile, and then he noticed Alec's eyes; and he knew then that hell would soon be considered a paradise for anyone standing against this young man.

ELEVEN

WHILE what was now being called the Third Universal War was raging between the larger federations and between Florencia and Marengo, all of them fighting for dominance, a small fleet consisting of some thirty large transport vessels—most of them made for transporting different types of fluids—escorted by six Crusher cruisers and their support ships slowed at the outskirts of the remote system of Samari, where they were met up by another fleet that included two Ambassador-class super-cruisers, another 20 destroyers, and well over 50 frigates. All of them headed inside the two giants, docking there to conceal their numbers. There were also four large support cruisers in the combined fleet, and as many large medical frigates, all heading towards an enormous oval-shaped platform ship nearby. Most of them docked inside large camouflage covers that disguised the ships, making them too look like different types of transport ships; and once the disguises we donned, they lined up with the other "freight" ships in a long column, while the two Ambassador cruisers—the *Drakh*, belonging to Bentor, and the newest Grisamm Ambassador cruiser, *Thunder*—kept station nearby. *Thunder* had been a gift from Alec to Grimm, which he had ordered a while back, after returning home from his terrible ordeal at the hands of Zorif af Sun and her Gormé friends. It was perhaps the best ship in fleet at the moment.

Crusher-5 remained Alec's flagship, to Captain Copola's dismay, and the acting "Mother" to the small fleet. It took the better part of the day to get the fleet organized, and many shuttles traveled back and forth to Samari, bringing on more troops and crew. Once the last shuttle headed back towards Samari, the convoy moved out toward their destiny. A large artificial singularity gate opened up at the behest of the *Crusher-5*, and after several probes had been launched through it, the fleet followed. Once the last ship had entered, the many hundreds of orbs that had expanded the gate followed, allowing the gate to shrink back to its normal microscopic size. Nearby lay a few hidden stealth probes and unobtrusive asteroids encrusted with sensors, guarding the secret gate.

Inside one of the enormous enclosed bays on the platform ship, *Carrier-One*, stood Alec, Miska, and Zicci. There were hundreds of fighters in the bay; some of them were being repaired, while others were undergoing maintenance. Thousands of people hurried back and forth; there was a strange, tense atmosphere in place, punctuated by nervous laughter and cursing. Orders were shouted, and the intercom provided updates and new orders constantly. Smoke and mist floated through parts of the bay.

"Remember, girls, that it's of utmost importance that you don't get yourself killed. Stay back and issue orders; these two fine gentlemen are both commanders, and will be accompanying you, helping with tactics."

Both girls cast each other sour expressions.

"Commander Saulk will go with you, Miska."

A young man Alec's age stepped forward; of the Krone species, he had a friendly expression and nodded his head, tendrils bobbing.

"And for you, Zicci, you'll have Commander Bess."

Another man with pure black skin and white eyes from the Mirana system stepped forward and gave Kirra a smile. It was supposed to be friendly, but that effort failed, since the little man had hundreds of fangs cluttering his mouth.

"Why is Zicci's battle group getting drone ships attached to their wings? Some even have those large mines, whatever they're called."

"They will need them, Miska, whereas you won't."

"I thought mines were illegal?"

"So is invading worlds, especially worlds that haven't yet evolved to the Space Age."

An alarm echoed through the bay, followed by a voice ordering the Second Battle Wing to stand by for launch.

"That's us. Bess, take the front; I'll be just behind you," Zicci ordered.

Bess gave her an odd look before climbing up into the front cockpit, while Zicci and Miska embraced. Crew helped the commander get strapped inside, and his helmet attached.

"Be safe, sister," Miska said.

"Always."

They held each other's forearms, and stared at each other for a moment.

"We're becoming fewer, aren't we." It wasn't a question.

"As long as we aren't extinct. Be careful out there, Zicci."

They embraced again, and then Zicci headed towards the aft cockpit of her fighter. She waved her support crew away as she jumped agilely into her seat and immediately began attaching her helmet. Suddenly Alec leaned over her, adjusting the helmet instead of the crew member who had handed it to her.

"Remember, Zicci, you only have 360 ships," Alec said quietly. "According to the experts, an action like this would normally require five or ten times that number—so be careful. Take no chances."

Zicci glared at Alec with an expression that told him that she'd heard this before about a million and one times. Alec just smiled and continued fixing her helmet.

The fighter was camouflaged in black and gray, stealthy looking except for the two much smaller drone ships that had temporarily been attached atop the wings. Both drones could be piloted by the crew on the fighters, or set on autopilot; they would then engage any enemy nearby, based on IFF transponder codes, and if set for self-destruction, could more or less act as missiles. This would be ideal if they encountered large ships that the fighters couldn't otherwise handle. Half of the ships also included two large missiles almost as long as the fighter itself—basically ship-killers—and the other half bore three large mines each.

The support personal hurried for cover as the ships lifted from the deck one by one and headed toward the exit in the aft of the ship.

Alec and Miska headed towards a large viewport, and Alec tapped a button on the wall to raise the blast shield, allowing them to look into the Big Dark. Soon, three large formations of 120 fighters each were hovering outside the carrier. Suddenly, one of the fighters made a dash towards Alec and Miska, followed by a laugh over the intercom from Zicci when both ducked and covered.

"Amateurs," Zicci shouted, and her words echoed over the intercom nearby.

"Bitch," Miska replied, but only got faint laughter in response as the fighters jetted off into the darkness. "You better make it back," Miska whispered, drying her eyes.

She felt Alec take her by her shoulder; at first she froze, feeling uncomfortable, but then she relaxed her head and body against Alec.

"She'll make it," he stated.

"How do you know?"

"I don't," he admitted, "but I believe she will, and sometimes believing is half the battle."

"Thank you, Alec." She looked up at him. "Do you ever think about Alexa?"

Alec shrugged and stepped away from her, holding up his hands in protest.

Miska shrugged and smiled. She had her answer.

"I didn't, I—" he stammered.

"I know, don't worry—and thank you for embracing me. Sometime a hug from a friend can get you through a lot."

Alec sighed and relaxed. "I miss Alexa every moment of every day, Miska."

"I and the others do too, but we won't allow what happened to her, Tara, and Nina to ruin our lives."

"Good for you. Now, do you have a moment so we can go over the details of your operation? Yes, again."

Miska inclined her head graciously, and the two of them moved to another hangar on the other side of the ship that was equally as busy as the first one, and twice as large, with hundreds of shuttles and fighters crammed inside along with thousands of people.

"**SECTION** leaders, diamond formation for each section, and report your wing status before accelerating to FTL," Commander Bess ordered, while Zicci looked over her flight board and scowled at a fighter flying a bit too close.

"Check your distance, Alpha-2," Zicci advised, and the other ship eased farther away, into its proper position.

"Section 2, all wings are go; I repeat, all wings are go."

"Section 3, all wings are go, all wings are go."

The fighters trembled as their engines grabbed the fabric of spacetime, accelerating them into the Big Dark and away from the safety of the fleet. As they breached light speed, they vanished. Zicci disregarded the strange flashing scenery outside the cockpit, though she caught some quiet "ohs" and "ahs" from Commander Bess. "First time?" she asked.

"In a small ship like this one, yes, Senior Commander. At super-luminal speeds everything seems much...closer. And smoother."

"Don't worry, you get used to it. It'll be bumpier when we drop to sublight or accelerate to attack speed. And lose the 'Senior Commander' shit, Bess, it's only us now."

"What about the others?"

"Who?"

"The other pilots?"

"We're all a team, sure, but in the end we're each alone in our little hyperspace bubble. And it's each ship for itself if everything turns to crap."

"You done this quite a few times, then." It wasn't really a question; Bess had heard about the rumors about the Vixens, and knew he was flying with one of them; however, sometimes rumors were exactly what they seemed.

Zicci ignored the question, deciding that Bess talked too much, and turned her attention to the main screen, which indicated they were closing in on the target. She made a few final checks on the console and then reconfigured her flight yoke to battle handles. The flight stick folded itself up and vanished into the console, while a hand-sized half-formed ball emerged near her right arm. The fighter's seat was constructed to reconfigure at need into something workable for almost any body plan and size, within certain limits, and to adapt to specific preferences. A joystick emerged on her left side.

The "ball" was for the fighter axes and fire control, and the joystick on the left was for speed and brakes. She also had foot controls for fine adjustments, and her helmet contained an advanced target and fire control for some of the weaponry systems, linked straight into the ship. It also contained eye movement and sip-and-blow backups of all the other controls, in case she or the main systems were disabled.

The fighters exited superluminal and quickly reformed into three diamond formations. Zicci's First Section took point, while the Second Section took up the right position and the Third took the left. Each section included two wings of 60 ships each, each wing consisting of ten flight squads of six ships each—six ships for the six fronts in 3-D space. Normally four ships would remain in two-by-two formations, while one ship each took station above and one below the formation.

As the ships closed in on a smallish world orbiting a yellow dwarf star, they activated their stealth and cloaking devices, disappearing from sight and sensors.

"No indications yet," Bess reported.

"Wait until we have them in line of sight."

"Aye, Commander Zicci. Everyone reporting in and all ships accounted for; radio silence until ordered otherwise."

"Fine, though soon enough everyone will be screaming and crying like a bunch of little bitches, I think."

"Like *what*?" Commander Bess turned his seat 180 degrees, looking at Zicci, who sat a bit higher and several feet away.

"Just a joke, bonehead. Don't worry about it."

"Ah. This is what's called a nervous conversation before battle, then, and..."

Zicci tapped a button, a bit frustrated, and Bess's seat turned back to its original position.

"I'm just saying..." Bess protested.

"Yeah, well, don't. And by the way, I hope you brought a shit bag, because things are about to get ugly. Here we go—and there they are."

Commander Bess's eyes widened as he saw what lay several hundred thousand kilometers ahead. The monitor station in the far distance was clotted with hundreds of ships and space stations. "That is far too many ships," Bess protested. "Our intel must be wrong. We must abort!"

"Shut your hole, or I'll abort your ass into space. Now, where are the gates?"

"There must be at least seven of them, and there were only supposed to be two," Bess complained, as if the universe itself had conspired to fool them. At this point, that wouldn't have surprised Zicci; but tiring of Bess's voice and attitude, she said firmly, while turning Bess's seat to face her. "*We will engage as ordered.* Is that clear? Now find me the bloody gates—and relax. If everything goes wrong, we only die."

Before the little dark-skinned man could answer, his seat was turned back around. Bess's mouth moved, but nothing came out; and then there was no time to say anything, as the fighter accelerated into attack speed, followed by the rest of the attack force.

A moment later, Bess choked out. "There are indeed seven gates, but only three appear to be fully operational..."

"Send encoded messages to Section Two to take out the nearest one, and for Section Three to take out the next. We'll change our mission orders; rather than Section One remaining in reserve, we'll hit the farthest black hole gate. Make sure that Sections Two and Three coordinate with us so that all three attacks are simultaneous."

Commander Bess quickly sent the messages as ordered, knowing full well that there was a small risk that the message could be intercepted, giving away their location. Once the pilots started to communicate, the stealth and cloaking effects of the fighters would be almost useless.

The diamond formation split as the three sections headed toward their separate destinies. Zicci stared at her console screen for a moment, thinking back, trying to remember her past before all this—before she had been captured and forced into piracy. Like most children taken at a young age, she didn't remember much; so instead she thought about her only family, the Vixens, now reduced to four; but instead of bringing her to tears, the thought of their losses infuriated her and snapped her back into focus on her mission.

Her eyes and mind were concentrated on the target she was closing on. It was an enormous singularity gate, large enough to transfer an Omega-class space station. Zicci disregarded the many ships on station around it, zig-zagging a course through the traffic, waiting for an alarm to be raised, warning her that they had been spotted. But nothing happened. *All too easy*, she thought as she slowed, allowing for any stragglers in her section to find their position in the formation. Her computer soon accounted for everyone; and when the target was only moments away, Zicci broke silence: "Demons, engage!"

Her words were followed by sixty sprint missiles leaping for their targets, various points on the constructs surrounding the wormhole, huge engines that had expanded it to such a vast size and held it stable. Less than a second later, the gate lit up the entire region—but not because it had been destroyed by any explosions, as none of the missiles had reached the targets yet. Instead, there were suddenly hundreds of ships before them, exiting at high velocity, leading an Omega station that was just beginning to emerge from the expanded singularity. Zicci remained calm, smiling drily at Commander Bess's expression, which she could see on a monitor on her console. She realized the danger all of them were facing, and barked new orders. "Fire everything you have on that big fat bitch—its shields are down! Drop all the mines and boost them towards that armada."

An alarm went off on Zicci's console, letting her know that they had finally been made—half a second before the first sprinters struck their intended targets, lighting up space with a ripple of explosions. The fighters of Section 1 spun around 180 degrees on their retrorockets, boosting at high velocity toward their rendezvous point.

The fighters of Section Three met them there. "Where's Two?" Zicci demanded.

"Middle of a dogfight," Bess said calmly, his hands flying across the console.

"All sections, prepare to melee-launch your drones, focused on the nearest cruisers. Split up into wings; wing leaders, independent command. Assist Section Two, and on my orders, boost for open space."

Her orders were punctuated by screaming and chatter over the radio, and she repeated them, adding, "Wing leaders take command, and prepare for a dog-eat-dog fight. Try and get away from this madness and rendezvous at the second or third rendezvous point. Acknowledge!" Acknowledgements came in as she locked onto one enemy fighter after another with her magma guns and blasted them into oblivion, as easily as if she were swatting insects.

The drones launched and veered to the sides, looking for trouble, while the rest of Section One merged with Section Three and went to assist Two. Zicci noted that thousands of enemy drones had been launched towards her formations—not unexpectedly—and immediately she accelerated her fighter toward the first dozen drones, locking her targeting system on them. She was just about to cluster-fire her point defense missiles to take them out when the entire region went white in an mammoth flash, like a sun had gone nova nearby. The explosion from the bisected Omega station as the black hole gate imploded sent shock waves through local spacetime, causing the nearest ships—mostly the Omega's own armada—

to either lose fusion containment in their engines and explode, or tumble uncontrolled in all directions.

The attack dissolved into a melee from hell.

"Watch your back, One-Actual," a voice from her helmet warned Zicci. She could see that her aft gun was auto-firing on a mix of several manned and drone enemy fighters, some of which seemed to be barely under control; her little fighter shuddered as she clipped the aft nacelle of a larger ship, and for a nanosecond, she too lost control. The autopilot saved them, thank Gull.

Heart in her throat, Zicci watched as explosions and flashes rippled through the space around her. The sensor console was useless; the instruments not fried by the EMP of the combined Omega explosion/wormhole implosion were too confused by the melee to make any sense. There were too many ships in local space to track accurately. Zicci shut it down and enlarged the battle screen, eyeballing the display to dodge her way through debris and ships, while continuing to lock on and fire at the enemy. She barely noticed as the kill total on her display scaled upward. Meanwhile, Commander Bess did his best, issuing orders to the wing commanders and updating Zicci.

"Ma'am, we have 52 casualties…no, make that 56…no, make that…"

"Enough! I can see the bloody casualties! Order all ships to do their best to pick up any survivors if the cockpits are still intact, and make sure that none of our ships are taken intact by the enemy."

Zicci veered hard to port, after an enemy fighter that was pursuing Alpha 2; and just as she had it locked on and fired, it too fired, sending Alpha 2 into oblivion. Zicci's fighter flew straight through the expanding debris and gasses of the two explosions, and she scanned for the cockpit pods of Alpha 2. She found one, and headed towards its location. Once her ship was near enough she launched a hook that grabbed the ejected cockpit, pulling it in and attaching it to her left wing. Just as it was attached, though, it exploded after being struck by a round from another fighter advancing from the front. Zicci cursed and spun a 180 on the retros, boosting to follow the bastard; moments later, she got a lock on it and took it out with her forward guns. As she bypassed the expanding debris cloud, Zicci raised her eyes and took in many additional ships advancing from all directions, as more explosions, large and small—marking deaths of capital ships and fighters alike—flickered around her in the distance. She noted one large ship headed towards the planet's surface, followed by a small space station.

"Bess! Order all our ships to sprint for open space and go to FTL. Get everyone away and..."

A voice overrode hers. "Zicci, get your ships out of there. Use our dropway."

"Alec, what the bloody Gull—"

A gray mass passed her fighter, and over a dozen large ships were hit with as many explosions a microsecond later. It took Zicci a section to realize what had happened: it was ships from Section 21, attacking at Galactic speed—a very dangerous, very reckless practice within a system, much less in the vicinity of a planet. Stunned, Zicci related Alec's orders to all her remaining fighters, and one by one they headed towards the spot where the Galactic strike had originated.

Suddenly there was another flash, and a singularity gate opened in front of Zicci's section, blocking their way. "Evasive maneuvers; evasive maneuvers! Make a roundabout and continue towards safety! Move to the dropway the fleet is providing for us!" Zicci ordered.

A smaller black hole gate emerged next to the single craggy moon orbiting the planet, and a massive, strange ship, oval-shaped with a ring mounted on the front, entered the fray. As it slowed, several larger ships and thousands of manned fighters emerged from the gate behind it, heading straight towards Zicci's ships. There came another gray flash between the two positions, causing a ripple of small explosions to descend on the new oncoming threat, even destroying one of the larger cruisers.

"Superluminal would be nice right about now, Zicci." Alec's voice sounded calm and almost humorous.

Zicci let out a sigh, and so did Commander Bess as the coast cleared and the fighters could finally accelerate past light speed.

Zicci noticed that there were at least two-dozen capital ships from Section 21 passing them. It was impossible to dock at this speed, but that didn't matter; they were safe for now. Zicci smiled, confident... and then she noticed on her holo-screen the number of fighters lost, and more so, how many pilots were either missing or dead. Her smile vanished.

ZICCI'S fighter was the last to dock aboard *Carrier-One*. Commander Bess was helped out of the cockpit by the maintenance crew, while a couple of crew members waited by Zicci's cockpit. Hers was still locked. She was staring in shock and disbelief at the casualty count on her screen. *The attack was an utter failure,* she thought, and felt like bawling like a child.

Someone knocked on the side of the cockpit; irritated, she gestured for whoever it was to leave her alone, but the knocking just got more insistent. She turned her head and saw an old man standing there, waiting for her. She had seen him before, but couldn't place his face...and then she noticed his rank: admiral. She immediately straightened and opened up her cockpit. The old Admiral helped her out of her helmet, and then he smiled at her. "Congratulations, Commander, your strike was a success."

Zicci could only stare at him, dumbfounded. "It was a disaster, sir," she croaked. "We lost almost one third of our fighters, and half the crew on those ships are either missing or dead."

The old man nodded, then helped her out of her seat and while carrying on, "Yes, Commander, the butcher's bill was high, the cost painful. But the objective was achieved; and your three Sections managed to destroy the generators holding open not one, not two, but *three* singularity gates. To top it off, your Section alone caused the destruction of an Omega-class battle station exiting your gate, as well as most of the battle cruisers escorting it. We followed everything from the command bridge; and when Alec saw what your rocket jockeys were up against, he immediately took part of the fleet and attacked to create a diversion." She noticed that he spoke of Alec as familiarly as she did, or as Alexa had; could this be his uncle,

Admiral Cook? He patted her on the shoulder. "I can't tell you how much I regret your losses, Commander. Had our intel been more accurate, we would never have sent you in alone—but these things do happen in war. I've never seen a battle plan survive contact with the enemy, I'm afraid."

"Are you telling me to get used to it, sir?"

A bushy gray eyebrow arched. "I wouldn't have put it so bluntly, Commander, but I supposed I am."

Zicci dried her eyes with a facial tissue the nice old Admiral handed her, not wanting the other crew to notice any weakness in her. He nodded sharply. "Now talk to your people, Commander Zicci, and remember that this is a victory. Look, there goes the rest of the fleet—along with your sister Miska, with her fighters heading towards our main objective, Omar. Wouldn't have been possible if your people had failed."

She was pretty sure now that this wasn't Hadrian Cook. He was supposed to be a crusty old bastard. Zicci gave the old man a puzzled expression and asked, "We *have* met before, haven't we?"

"Indeed we have—the first time with Alec on board his little ship *Predator,* at New Frontier-16. Admiral Busch at your service." He clicked his heels and bowed his head as she saluted.

She gave his name some thought, and then remembered, "Sir, weren't you supposed to be stationed with the regular Nastasturian forces?"

"I was, Commander, but Admiral Cook managed to get me back under his command again, thank Gull, and I was able to bring my attack wing with me, thanks to Alec's father. At least now Section 21 has a few more battle cruisers."

"Were those the ships that came to our rescue?"

"Some of them. Anyway, time to gather your troops and head towards the debriefing, young lady. I'll be the new Admiral commanding your sections, and we'll soon head after the rest of the fleet for Omar."

Zicci nodded and then saluted the Admiral again; he returned the salute and then walked away toward a group of waiting staff officers, who were inspecting the fighters. Before he got far, he turned back and said, with a twinkle in his eyes, "Don't expect any special treatment from me, kid, just because I like the way you dance."

Remembering the seductive dance she and her friends had performed on New Frontier-16 several years ago, she blushed from the crown of her head to the tips of her toes. She had no idea she was still capable of that.

Zicci was still in shock as she looked out one of the large bay windows, on several capital ships passing the carrier. Hearing movement behind her, she turned and faced the survivors of her Section, all of them lined up, waiting for her. She took a deep breath and marched over to them.

"Division Commander on deck!" Bess shouted.

Boots hit the steel in unison, and all the pilots stood at attention. At first, Zicci dared not look anyone in his or her eyes, but eventually she did; and she noticed that all the pilots and navigators looked satisfied, and stared back at her with what appeared to be calm respect.

TWELVE

THE concentration camp was just one of hundreds on Omar, where over seventy percent of the surviving population were held like cattle—while the remaining population, all quislings and collaborators, had taken local control and lived in luxury in homes stolen from their betters. The new leaders, all representing a minority race and religion, couldn't care less about their fellow Omari, and allowed the invaders to do as they pleased and help themselves to the planet's resources. What the idiots didn't realize was that in due time, they would suffer the same fate as the people they had betrayed.

Learning Center 93 had dozens of chimneys that belched thick, dark smoke, covering the valley with toxins. In the far distance, near a mountain range, was one of the enormous factories, drilling away into the core of the planet, extracting Tritonium silver and, by doing so, ruining the land and atmosphere with pollution. The invaders had brought in their special mobile factories for this particular purpose; they were also referred to as Population Controllers. Next to Learning Center 93 was the headquarters of the Handover occupation forces.

An enormous but temporary airfield made of giant steel grills had been laid on the far side of the camp. Over two thousand shuttles and transporters were neatly lined up on it. A few dozen large hangars and maintenance buildings were spread out around the airfield. Anti-aircraft guns were mounted all over, but most of them showed signs of being taken down and prepped to be transported away. East of the concentration camp, which could hold over a million people, was a vast military base for coordinating and housing half a million Handoverian troops, most of whom were spread all over the planet, conducting their various duties; shuttles constantly trafficked the many soldiers back and forth.

North of the Learning Center was an even larger camp housing allied troops and domestic aliens. Thousands of ground and hover tanks, mobile artillery, and missile launchers were lined up there for cleaning and maintenance. All the equipment had been used during the short "war" that conquered the world for Florencia.

Most of the prisoners and military forces were still asleep, as a new morning was about to begin. All that could be heard was the soughing of the mild storm and the strange tapping sounds from the factory. The stench of burnt flesh had settled over the entire region, and the guards who were awake, or the ones torturing prisoners, mostly wore protective helmets that filtered their air.

Several large domes arose from the ground like fat blisters on seared skin, and all were limned with pale yellow protective shields to keep the people and objects beneath them safe from any unpleasant surprises from above. The shield barriers had a distinct darker and dirtier color than normal, the result of all the smog and toxins in the air. Antennae attached to fusion power generators, some small, others as big as a house, kept the shields up and in place. From time to time there was a sparkle and an electric *zap* as rare surviving avian or reptiloid flew into one of the shields and was incinerated.

On the east side of the camp was a large mountain chain; to the south were dying fields of grass that stretched for thousands of kilometers to the Southern Sea. North of the entire blighted region was a particularly steep mountainside topped with a flat plateau, which dropped off sharply into an ocean. Clouds covered the sea far below like a white thick blanket, but they couldn't muffle the sound of waves breaking on a rocky shore.

The mesa was covered by a thick forest, which spilled over onto the opposite mountainside and continued on to the edge of the plains, where it cut off sharply. The entire region was located on a natural peninsula that ended in the cliffside headland.

Major Asshamn thought it was beautiful. He daydreamed about asserting his dominance again, knowing that his ironclad boot would strike the target with deadly precision, crushing the infant's skull and sending its brains and blood splashing in all directions. The small, ugly Chingaoan, whose face looked like a bucket of bloody worms, relished the thought. Unfortunately, such an action would end the squalling of the little non-believer; he really enjoyed the sound of suffering. The good news was that the loathsome infant's mother would no doubt wail at the top of her lungs, even as his troops ravished her.

Ah, what a beautiful day, he thought as he scampered over the muddy ground barefoot, cursing aloud just for the sheer joy of it. His toes, which ended in centimeter-long claws, couldn't be contained in standard Florencian-issue boots, and his people had evolved in the equatorial swamps of Chingao; so the muddier and filthier the ground, the better he liked it. Sniffing, he raised his head and noticed that the protective shield overhead was flickering—again. Nothing worked as it should on this stupid world, and no wonder, because of the bloody rains filled with Poulsa particles. He liked mud, but the staticky Poulsa rain, the result of the super-weapons used in the war, was the only thing that could penetrate the shields—and it stung when it struck unprotected skin. The rain also made it very difficult to communicate with ships in orbit. A tall radio tower had been erected on top of the mountain in response, providing the only secure ground-to-orbit communications link in this region.

Unfortunately, the Poulsa rain degraded the tower's exposed transceiver components, so currently, dozens of engineering troopers cluttered it while conducting repairs. A dozen hover speeders were parked at the bottom of the parked peak, and as he watched, several maintenance androids flew upward toward the antenna, preparing to add their expertise to the repairs.

The rain intensified as the wind increased, and the full power of the storm hit, bringing with it a wintry mix of freezing rain and snow. Some of the protective shields flickered and gave away due to the sudden increase in Poulsa particles or, just as likely, poor maintenance. Just another beautiful day on Omar. Major Asshamn sneered and paused for a moment, wondering if he should issue new maintenance orders. He decided against it; the idiot slugabed General was still asleep and wouldn't call for any reports until midday, because the bastard would sleep in and then he would have his usual hours-long breakfast.

No, nothing was going to change Major Assham's plans to entertain himself, and perhaps collect a head trophy or two from the locals. Besides, he had made promises to some of his more loyal troops that they would be awarded for destroying one of the rebel nests that had annoyed the HQ since shortly after it had been built.

The storm intensified, and with it came a fog from nowhere that grew thicker with every step he took. Just like home, though it annoyed him that he couldn't see a meter in front of him, even with his infravision. He finally reached the edge of the large encampment, which was protected behind one of the many shield walls made from large overlapping metal plates—a by-product of the factory—to keep local animals and the locals away from the camp. You couldn't always relay on high-tech for protection, as the failing dome shields had proven. His men and women were waiting for him, and they had brought with them eight women and their infants. Perfect. The women were being tied up along a long wooden rail and stripped naked. Ugly things, all muscular legs, because they bonded instead of walking. All screamed when they saw the rough treatment their little ones received, and those screams were like music to Assham's ears.

Everything would be fine, just fine, if it weren't for the fog; and they also had to hurry in case an MP patrol showed up. The General didn't like some of his Major Asshamn favorite activities, and had lectured him about them on numerous occasions.

"We're ready, major," a young woman said, smiling sadistically.

Ignoring her, the Major sniffed the air. Something wasn't right. Then a faint noise reached his twitching ears, and he said, "Did you hear that, lieutenant?"

The young Oman looked puzzled; not surprising, since Oman senses weren't worth a damn. She turned into the strong wind, holding an arm up for protection. After a moment she shook her head—but there it was again, a faint sound, a kind of rhythmic pulsing.

Everyone heard it this time. They looked towards the sound and squinted their eyes to see better, but the fog was too thick. Now the lieutenant said, "It sounds like drums or trembling, perhaps a horn sir. I'm not sure."

"More like hoofbeats," another said aloud. Asshamn nodded; that's what it was, he realized. He was annoyed, because his instincts told him it had to be investigated, which would delay his fun; so he ordered the young lieutenant and the soldier who had made the horn comments to check it out. Both hurried away over a small bluff, and as they did, both were engulfed by the thick fog.

None of them were aware that there were no hoofed animals native to Omar. Their job was to kill and oppress the Omarians, not to learn the planet's biota.

Moments later, there was a choking and gurgling sound; then several enormous beasts suddenly charged from the fog. The larger one in the front had his two people skewered on the meter-long horn jutting from its forehead. Too late, Asshamn realized what was happening; and in a handful of seconds, he and all his friends were decorating the horns on a menagerie of even stranger beasts.

The lead rider raised her arm, fist clenched, and the others reined their mounts to a halt. With snorts of disgust, the K'Draks slung the dead Fish Fuckers from their horns, flinging colorful blood and ichor in all directions. Keeping her voice low, the leader made her sitrep into her wristcomp.

The landforms of this region were perfect for a ground assault; where the Florencians hadn't flattened and paved the area for their own purposes, there were hundreds of low bluffs rolling like waves to the shallow forest at the bottom of the mountain range. On one of the bluffs in the distance lay two camouflaged soldiers, spying on the encampment through infrared binoculars that pieced the fog with ease. Behind the bluff below them were two more scouts tasked with handling a large communicator designed to pierce the Poulsa interference. Meanwhile, hidden in the forest were several hundred infantry, all of them heavily armed and each with a specially constructed targeting device for marking or "painting" a target through the fog, which had been encouraged, if not created, by their own engineers. In this case, the term "fog of war" was going to be quite literal. A ring of mortar-men were stationed around the facility; their job was to continually launch small bombs that silently flew half a kilometer into the sky before quietly popping, releasing a cloud of particles that generated a dense fog from the moisture in the air.

The fog continued to intensify and thicken.

Movement occurred on the northern side of the plateau, just below the dense white cloud. A large, muscular limb extended from the cover of the cloud. Its hoof, aided by stubby opposable digits, grabbed hold of the basalt and pulled yet another K'Drak upward, towards the plateau. Hundreds of similar arms extended up through the cloud, fingers opening like flowers blossoming, reaching for an edge to grab hold of.

On top of the mountain, the radio tower stood unmanned. The hundreds of maintenance workers who had been there half an hour before were gone; whether organic or android, no evidence of them remained. This couldn't be seen from the camp in the valley because of the fog, and they had therefore been the first targets of the invaders.

Down in the camp, a group officers, most Oman, trooped through the confusion towards the main command bunker located in the center of the camp. Their transport had failed to appear, and to a being, they were angry at having to soil their shoes and wet their fine uniforms in the rain. A flash of lightning, followed almost instantly by a peal of thunder, warned that the storm was about to reach its peak. The officers hunkered down, holding onto their hats as the hostile weather and powerful wind made them struggle to get inside the command bunker. The rumbling of the storm increased. The shields did nothing to protect them from the wind; besides, they were of an older type, and not very reliable.

On the outskirts of the occupied region were andy guards, commanded by squads of five soldiers per group. Each group guarded a shield generator, but at the moment all the living guards were doing their best to protect themselves from the storm, hiding inside their armored personnel carriers. There came a faint musical sound from the northern plateau; one guard put down his cards and told his fellow soldiers to shut up and listen. The squad leader joined him as he eased out of the carrier, and both soldiers shielded their eyes as they tried to look through the storm.

Hundreds of shadows emerged from the cliff side, and were suddenly all over the plateau. They resolved into riders on monstrous beast to those unfortunate enough to witness them; they charged in lethal and stealthy silence, killing all the guards protecting any shield generator. In many cases, it was a simple matter of tossing a fragmentation grenade into a carrier, and letting it do its work on the fragile soldiers inside. The androids were a little more trouble, but the soldiers bore EMP rifles and grenades that fried their electronics instantly, "killing" them. And somehow, the beasts moved straight through the protective shields without causing any damage to themselves or their respective riders, or setting off any alarms.

As the last of the shields vanished, clearing a path toward the center of the encampment, the enemy finally realized the danger, and alarms brayed from speakers across the vast facility. Either someone had noticed the lack of shields, or the corpses of Assham's group had been discovered. As the alarms went off, hundreds of infrared laser beams, each aimed at a specific target, pierced the fog, and hell rained down from above.

"Drop your payloads and head for the next target," Miska ordered her section, while bearing down on several painted targets. On her console, half a dozen target-lock lights blinked, and she pressed the FIRE toggle on her joystick. Missiles detached from beneath her wings and sprinted toward their targets. Just before they impacted, she herked back the stick and accelerated upward and starboard, away from the explosions that bloomed like lethal flowers in the midst of the grouped Florencian ships. As she leveled off a thousand meters above the plateau, she checked the damage reports and the status of her attack wing. All ships present and accounted for.

Veering and diving like a rollercoaster ride from hell, she led her ships through the battlefield, spearing any enemy she could spot with heat lances. They reached the airfield, and again a hail of missiles and magma bolts rained down, destroying hundreds of enemy ships and shuttles. Pilots and maintenance crew ran for cover; the bravest of them hurried to their ships in a futile attempt to get airborne before it was too late. Miska made sure they remained earthbound, a hard expression on her face as she slowed to take out specific targets, jinking occasionally as some of the better shots split the air nearby with their own energy beams and magma blasts. Muttering under her breath, she hit the accelerator and zoomed upward, before circling the camp again to support the incoming troops.

The airfield became a field of bright burning flowers as thousands more missiles and magma blast showered down, crippling the Florencian airpower for the region. When the dust settled, their vaunted air superiority had been lost; any fighters or shuttles they used would have to be brought in from hundreds or thousands of kilometers away. From the forest advanced thousands of infantry, running towards the encampment in a silent horde. Portable artillery advanced, continuing to pound the airfield, finishing off the Florencian air and spacecraft and cratering the tarmac and metal gridwork with rounds after round. Mobile missile units followed behind, sending their deadly loads into the military base itself.

As the natural storm intensified, so did the battle storm. Stealth shuttles dropped all over the region, delivering armored assault vehicles and thousands more infantry. From the southeast roared in 300+ great hovertanks, arrowing in towards the outskirts of the base. As the first line of tanks came to a halt, their hover-cushions automatically folded in under their glacises, allowing their tracks to touch the ground as they converted to ground-effect. They advanced more slowly now, firing simultaneously in devastating waves of destruction. Behind the tanks followed hundreds of fast-moving armored personal carriers, bringing more troops to the fray.

Hundreds more small, heavily armed troop transports descended from orbit, followed by a pair of enormous ovoid ships escorted by dozens of fighters. Fifty ports irised open on the each side of each ovoid's hull; from each emerged ten metallic eggs, which pierced the surviving force shields and the metal shield wall like they were tissue paper before landing hard enough to create a crater. They split open, each spilling an armored soldier in a flood of deliquescing shock gel, which had protected them from the high-gee impacts. The shock troops took care of the targets in their immediate areas, then joined into squads to attack any surviving shield generators or grounded vehicles.

As the deflector shields failed one by one, another wave of larger transports approached, laying down a withering field of suppressive and cover fire as each dropped either one or three tanks and personnel carriers to the ground. Once they dropped their cargo, they exited the scene.

Troops on both sides fell in droves, but the attackers had the element of surprise and copious numbers, and methodically wiped out the Handoverians and any strategic positions. Meanwhile, the aerial fighters split into small groups and swarmed the base, emptying their missile launchers and exhausting their magma tubes and heat lance batteries on topic after target. The entire region ahead of the infantry's advance was engulfed in fire and explosions, like some real-life version of the mythical hell.

The Handover defenders and their quisling allies were taken entirely by surprise, and the battle soon escalated into a slaughter. Low-ranking soldiers were killed or executed on the spot, while the officers surviving the initial assault—and there were many, in the typically top-heavy Florencian military fashion—were rounded up. Some of the more hardened Handover soldiers put up a last-ditch resistance near the central command bunker, but were scattered and destroyed in detail by the K'Drak cavalry, which impaled them on their horns and tore them to pieces. Some of the beasts, with their riders clinging on stoically, stood on their hind legs and tore into the enemy with their front hooves, which were shod with sharp iron shoes, while emitting a horrible and debilitating call from the tips of their horns. The fighting was fierce but brief, leaving not a single Florencian soldier alive at the command bunker.

Hundreds of medical shuttles descended and joined as they landed, forming into Mobile Army Surgical Hospitals at five separate locations. A command craft hovering above each, and protective shields—these truly impenetrable, much superior to the Florencians'—fell over them like umbrellas. Thousands of combat medics ranged outward from three of the hospitals, locating and attending to their injured soldiers; the other two MASH units formed on opposite sides of the huge concentration camp, and began treating the starved and abused Omarian survivors.

Everything went like clockwork, the result of careful planning and endless rehearsal. The assault took less than an hour from the first shot to the last, and was more effective than anyone had dared dream.

Several command shuttles and their fighter escorts settled on a remote hill south of the battle, while fifty fighters secured the region from above and a command platform projected a protective shield over the hilltop. One soldier stood atop of the hill next to a single tree; behind him, below the hillcrest, stood several of his officers. One of them moved towards the man by the tree, as two black-feathered birds sat in silence on a long-dead branch and observed. Behind the man on the hilltop was a standard, its pole jammed into the ground. Atop the standard was a silver bar, and from it hung a black flag dominated by a large red circle; inside the circle was a triangle, and inside the triangle were a large eye with a deep blue iris, flanked on its left side by two straight lines and on the right side by one line. This was the battle standard of Section 21.

The sound of the banner snapping in the wind was interrupted by General Grimm. "Congratulation, Admiral von Hornet. It appears we caught them with their pants down." His comment was followed by laughter from the officers who had followed Grimm.

Explosions and distant small-arms fire, peppered by the occasional K'Drak roar and Handoverian scream, rolled across the hilltop as Alec peered down through high-powered binoculars. He watched, not taking part in the self-congratulatory laughter, as lines of marching troops and convoys of tanks and other support vehicles moved towards specific targets, occasionally spitting fire at the enemy in the form of heat lances and magma bursts. Tracers marked out the paths of old-fashioned but effective heavy-metal ammunition. Alec lowered his binoculars at last, attaching the instrument to his belt.

"It's all thanks to you and the Grisamm instructors, Grimm," he answered belatedly, in a quiet voice. "Not to mention our fearless soldiers from Samari. The new recruits did well."

Grimm replied, "You do realize we've just done something unheard off, don't you?"

"You mean liberating an entire planet in less than a day?"

"Yes, just that, and with less than a quarter of a million troops at our disposal."

Admiral Busch, listening to something on his earbug, shouted, "All sections report victory, sir—except for some of the smaller enemy Elite units, we're pretty much done."

"Make sure all those *tiny* units are well taken care of Admiral," Alec said to another officer, who nodded and began barking orders into his wristcomp.

Alec touched his headpiece, then tapped a button on his own wristcomp to reveal a rotating holographic image of Omar, displayed with many multicolored tags. He touched his left ear and listened; he then ordered, "Miska. Take your Vixens and wipe out the enemy fighters approaching us. Sending you their coordinates now."

"Wipe out approaching fighters, aye," Miska confirmed with something approaching decent communications discipline. "Coordinates received. Miska out."

A flight of some forty fighters dropped from the sky, heading west, and abruptly veered headed towards the hill, piercing the protective dome with ease and forcing everyone to duck. As her wake wash buffered them, Alec could hear Miska laughing in his earpiece, and could only shake his head. "Those girls!"

"She should be disciplined for that," a general muttered in the background, as she leaned towards the ground to pick up her hat.

Busch nodded to Alec, then turned to several subordinates, issuing a string of orders before turning back towards Grimm and Alec. He actually rubbed his hands together with glee. "Love it!" he bellowed. "We're the only active Galactic fleet with an infantry—at least until the shitheads back home hear about this one!" The Admiral laughed at the top of his lungs.

Alec turned to his officers. "Florencia has never sanctioned the invasion of Omar, because even their politicians were aware of the possibility of backlash from other polities if they broke the very strict Universal laws preventing contact, much less attack, of any world that hadn't yet evolved an advanced spacefaring race. Then again, unofficially they weren't against it, and let their membership worlds do more or less as they pleased, as long as it favored their God."

Grimm replied, "And we all know the real reason why Florencia haven't objected or tried to stop Handover: this system is a hub for hundreds of natural singularity gates. And now *we* control them."

Tyrussan General A'Hirra objected, "Not so fast, Grimm," its pearlescent tusks shimmering in the dim light that filtered through the polluted skies. "I'm sure they'll send a fleet or two to try and take it back."

"But soon we'll inform Nastasturus High Command, and they will surely send sufficient forces to secure the system," a Colonel said. As her culture dictated, she wore a tight-fitting outfit that covered everything but her oversized catlike ears, which were pierced with multiple rings and studs indicating her rank.

A'Hirra gave the younger officer a stare that shut her up quickly.

Meanwhile, several hundred K'Drak cavalry escorted thousands of Handoverian and quisling Omarian prisoners to the foot of the hill. One rider, their leader, rode up the hillside to stop in front of Alec and saluted him. The grizzled Samari major gazed at her young commander-in-chief with undisguised respect and admiration. "My lord, what do you want us to do with them?" She motioned her head towards the prisoners, who looked up at Alec's group in defiance.

"Don't call me that!" Alec hissed at her angrily; but that only lasted a second before his expression softened and took on a dreamy cast. He spoke softly to himself, but still loudly enough for anyone to hear: "Cut off the bird's wings...yes, cut them off. Make it a bird no more."

The major ignored her leader's comment; he was known for thinking out loud, in ways that often left his subordinates confused. Alec looked down at the enemy combatants, a wide range of Oman, omanoid, and other species from many different Florencian worlds, making their origins obvious; Handover's population was almost exclusively Oman and omanoid. Huddled among them were many of the opportunistic Omarians who had been taken in by Handoverian lies.

"Who are they?" he asked, pointing at half-a-dozen Tza-Tza. The mid-sized reptilians, who looked svelte next to their Samari captors, stared back; one of them took a few steps towards the hill, but was stopped by a guard, who pounded the Tza-Tza in the gut with his rifle-butt. The alien hiss-screamed and shouted, "You have no right to treat us this way, trespassers! We are emissaries from the Federated Traders, and we are here on business!"

Alec looked down at the Tza-Tza and said decisively, "Slavers. Impale all of them through their anuses. Make them slide down slowly toward their destinies. Spare none of them. Do it here—right here, on this very hill. Make this hill a forest of them, and make sure the rest of the universe knows."

Alec looked almost insane as he stared hatefully at the mass murderers below, most of whom, despite their predicament, met his stare with equal hate. They didn't believe he'd do it, so they showed no signs of fear. The local combatants, who had seen (and participated in) the atrocities offworlders were capable of, reacted quite differently; they fell to their multi-jointed knees, praying and begging for their lives. The slavers, who knew of Alec's reputation, joined them.

One of the prisoners tried to bound away in a futile attempt to escape; a K'Drak snapped off his head in one bite, swallowing it whole. The body bounced twice more before tumbling in a heap, splattering a wide arc of crimson blood over some of the cavalry, who reeled back in disgust.

Alec grabbed the mane of the major's beast; the wild snorting head shook at first, and then settled immediately. Warm, friendly eyes looked down on Alec as he caressed the large, fearsome head. He scratched the beast behind its pointing ears, and the beast tilted its head to the side while Alec whispered softly to it. He peeled some skin and dried blood from its short horn, and the beast started to purr like a cat.

"Look, your horn has almost grown back," Alec murmured. He kissed the animal's large head and glanced up to the major, who sat astride the beast, proud and herself still bloody from the fight. Another horn hung from her left shoulder on a leather sling, similar to the new one emerging on the forehead of the beast. "It's a very nice K´Drak you have here, Major. Was she hard to tame?"

"Yes, my lo…er, yes, Admiral. It took quite some doing for her to get used to me."

Alec petted the K´Drak a few more times, harder this time, and it made a strange, baritone keening, soon taken up by the other cavalry K'Draks in what sounded like an alien hymn. Alec listened for a while, and then cleared his throat and gestured for the Major to proceed. He and his fellow officers watched the K'Draks as they moved on in a long procession, escorting all the prisoners elsewhere for the moment. The Handoverians snorted in derision and the Omarians and Tza-Tza scrambled to their feet in relief, all convinced that Alec wouldn't go through with their punishment. They were wrong; the cavalry was merely waiting until the officers cleared the hill before proceeding with their orders.

The weather begun to clear up—all the awful factories had been deactivated in this hemisphere—and a warm, bright sun greeted another dawn on this side of Omar. As the first rays pierced the force shield, an officer hurried to Admiral Busch and reported, "Sir: Admiral Vito reports that he has have captured eighteen megatransports heading into the system, and Captain Copola has captured two similar ships trying to leave. The outgoing ships were overloaded with Omarians and crewed by Tza-Tza claiming the fealty and protection of the Federated Traders."

Busch answered, "Release all the prisoners, render medical aid as necessary, and then return them to Omar. Dispatch a Rebuild Team to help them salvage and rebuild their infrastructure, and be sure to provide them with a company of psychologists. They'll all probably be in some sort of shock."

The messenger said, "Release the prisoners, render aid, and return them home with Rebuild and Psychology teams, aye." He hesitated.

"Well, what is it, man? Spit it out."

The young Oman nodded decisively and said, "Sir, Captain Copola has noted that at least a third of the liberated Omarians have volunteered to join us in our...'crusade,' as he put it."

Alec, having overheard them, turned towards them, his face expressionless. "Excellent. Any adult Omarian is welcome to join our force in any capacity in which he or she cares to serve—volunteers only, and only after clearance by the psychologists."

The young officer snapped to full attention and saluted. "Aye aye, Admiral."

Alec turned to his Grisamm ally. "Grimm, we're done here for the day. I'll leave the rest with you and the locals, but hurry—I want to move on as soon as possible."

"Sir, there's more!" the young courier burst out. Alec turned back to him, lifting an eyebrow. "My lord, we've had problems with communications after the initial assault, and..."

Alec shook his head, not liking the "my lord" bit, but decided not to reprimand the young soldier. "I know all about the communications problems. Now speak up: what is it?"

"There appears to be a new threat approaching the system via hyperspace, sir, and it's only a light year or so away. An Omega class battle station. The analysts say it will be here soon."

Some of the officers couldn't hide their expressions, and more than one of them began to talk about the possibility of retreat. When they saw Alec's expression, they stop talking like their vocal cords had been cut.Alec just looked at the slavers and smiled. "I have another little plan."

Busch and few of the others who had grown accustomed to Alec's style rolled their eyes as the young commander smiled calmly. Grimm just nodded toward Alec, who hurried back to a fighter waiting below the hill. In less than a minute it was in the air, followed by a dozen elite fighters flying escort. They made a large circle over the battlefield, then shot straight up until they left the atmosphere and cleared into the deep darkness of space.

Then the cavalry began their grim work with the captured Florencian officers, slavers, and quislings.

"Divide the fleet? No, Alec, no, no, no!" Busch sounded very concerned.

Alec and his senior staff had convened inside a large conference room aboard *Crusher-5*. Captain Copola, still a bit upset, sat with his hands clasped, counting his fingers and shaking his head.

"What's this I hear about dividing the fleet?" Admiral Vito entered the room, followed by several aids.

There was a brief silence and then Vito looked at the battle plan laid out in front of his seat. He sat down, flipped through it, and shook his head.

"Alec"—it was customary to address each other without rank during open staff meetings—"liberating Omar is all well and good, because it's anyone's duty. Attacking the Omega station closing on Omar is also fine, given its obvious intentions. But attacking Handover is a big no-no. We must have a commission for that, and I need not remind you, the fleet has not yet been commissioned. If you attack them now, then Handover will accuse you of piracy, and Section 21 will be terminated before we've even begun."

"That's what we been telling him," Busch said.

Alec leaned his jaw on his hand, thinking aloud. "When is that inauguration ceremony for our fleet?"

"In two days, and I suggest that you return to our capital and represent us well." Busch sounded nervous and very concerned.

"Once we're an official fleet group, we'll be attached to a fleet and have to follow orders, right?"

"That would be normal," Busch said, raising his eyebrows and obviously wondering what Alec was getting at.

"No," Alec said.

There was an uproar as everyone tried to talk at once. Alec only smiled, then raised his hand for silence.

"Admiral Cook will represent us at the inaugural crap," he announced, "and the moment we have our commission, we will follow up on this plan—and I expect all of you to do your duties. If you don't like it, you're welcome to leave—*after* the plan has been executed."

"At least by then Mother should be ready," Vito concurred.

"Bentor, inform Frances to prepare your Elites and General A'Hirra's. Give him anything he needs, including some of your own troops if necessary." Alec noticed that Bentor was about to say something, and he held up his hand and continued, "I'll need you and your people with me during the second phase of the plan."

Bentor took a deep breath and nodded, brow furrowed in thought; then he smiled and nodded again more firmly.

Alec went on, "This war has been a joke thus far, because our politicians are holding back our standard armed forces while increasing this new Federation Force, making it literally impossible for our high command to act independently. We have a chance to strike a severe blow against both the enemy and the politicians back home. It's time for an eye-opener. Ladies and gentlemen, prepare your forces. I'll give in on one point: we will *not* divide our fleet."

A wave of relieved sighs echoed through the room as the officers finally realized that perhaps their commanding officer wasn't mad after all.

"First we take the Omega station," Alec said, "and shortly thereafter we will conquer Handover." Before anyone could object, Alec raised his hand and his eyebrows. "You have your orders. Execute them."

An eerie silence fell over the room as everyone stared at their young commander, wide-eyed with shock. Again, he met each stare calmly. "We *will* prevail, trust me," he said, and cutting the large

Grisamm off, went on, "Bentor, look on the bright side. Now you finally get to use that hammer of yours."

Suddenly Grimm started laughing, and eventually most of the other senior staff did too, though there were a few individuals who couldn't hide what they thought of this mad plan hatched by their mad commander-in-chief. Alec memorized the names and faces of each one of those doubting him. He never joined in the laughter; he only smiled.

THIRTEEN

THE three tightly packed megatransports, each carrying tens of thousands of souls who would soon be broken for slavery, dropped out of superluminal velocity to the standard cruising speed of a quarter-c as they arrived at the rendezvous point. A distant cloud of movement soon resolved into hundreds of battle cruisers and other capital ships escorting an enormous Omega battle station, like a swarm of moons around a gas giant; beyond them was the grayish smudge of a Galactic Fleet, protecting the six of the armada gliding toward the Omar system in all its deadly grace. A large frigate from the outer rim of the swarm of ships around the Omega station boosted suddenly to the point position; a moment later, the comm officer of the flagship of the slaver convoy piped an incoming text message to his captain's console.

It was brief and to the point: *Follow our course and do not deviate or your ships will be destroyed. Acknowledge.*

"As ordered," the distinctly non-Tza-Tza captain responded. The compsys converted it to text and responded in kind.

"They didn't even greet us on screen," Commander Vega mumbled, shaking her head. "Overconfident fools."

"Of such things are victories made, Commander," Frances said dryly, peering at the several holo-imagers facing him, looking over them to focus on the crew members from time to time. Occasionally, he flipped one of the imagers to the cargo bay cameras, and studied the thousands of prisoners bound in the slave blocks, all covered by large blankets that he would provide "punishment" for an attempted insurrection, if asked. Omarians had trouble regulating their body temperature; when too hot, they went into a form of semi-hibernation until they were rehydrated. This was a simple and inexpensive way of making them torpid without drugging or damaging the merchandise.

"Think it will work?"

"Having doubts, commander?"

"No doubts, sir; we're doing the right thing. I do have concerns, of course. This is pretty much a suicide mission, if you ask me."

"Good thing I'm not asking, then."

Their conversation was interrupted by a voice over the intercom: "Proceed along the following coordinates, and follow all instructions as you enter the base."

"Oho, we get a voice this time. They must trust us." He tapped a key and said in the Tza-Tza dialect, "Coordinates received and programmed. Order received, will comply."

"Have a nice day."

Frances and Vega shot each other puzzled glances; they hadn't expected such a nice, *normal* comment from an invading armada.

"Could it be a test?"

Frances ignored Commander Vega and responded, "Thank you. Have a nice day, too." He then turned to the nervous Commander and smiled toothily as he said, "Doubt it. Take over this station, and stick to the plan as scripted, no matter what. Understood?"

"Sir yes sir!" Vega assumed Frances' former position in the command seat, and observed the gaping maw that opened in the side of the Omega station. It was large enough to handle ten of the megatransports, and she observed tensely as the three ships were swallowed by the monster. "Oh my," she muttered, raising her hand towards her mouth, not realizing that her nervous action had been displayed before the entire bridge crew.

Inside the space station were hangered hundreds of capital ships of various classes—interspersed, oddly enough, with hundreds of civilian luxury yachts. It appeared the Florencian Elite Clans had accompanied the armada in order to stake their claims on what they expected would be the new "homeworld" of the Handoverians.

"Their guidance computer has assumed helm control," a lieutenant reported.

"All too easy," a major muttered.

"Don't jinx us, Major. Now come along." To the rest of the officers on the bridge, Frances commanded firmly, "Unit Commanders: Order your troops to stand by and wait for the sign," as he left the bridge with the major following him close behind.

"Wait, sir! Something's happening!" Vega shouted.Both the Major and Frances stopped and turned.

"We aren't being directed heading towards a regular cargo port, sir; it appears we're heading towards one of the VIP docks further in towards the center of the station."

"Perhaps you're right, Major," Frances rumbled.

"Sir?"

"All too easy. Commander, proceed as ordered and follow the plan to the letter. Should anything go wrong, use your judgment; it's of the utmost importance that we succeed here."

The megatransport convoy split as each ship received different docking orders. The first ship was ordered to dock on a vast landing platform, while the other two were directed to separate docking bays. Massive docking arms latched onto their hardpoints, while clamps slipped into slots on the sides and undersides of the ships to lock them in place.

Frances, followed by several officers—all wearing civilian shipsuits—took the long trip down to the cargo bays via turbo-lift. As they entered Cargo Bay Ten, the last and largest, they were presented with the sight of many hundreds of slave blocks, still covered to "punish" the Omarian captives, which the android crew were quick to line up for inspection. Just as Frances and his colleagues reached the platform outer lock, the door hissed open and a horde of hundreds of civilians rushed towards them, eager to review and purchase the new meat. The delegation was led by a self-important ninny in a fur-lined cloak that dragged the deck.

"That can't seriously be the Governor himself, can it?" the major whispered to Frances, which was pointless because of all the background noise from the advancing slavers and the shouts from the poor "slaves." By now, the andies were removing the covers.

Governor Rimez had a good lead on well-nigh one thousand of his closest friends, all of whom were eyeing the slaves hungrily; and to his bemusement, Frances actually heard the self-important little prick giggle when he realized that most were female. Rimez clasped his hands and practically ran towards the first slave block. He looked a bit disappointed when he didn't notice any men right off. Apparently he liked a little variety. He hurried further down and saw that yes, there were several blocks filled with males, too.

"Vera, Vera...where's that stupid cow gone to?" Rimez looked around for his servant, but the old hag was nowhere to be seen. He sure as hell didn't *need* the old bitch, but it wouldn't hurt if she were by his side to help him straighten up a little after he'd rushed down here straight from the party so he could inspect the cargo. His hair was surely a mess. Well, no matter; he would pick the best specimens and then allow his friends to pick a few of their own. The lazoids still several levels up could pick from the leftovers later on. No reason for everyone to leave the party.

"Why are they all covered up?" Rimez shouted angrily, as he noticed that the andies were still working to uncover most of the blocks.

No one responded; the slaver crew just blinked at him like the dullards they were. Odd; he had been told the crews were mostly Tza-Tza, who were usually more reasonable when dealing with Elites of Rimez's caliber. Fuming, he looked with a murderous stare for a scapegoat. Some of his friends had heard him, and stopped a few paces behind him; but the many who didn't hear his little outburst pushed on, generating a slight commotion and a few shouted tantrums that echoed through the cargo bay like the squeaking of bats in a cave. Rimez finally noticed a few guards and officers heading towards his location, and he readied himself to let the idiot officer in charge know what he thought of this ill-prepared slave display.

"My lord, my lord," said the scaly officer who was their spokesbeing; the convoy's leader, by the flash on his sleeves and collar. "These slaves have been difficult, and were undergoing punishment; they are docile when covered. We have just arrived and have yet to shake off the chill of the Big Dark, my lord; if you give us a few moments, we will soon have them uncovered and at full vigor. As you no doubt know, we are very concerned for the wellbeing of the merchandise."

Rimez waved his hand in the air for the old commodore to shut up; he had laid his eyes on an exquisitely attractive female who seemed more Oman than Omarian. Her seductive smile told him he had to claim her immediately. He headed straight towards the slave block; he couldn't wait to see if she had beautiful feet he could twist and break and lacerate. He'd heard that the Omarians had powerful legs; surely they had feet to match. His eyes widened as his manhood grew.

"Remove that stupid cover," he ordered as he stared at the beautiful blonde Oman. Oman...? Rimez had a vague feeling that something was wrong. The people of Omar were omanoid, but not as omanoid as this; they certainly weren't pure Oman. As surely as a blue-white giant would supernova, this slave was not from Omar. He gave her a suspicious look.

"My Lord, my dear superior lord."

The captain, who was larger than he had first appeared, approached him in the company of several Omans, a Crested Marengan, and omanoids with shockingly blue skin and heavily muscled legs with knees that appeared to point backward. Though Rimez wasn't a terribly perceptive man, he realized something was off-kilter.

"Where are the Omar slaves, and why are there regular Omans among this batch?"

A young man wearing a shabby civilian coat prepared to address Rimez; Rimez looked the young man up and down, deciding that he didn't like this particular slaver. The larger person behind him bore a slightly haughty expression on his face, so Rimez didn't like him either."My lord, we..." the younger man said nervously.

Rimez interrupted him before he got far. "We ordered that the Omar slaves be taken here. The others were to dock nearer the party, so my regular guests could grab whomever they wanted. All the non-Omans should be in this third ship. And...VERA, VERA! Someone find my stupid assistant for me!"

Rimez shouted into one of his guest's wrist-comps, since he lacked one of his own.

"Are you Governor Rimez?" the large man demanded impolitely.

"In person, and you'd better watch your tone..."

All around them, there was swift and sudden movement. The slaves exploded out of the blocks they were supposedly secured in, the blankets hitting the deck in their hundreds. Formations of androids swept from the cargo bay of the ship to take up stations at points all over the docking platform and in the air above. One of the sycophants next to him shrieked, "Battle androids! We're under..."

The old man never finished his sentence, because it's impossible to speak while your head is rolling across the deck like a bocce ball, and your body is reeling toward the horizontal, fountaining blood in all directions. A warm fluid hit Rimez in the face, instantly dying his beautiful white outfit in scarlet splotches; it took him a moment to realize it wasn't dye, but blood. The insolent shit who seemed to be in charge was slinging blood from a long wrist blade attached to the underside of his arm.

Someone shouted in alarm, and then all hell broke out as shots were fired and people screamed. The "slaves" had tossed their blankets away, and proved to be comprised of a mix of races—mostly Omans—dressed in strange looking battle fatigues. They waded into the fray, making short work of Rimez's slaver friends and their woefully inadequate bodyguards. Someone placed large hands on Rimez's shoulder and turned him around, so that he faced the hateful ship's captain, whose large face was set in a creepy smile.

An explosion ripped through the middle distance, where one of the other slave ships was attached to a docking arm, devouring the party-goers who had congregated there. Moments later, a horde of those badly dressed soldiers poured onto the party deck, really upsetting Rimez. "How dare you burst in uninvited to one of my special functions!" he shrieked, appalled by the gaucherie of it all. "Why, I—"

Rimez hit the ground as hard as the backhand he'd just received from Frances. He lay there in disbelief, not recognizing the stunning pain in his jaw for what it was, rarely having experienced anything like it. He'd lived such a protected life that he'd never even skinned a knee as a child; and even if he had, andy medics would have assuaged the pain in seconds and erased the memories of it soon after. Rimez was in shock.

The brute leaned down and whispered pleasantly, "Now, Governor Rimez, let's discuss your unconditional surrender."

The fighting on the station was brief and the bloodshed relatively minimal, which surprised the attackers; a station this size could easily hold a million armed troops. Aside from the occasional bodyguard, no one fought back; and even most of the bodyguards laid down their arms when they saw the slavers mowed down and realized what they faced. When the surviving VIPs were gathered up and lined up, several hundred of the former Omarian prisoners volunteered to install their erstwhile masters in the slave blocks. They'd learned quite a lot about their capabilities and operations over the last few days.

There was very little resistance by that point, and the Omarians didn't hesitate to stomp to death those who did so much as twitch as the tables were turned on them; those powerful legs were potent weapons. After the invasion moved on, the only resistance they faced was a Marine detachment guarding the station's main bridge, located in the well-protected center of the docking region.

The Florencians put up stiff resistance until the Governor's assistant arrived with the wrist-comp that should have been on the Governor's arm in the first place, and began screaming contradictory orders into it. Then their resistance began to fall apart as they tried to interpret what the hell she wanted them to do. Meanwhile, Frances worked to get his megatransport's computer to mesh with the station's, trying to rig an override to open the blast doors that led into the bridge.

Suddenly, they opened on their own. "Florencian troops! Stand down!" a battle andy ordered flatly as it flew into the docking region, followed by dozens of marching battle androids hurrying after. Frances' troops just stared, remaining at attention, even as the surviving Florencians reluctantly dropped their weapons and, one by one, knelt with their hands behind their heads.

"Florencians! Surrender or die!" a voice bellowed from several intercoms. As Frances entered the bridge and noted that the dozen or so officers inside were already surrendering, he saw the image of an angry man gesticulating on the main viewscreen. He wore an Admiral's uniform, and seemed familiar; Frances squinted, and tried to remember the old officer's name. Mass? Noss? No, it was *Nass*. He had met Admiral Nass while aboard the *Predator* at the Battle of the New Frontier-16, when Alec had taken command of both Florencian and Nastasturian fleets and destroyed several attacking pirate clans consisting of several thousand ships. It was Admiral Nass who had apparently ordered the senior staff to surrender.

Frances walked over to one of the viewscreens and stared at the Admiral, who stared back with a puzzled expression; then he said, "Frances af Grisamm, correct?"

Frances nodded sharply.

The old Admiral stared in silence for a moment, then asked, "Should I assume our mutual acquaintance is nearby?"

Before Frances could answer, an alarm hooted in the background and someone shouted "Incoming!"

"That should be him now, Admiral," Frances assured Nass.

AN enormous new class of battle cruiser Nass had never seen before blinked into existence as it dropped out of superluminal space. Nearly a quarter of the size of the Omega station, it was very different in form, harsh and angular where the station was spherical and moonlike. Accompanying it but well in the distance were two equally large but much simpler ships that looked like little more than flat platforms—ship carriers of some kind. Behind those was a cloud of hundreds more ships not currently visible to the naked eye, though Nass could follow them on the radar holo-imager before him.

Someone behind his cleared his throat. "I think we can take them, sir," the man said aloud when Nass ignored him.

Nass settled back in his chair. "In your dreams, general. You don't know what this kid is capable of. He's practically a Silver Guard Sentinel all on his own. He'll have some tricks up his sleeve."

The comm officer announced, "Sir, they're hailing us."

"On screen, Commander."

Alec looked at Nass, who looked back at him.

"Lunch?"

Alec's voice sounded so innocent that Nass couldn't help smiling. He nodded and said, "Sure."

"My shuttle will bring you over."

There was a flicker in space-time right next to Nass's flagship, and a black shuttle appeared at the docking bay nearest the flagship's bridge.

ONCE idyllic, the world of Handover was now sheathed in a perpetual orange smog. If not for the power satellites and materials brought in from all over Florencia and its territories, the population would have died long ago; they lived in a perpetual twilight where only the hardiest of wild plants and animals could survive, and its inhabitants had to wear breathing devices to move from one place to another. Most just stayed inside, using the complex of subterranean tunnels between points when they absolutely had to travel. The tunnels, and most homes, were equipped with chemical and nuclear breathing systems that produced fresh air, ancient inventions constantly tinkered with to improve them.

But their output was never quite enough; and as nature has a tendency to do, it removed what was killing it. Over ten billion people had died from asphyxiation in the past ten years alone. Given that the world was groaning with a population of over one hundred billion, the planetary leaders had welcomed this nature disaster—as long as it didn't affect them personally, of course—but it wasn't enough. The planet was dying, and experts had long proclaimed that without a miracle from Gull, Handover had one, or perhaps if they were lucky, two more centuries before the biosphere catastrophically failed, killing everyone. The planet might yet be saved, but only if all Tritonium silver mining ceased, and 99% of the population was moved offworld. Domes had been erected to protect key cities, of course, but they were expensive to build and there weren't enough of them.

The atmosphere was degrading rapidly and the Handoverians were desperate for a new homeworld—especially their leaders.

The Florencian Federation had ordered thirty fleets to be mustered for the war: twenty InterGalactic, ten Galactic. It was an enormous expense, resulting in the drafting of over five hundred million citizens. That would ease the overstressed planet temporarily, and those drafted were actually relieved to get offworld, where the air was recycled but clean. But it wouldn't be nearly enough to save Handover. Once Omar had been taken, the exodus would begin. Only engineers and scientists would be left behind to save the world, living in the domes. One day, it might be reclaimed by their descendants.

Like many of the worlds in both Florencia and Nastasturus, Handover was an odd mixture of dictatorship and democracy. The Elite, consisting of some one million citizens, not including their families, could never be replaced. Their leadership was inherited, and the highest positions in the government were voted on only by the Elites. The rest of the populace had regular regional elections and their Congresses of the Common. Ultimately, the Florencian federal government cared very little about the infrastructure on any particular world they controlled; some were full democracies, many were dictatorships of various flavors, and a few were functional anarchies. Florencia's basic structure was oligarchical, though eventually most worlds turned towards capitalist democracy; the economics didn't work well otherwise. Much blame of this was due to the leadership in the galaxies of Yaharra, controlled by the Federated Merchants; and Sabaza, aligned with the Traders, both of which wielded too much power.

Just another reason why both galaxies must be conquered by Florencia, and all the Brakks—who totally controlled both the Merchants and the Traders—must be erased from the universe.

Chancellor Rock Belim of Handover woke up for the third time since he'd lain down the night before. This latest earthquake had been stronger than the others, but shorter. He blinked his eyes a certain way, and a holographic image of the time appeared before his eyes; it was still another hour before he usually got up. He blinked again to banish the image. He hated the biochip that had been installed in his brain as a child; he imagined that it caused him headaches. But the complink in his mind, unique to him alone, was standard among most clans who could afford them, especially the Elites. Most military personnel had them too.

No need to continue this charade of sleeping. He jammed his feet into his morning slippers, and a hovering android placed his robe over his shoulders. After he'd donned the robe, he motioned for the little andy to return to its docking station.

Belim turned to look at the empty side of his bed. His wife had died years back, leaving him to raise their son, Rimez—a useless little bastard if ever there was one, but still his son, and perhaps the next leader of Handover if Belim could convince his friends to vote for him when the time came. He hoped and prayed that Rimez's new position as Lieutenant Governor of Omar, their promising new homeworld, would settle down his boy and improve his sons' chances, especially after the disaster at New Frontier-16. The idiot hadn't even been present at the battle, yet still demanded that it be credited to him—when anyone with any sense knew it was the doing of that frightening von Hornet heir from Nastasturus. Well, there was no help for that; Rock Belim could do many things, but that was something he could do nothing about. If the incident at the New Frontier had occurred in space that Handover controlled, then perhaps he might have been able to spin it to his son's favor;

but because the battle took place in a neutral sector, there were far too many outsiders who knew the truth.

Rock looked at the large painting of his dead wife on the far wall. His eyes turned red, and for a moment, he shed tears in her memory. He quickly stopped when he heard himself sobbing. He was upset with himself; how he could display such weakness? He glanced quickly about the enormous bedroom his wife had decorated, looking for any witnesses, but the only thing he saw was a guard android still attached on its place in the ceiling high above.

A ping from the double doors made the red light on forehead of the guard andy light up. An image of Basita, Rock's personal butler, appeared.

"Would you like your breakfast, sir?"

Rock nodded, ducking his head and drying his tears with a spider-silk handkerchief.

"Would you like it on the morning balcony, Sir? The House Astronomer tells me that the year's third solar eclipse is expected within the half-hour. It will be quite a sight, he assures me."

"Sounds fine. Thank you, Basita."

For an instant Basita looked puzzled, and then the image vanished.

Basita, First Butler of the House of Belim, moved with a feline grace, despite being one hundred and five years old. Behind him flew a dozen small andies in a tidy line, each carrying a different dish. Given the current food shortage on Handover, it wasn't the normal one hundred dishes to choose from, but this would have to do.

The enormous balcony, with many stone pillars lifting towards the sky, shone pale white with red reflections from the rising sun. The only furniture was one chair and a small table along the right rail. Basita, who hated breaking protocol, noted with some disapproval that his master wasn't already seated; instead, he stood leaning on the stone rail, looking towards the horizon, still dressed in his morning robe. Strange; he normally wore his bath robe for breakfast. Basita cleared his throat.

"Is there any news about the earthquakes?" Rock Belim asked, without turning around.

"No, my lord, nothing yet."

Rock squint his eyes towards the red sun, thinking he was lucky they could see it at all. That had taken one of his few remaining Aridity Seeds, which sucked all the moisture out of the air over the continent, taking the smog with it. The effect would last a day or so, long enough for this event, whereupon the clouds would roar back with a vengeance, shrouding the capital and soaking it with centimeters of rain. He gazed at the large crowd that had gathered on a park in the distance just outside the magnificence of his lawn to observe the eclipse; they were clearly excited, as it was a time when the people thought their wishes would come true. A nice little tradition, among the very few they had left on Handover; after all, too many old traditions often led to disruption among the populace. He used his eyeball comp to zoom in on the crowd, but quickly got bored and canceled the zoom.

Again Basita cleared his throat. This made Rock smile, still with his back turned; he knew how important protocol was for his old Butler and friend. Perhaps today, he could convince him to retire and enjoy what remained of his life. Rock had a special surprise for him: his own palace on a remote island, where Basita could be taken care of for once. The palace was, of course, only a temporary gift—after all, it was very expensive—but Rock thought he deserved it; and besides, he would only live there for a few more years anyway, before he either died of old age or lack of air. Rock didn't need the palace at the moment; it was only one among his collection. He owned well over two hundred different estates on Handover alone.

Finally, the Handoverian leader deigned to seat himself, and nodded at the fourth dish. Basita quickly took the dish from the hovering andy and then signaled for the rest to leave. The dishes they carried would be put in stasis, where they would be frozen in time until the next day's breakfast, still as fresh as they had been when prepared. Even in the Supreme Leader's home, "waste not, want not" was the catch-phrase.

Basita thought briefly back to the days of his youth, when the sun could still be seen without Aridity Seeds, then dismissed the thought lest it unman him. He served his master as he always had done; and while he was securing the large white serviette around Rock Belim's neck, there came a strident peep from a communicator. His eyes widened in horror and disbelief; no one dared interrupt the Master while he had his breakfast, not even family! It was unheard of! Why, the Missus had been executed for less!

He waited, trembling, for his master's instructions. The annoying beep kept sounding until, with a frustrated snarl, Master Rock waved his hand and Basita activated the communicator with his wrist computer. A holographic image of a woman with the rank of General appeared, abasing himself before her world's Supreme Leader in what might be the last act of her life. Nevertheless, her voice boomed out strongly: "Chancellor, I most sincerely apologize, but I must see you at once. You have received an extremely urgent message I knew you would want to know of immediately."

Rock frowned towards the image and nodded his head. He then motioned for Basita to shut it off, and started his breakfast with his Butler waiting the standard four paces behind him and to the side. Steps echoed over the marble flooring as several people hurried into the room. This was highly unusual, and definitely not protocol. His young chief of security, Azima something, stopped behind Basita, and several other people ranged out behind her. Belim spun his chair to face them.

"My lord, I…"

He raised his right hand, ordering her to stop, still trying to remember her stupid name; thank Gull these idiots had ranks. "General, it had better be truly urgent. I get little enough time for myself as it is."

"It's very urgent, sir. It's a message from your son."

Knowing that had to be dire news, Belim suddenly lost his appetite. He tore off the serviette, threw it on the table, and stood. He marched over towards the railing and leaned on it. The crowd out there was much larger now; he supposed they weren't afraid of earthquakes. He bit his lower lip trying to control his fury. He closed his eyes.

"Well then, General, play the message for me."

He didn't want to see the image of his son and be reminded of his utter failure. It wasn't that his son preferred men for his body games; that he cared little or nothing about. Most people were naturally bisexual, and if an heir had to be produced through natural means and not through a bloody test tube, that could always be arranged. What made him sick was that his idiot son would never be Chancellor, because he was indeed an idiot; merely the mention of Rimez's name angered him these days. "Well?" he snapped.

"It...sir, it can't be played. It's...not that kind of message."

Rock interrupted the young general harshly. "Then read the damned thing."

"It can't be read either, sir...I'm afraid you have to see it."

Rock opened his eyes, still looking towards the horizon. He exhaled, calming himself, just as the ground trembled like there had been an explosion in the distance. He had to hold onto the railing to stay on his feet. The building shook like a rag doll in an angry child's hand, and some of the pillars reaching toward the sky cracked; one shattered like glass, sending stone slivers sheeting across the balcony like shrapnel. The General and his staff were knocked from their feet as battle androids surged out of openings in the pillars; some were crushed from the debris of their hiding places, but the others hurried to protect Belim, who had lost his grip and fallen to the floor.

"Rock! Look out, look out!"

Rock Belim was surprised and shocked when he heard Basita call him his first name for the first time ever, and looked towards the warning. Basita flew through the air and landed on top of him. "What in Gull's name are you doing...?"

Stones rained down on them, followed by some minor explosions—gunshots?—in the distance and shouts from many throats. After an endless moment, the trembling stopped. It took them all a few moments to get up.

"Secure the Lord Chancellor!" the General ordered as she brushed dust off her uniform.

The andies moved swiftly towards their programmed mark as Rock Belim knelt over his only friend, Basita, and held his head in his lap. A trickle of blood from the old man's lips and his awful still-ness was the only visible indication of injury.

"My lord, let us help him. Medic!" the general shouted; and then she noticed the pool of blood widening around the knees of the Chancellor.

Rock was trembling, and he no longer cared about what others thought of him as his tears poured down like a flood. He embraced his old friend's head, feeling the bones shift under the skin, and rocked back and forth, sobbing.

"My lord. Please."

Rock first glanced at the General's hand as it touched his shoulder, and then his glare seared into the General's eyes, making her let go. His voice icy, he said, "The message, General."

She closed her eyes and stood, nodding, knowing delivering this message might be the last thing she ever did. Struggling to keep her dignity intact, she gestured, and someone from the rear moved through the debris, carrying an old-style woven basket. Rock didn't pay any attention to who brought him the basket; all he saw was the black boots, now with quite of bit of dust on them, ruining the shine. He still held his friend's head in a one-armed embrace as he reached over with his left arm and removed the basket's lid. He had to pull the basket a bit closer so he could look into it; and there it was, his son Rimez's head looking back at him, perfectly preserved and bearing a surprised expression. The eyes looked in different directions, and the swollen tongue poked out the side of the full-lipped mouth.

For a moment, all was silent save for the rumbling of the after-shocks and the distant cries of the injured. Then Rock let out a loud cry of agony as he embraced two heads, one in each arm, one his best friend's and the other his only child's.

There was another earthquake, followed by explosions. Some-one shouted over the alarm: "Look, look!"

The quake lasted only a few seconds. Belim tossed the basket with the cruel contents aside, and then ordered the General to take care of his dearest friend. Two guards carried the old man between them, while a third reached for the head of Rimez, which who had rolled out of the basket. He missed the head as someone kicked it away. Flabbergasted, he looked up and into the Chancellor's staring eyes.

The General looked towards the horizon, pointing towards the rising sun. The enormous park just outside the palace grounds was pockmarked with craters, smoke half-veiling the thousands of crumpled bodies and just as many survivors scrambling for safety.

Rock peered at the onslaught, irritated, but then something caught his eyes on a hill in the far distance: two enormous, perfectly round holes piercing the hillslope. They looked too regular to be natural. Flicking on his eye-zoom, he looked closer; but overhead there was a bright flickering, then a flash, and the dome protecting the capitol vanished. Dark clouds moved in swiftly, dropping a torrent of rain as the air went foul. The rain was too dense for Rock Belim to see through; he held out a hand, and the general handed him a pair of mil-spec binoculars.

Standing on the broken terrace, Belim looked towards the horizon, the sensors on the binocs piercing the rain as if it weren't even there. The sounds of the wind and storm increased, and from the direction of the hill came a faint sound...or so he thought. He nodded his head to increase the acuity of his hearing.

"What are your orders, my lord?" the general's voice thundered.

Hundreds—no, *thousands* of small ships dropped from the sky, heat lances and magma blasts razing targets in all directions, as far as his eyes could see. They were followed by hundreds of larger ships, bombers, dropping their payloads and firing their missiles.

"Sir, your orders...?"

A brace of missiles arced toward the terrace. Rock Belim never answered the General; he knew this was the end.

FOURTEEN

ADMIRAL Nass ducked under a beam that had fallen from the ceiling as he picked his way through the carnage of what had once been the Supreme Leader's Palace of his homeworld. Dust sifted down onto his shoulders as he headed towards the sound of voices further down the long corridor, which was mostly clear. Fires still burnt here and there, but the invaders seemed to have things under control. The sounds of distant explosions intermingled randomly with nearer screams, and occasional hysterical laughter, punctuated with the clatter of broken glass as people moved around the palace ruins. There came a strange rising whistling sound from above; it ended in an explosion that shattered the outer wall of the ballroom Nass had just left. He instinctively hit the dirt. After rising and dusting himself off, he saw the wreckage of what remained of a Florencian fighter through the eddying dust and smoke, half-embedded in the thick stone wall.

Nass watched, blank-faced, as his followers rose from the ground. A few Section 21 soldiers hurried toward the wreckage, eyes bloodthirsty; when they attempted to retrieve the pilot, the ship came loose and fell towards the ground a thousand feet below, exploding as it hit.

Nass straightened his once-white uniform tunic, brushing dirt from it as he wrinkled his nose at the smell of burnt flesh. He swallowed hard. His eyes stung from the smoke, and he cursed silently as he wiped away a tear. He didn't want anyone to see and think he was weak enough to weep; that he would never do, no matter how he felt. The tear was an autonomic response to the increasing smoke in the air, and it was just getting worse. He held his hand over his mouth in a futile attempt to suppress a cough that came anyway. He stopped, thinking to pull out his spare breather mask from his battlepack, but decided against it. He glanced at the people following him, noticing that most of them wore their masks.

The sound of arguing voices grew louder as they reached what once had been a large entrance to some sort of hall, with four enormous staircases circling each other in a double helix. He had never been to this part of the palace before, and he was as lost as anyone. Suddenly he and the others froze, for far above them was one of those strange monsters—standing *on the vertical wall,* its claws buried in the rose-colored granite. It stared at them, and for the briefest of instants, Nass could have sworn it smiled at him.

"Admiral Nass? This way, sir."

A young woman stood before him, dressed in strange armor, something like an ancient knight's but made out of a modern composite. A pale blue glow followed the contours of the uniform, and some parts were decorated with strange sigils. Behind her were a number of Grisamm soldiers in their plain gray-brown fatigues. As they turned to follow, the monster on the wall smoothly worked its way down to the floor, where it followed along behind, as silent as a snake. Nass could feel its glare from behind, and it gave him goosebumps.

The lady knight and her retinue led them through many rooms, and here and there they encountered groups of soldiers, laughing and pillaging. A sudden scream got everyone's attention as they passed an enormous dining room. There were several servants of various species there, still wearing their House Belim livery; having worked more or less as slaves at the palace for years, they had apparently decided to get back at some of their former masters. It sickened him to realize that they were raping and torturing their victims, who from the look of them had been Elite citizens. *You reap what you sow, I suppose,* he thought.

The young woman leading then whistled and nodded, and the monster set upon the rapists, who fled for their lives—some not fast enough. Several Grisamm detached themselves from the escort and saw to the victims.

"There is no order here; everything is chaos," an old colonel in his retinue groused. "And look at these troops! All of them wearing different uniforms, and hell, look over there," he complained, pointing at some of the invaders, "For Gull's sake, some of these so-called soldiers seem to be wearing civilian clothing!"

Nass thought it symptomatic of all that was wrong with the Florencian military that the colonel complained about what the invaders were *wearing,* of all things, and said not a word about the rape and torture—as if it were only to be expected, perhaps even acceptable! Even he didn't give a damn that they were killing the Elites, as long as his troops were left alone. But Nass looked in the direction the colonel pointed at, and yes, his old colleague was right; Alec's army seemed to be lacking in discipline, not to mention uniform dress. In an epiphany, he understood what Colonel Adiss meant: lack of a unified command wasn't good at all, and would surely lead to trouble in the future if not corrected immediately. He made a note to bring the matter up with Alec von Hornet once they were alone.

He found Alec standing under a temporary canvas awning on a large balcony with marble pillars that were encrusted with green ivy and stone plant. He and his staff were milling about a large, circular table made of the same marble as the rest of the balcony. Parts of the balcony were ruined, and so was half the table. Corpses lay scattered across the balcony, most wearing civilian clothing; several soldiers were in the process of removing them by tossing them over the side, letting the bodies fall over a thousand feet to the ground, clearing up more space on the balcony. Nass only had to look towards the pillars to see more of the monsters, all looking different in detail and yet similar to each other in design, their skins various colors. One very large beast, as light-drinking black as the space between the stars, lay behind Alec, head on its forelegs like a huge dog, seemingly asleep.

As the Admiral approached the table, he saw that several large holographic maps were on display, though he gave them little or no attention. Two young officers wearing flight suits, holding their helmets under their arms, stood by Alec listening to his instructions. Nass decided to wait until he was summoned. He looked for the woman who had escorted him and his friends, and noticed that she was seated astride what was apparently her own monster—the one that had followed them from the stairway hall—and they were heading up the wall towards another level. As they reached an enormous window, the beast and its rider vanished through it, sending glass crashing toward the ground.

"They're called K'Draks, if you were wondering," a youthful voice called out. "They don't like to be thought of as monsters."

"Good to know," Nass said, turning to facing Alec again as the young warlord waved his arm for him to join him. Nass looked back and motioned for his retinue to remain; then, as he moved forward, he bumped into one of the pilots. He recognized her, and her name popped into his head an instant later. One thing Nass was good at was matching names to faces he remembered.

He smiled. "Ah, Kirra, was it? And your friend must be Miska... no, no, that was one of the twins. Zicci, right?"

"*Nassie!* What's up with you, old man? You're right on the names...Miska had to join up with her sister at HQ. Bloody twins are useless whenever they're separated," Kirra smiled sweetly, holding her arms behind her back with her helmet in them, just standing there waiting for something to happen, like the little troublemaker she was.

Nass could only grin; he remembered all too well how these girls had affected the crew of the *Predator* at the Battle of New Frontier-16. Without thinking, he grabbed her by the shoulders and squeezed fondly, then blushed and removed his hands. "Still following young Alec?" he asked, flustered.

"We couldn't find anything better to do, so yes, I guess you could say that."

"How are you girls doing?"

"Fine for the most part. You?"

"I'm doing better every day, thank you for asking. Especially after today." He paused and looked around at the carnage. "Who knows? Perhaps this will be a new beginning for Handover, for my people. Thank you for helping us—for liberating us from ourselves, it seems."

"Anytime, old man. Just give us a call, and we'll fall down from the heavens like demons. What's wrong, Zicci?"

Zicci was staring hatefully at Nass, he realized; and it took only a moment for him to recognize that he was seeing something he had seen far too many times in young people's eyes; the pain of someone who had seen death one time too many. Zicci's physical appearance was that of a late teenager, but her eyes were as pained and experienced as a hundred-year-old slave's who had lived through hell and survived.

Kirra elbowed Zicci, feeling uncomfortable over her friend's behavior. Nass was practically an old friend. "What's wrong, Zicci? That's no way to greet someone, you know?"

There were an awkward silence and Nass decided to move forward to the waiting Alec; so he cleared his throat and was just about to advance when Zicci stepped in his path. "You're wearing the uniform of the enemy," she growled.

For an instant, Nass thought that his life might be over; but then he came to his senses. This was a young person who was going through the hard lesson of war, and she must have experienced something over the ordinary. Then again, no experience from any war is ordinary.

"I'm not your enemy, and..." He stopped himself, and then he smiled. He took a step back and unbuttoned his filthy white tunic, the fruit-salad on the breast glistening in the light, and handed the jacket to Zicci. "Here, keep it. A souvenir, perhaps?"

Zicci gave the tunic a suspicious look and studied it closely. Several people in the background had noticed the minor commotion, and looked on, puzzled, trying to figure out what was going on. Grimm started to walk towards them, but Alec stopped him with a gentle hand on Grimm's arm.

Nass had to wave the tunic at Zicci for a bit before she slowly tried to take it. He pulled it away swiftly and tossed it over her shoulders, brushing off some dirt while patting her shoulders.

"There you go. Now you're the admiral."

Zicci looked at her souvenir, then faced Nass. She tilted her head and said, "Thank you. I'm sorry, I feel…"

Nass wrapped her in a warm, fatherly embrace and whispered, "War is hell; please be strong. You remind me of a daughter I once had…if you or the other Vixens ever need a friend, then I'll be there."

He then pushed her away, still holding her shoulders in a firm grasp, looking down at her young, sad face; he would have thought "innocent," but she was far from that. She looked very confused; and wearing his tunic, which fit her like a cloak, she looked even younger. Nass felt so sad for her at that moment, knowing some of Zicci's and the other Vixens' past. He dried a tear from her eyes; and to his surprise, she did the same to him. She then fumbled with her helmet and headed towards a waiting fighter hovering next to an edge of the balcony. When Kirra turned to go, Nass reached out his arm and grabbed hers. "Look after her, will you?"

Kirra looked over at her friend and then back at Nass, nodding. She hurried towards her waiting fighter, climbing into the cockpit. The two fighters took off straight up into the sky; and a moment later, another thirty or so fighters joined them.

"She's had some bad experiences in battle."

Nass jumped and then looked at Alec, who had suddenly appeared next to him. "Haven't we all, Lord Hornet? I hope she'll make it. Some don't."

"She's a Vixen. Of course she'll make it." Alec gestured to Nass to join him by the broken marble table.

"So, what will happen to your people now?" Grimm asked, looking suspiciously at Nass.

"I'll move them to the Caranass system. Mass exodus."

"Never heard of it," Admiral Vito said.

"Doubt anyone has."

Nass gestured toward one of the holo-maps and looked at Alec, who nodded his head in consent. Nass tapped a few buttons and the image changed, zooming in on a system on the other side of the galaxy.

"Caranass is a closely guarded secret. An environmentalist who conducted research there over five centuries ago passed on the information." Nass noticed some skeptical expressions. "He was one of my ancestors, so House Nass is well aware of its existence. The Elite illegally annexed the system long ago for their own comfort. The inhabitable fourth planet is where they retire; very few Florencians even know about it. The planet is mostly wilderness. There are no traces of any Tritonium silver in the planet's core, so the world's environment remains very clean."

"And still you bastards decided to invade Omar and make it your next capital! The third one so far, I believe," Bentor broke in. "Worse, your Elites had already begun excavating for more Tritonium silver, and in this short time have polluted the world so thoroughly that it will take almost a century for Omar to recover. After only months of mining!"

Nass ignored the sardonic but very true remark; he knew his people would have to prove to the universe that they could change.

"Will you have to invade it?"

Nass looked up at Alec, and saw him smiling for a change. "No," he replied hastily. "No, I don't think so. I hope it will not come to that. Not many people live there; perhaps five hundred families and about ten million servants. Slaves, really."

"I thought your world was a democratic one, and you hated slavery. As of a matter of fact, isn't Handover supposed to be one of the few worlds in Florencia *without* any slaves?" taunted Bentor.

"Yes, ideally, but the ideal doesn't match reality. And we still sell slaves to other worlds, unfortunately," someone interrupted.

"General Watt-Henley—you made it! You're still alive," Nass burst out, as he noticed his old colleague standing near Bentor. She looked tired and gaunt, and a cloak covered her entire body.

A medical andy followed her; and when she shifted, he noted that she moved stiffly. "What have those monsters done to you?" he demanded, alarmed.

"Our beloved leaders didn't like my attitude, so they had me...'interrogated.' Good to see you too, old friend." The two of them embraced, and Nass supported his old commanding officer as she coughed.

She stepped back. "Nass, let me take care of Caranass as we've discussed in the past, while you prepare and organize the evacuation of Handover."

Alec broke in. "You think it will be that easy, my lady? What about your former masters in the rest of Florencia?" He gave the two old officers a puzzled look.

"There is only one way to the Caranass system, and we have sufficient fleets to make it," the General said. "Soon, we will order all our troops and fleets to rejoin us there."

"What about any retaliation?" Vito wanted to know.

"Anything is possible, but I doubt Florencia has enough forces left after attacking Marengo. The Siege of Marengo was a mistake in everyone else's favor, you see. Besides, we want to join forces with Section 21 when it's possible."

"That will be for later. For now, help your people relocate to your new world. You have an entire planet to settle...and try not to ruin this one."

"We'll do our best. I think, I hope, we have finally learned, once and for all."

"We just need to make sure the entire Elite class, and anyone sympathizing with them, are dead and gone as soon as possible," General Watt-Henley broke in.

"You're talking about genocide!" General Vito said angrily.

"Do you have a better suggestion?" the General replied, just as angrily. "Those monsters have ruled and murdered for thousands of years, not to mention all the worlds they've destroyed in search for Tritonium silver—the most useless metal in the known universe. So yes, we will have genocide; but I would rather have *them* killed than more innocents like the people of Omar. And look around you; you too have suffered casualties today, here in our former *capital.*" She spat the last word like it was an obscenity.

"Vito, please," Alec said calmly. "Forgiveness, my lady. War is war, Vito; let them deal with their own without outside interference. But please, spare the children. Admiral Nass, let me know what you need from us."

"Thank you, Alec. For now, we need to re-organize our forces and start with the evacuation. Should Florencia make a move you'll know, correct? Do you expect it?"

"I think they will," Grimm stated flatly. "They can't afford to let anyone secede from their Federation, much less one of their capital world. Other worlds would surely follow."

"You're probably right, Grimm, but this is the situation we're facing—and we'll deal with it," said Alec.

"I suppose you're going to target specific religious and social groups, too, aren't you?" Nass demanded angrily, almost shouting.

Before anyone could respond, Alec brought his hand down hard on the table's surface, generating a loud *crack* that echoed across the ruined balcony. The K'Drak behind him whipped its long neck around, bringing its head beside Alec's, staring balefully at Nass, whom backed up.

"Nass, what do you *think* they're going to do? They've lived under an oppressive lie for centuries, and finally they have come to their senses. Should they bring with them the old ways, and start the same shit again? Yes, Rock Belim and his son are gone, and good riddance." Alec motioned towards the two impaled heads on the railing of the balcony nearby: Rock Belim's and that of his son, Rimez. Further away were several other heads—and for the first time, Nass realized that several soldiers were beheading many of the prisoners, and decorating what remained of the balcony with severed heads. For a moment he was nauseous, but he clamped down on the reaction and controlled himself.

"Belim is gone," Alec continued, "but he will be replaced; and bear in mind that even though we believe the majority will follow you and General Watt-Henley in this endeavor, don't fool yourself: you have a civil war on your hands. If you can get more than half the troops on your side, then we've have already dealt a severe blow to the enemy. Besides—it won't hurt if the day comes that 'good' side of Handover is part of Section 21."

Alec held up his hand towards Grimm, who was about to intervene; Alec knew full well that the majority of his staff were against any part of Handover joining Section 21 anytime soon, and for now Alec had capitulated in the matter. "Now, for some more—"

"My lord, my lord! Urgent message," a voice distorted by electrical interference interrupted Alec.

"Stop calling me lord! *I am no one's lord!*" Alec shouted, looking supremely irritated.

"Of course, my lord, but the message is from your father."

"What now?"

"He's wondering how your training mission is going, and would like to inspect your fleet before the great inauguration this week when you will receive your commission, so that you can join in on the war effort."

Nass looked flabbergasted. *"Training mission?"*

"A convenient fiction," Grimm rumbled.

Alec ignored Nass and gave the messenger, which happened to be an android, a gift from his father: an evil smile.

GALL lay on the outskirts of the universe's largest known and most densely inhabited system, Marengo. Although the Sun Empire was now limited to the Marengan system itself, it still had enormous resources and manpower behind it. The siege of Marengo had become a nightmare for even such a glorious commander as Hoff, who was used to stand-up fights rather than sieges. Time and time again, she had considered returning to the capital to remove her co-Marquessa permanently, but that *other her* inside her had held her back. If only her second self would shut up and back off!

Someone cleared his throat behind her. She motioned for the person to proceed—and then she noticed the last two messengers lying on the deck, gory and dead. *Oh. Yes.* She turned facing a trembling young officer, a lieutenant; apparently the cowardly generals and admirals had started sending these poor creatures to her whenever there something bad to report, and that had been happening quite often lately.

The monster only shook her head, staring at her reflection on the shiny nano-wall across the room. She didn't remember killing the messengers, and she certainly couldn't remember where the blood that covered her from top to toe came from. She turned to the waiting lieutenant, a groveling Red Chinnick. "REPORT!" Her shout echoed through the command bridge.

The little male said nervously, "My lady, we think we might have some information about a fleet commander named Alec von Hornet, and—"

Before the lieutenant could say another word, Hoff was standing in front of him, less than a half-meter away, listening intently. She twisted her head and gave him a stare that ordered him to proceed with his report.

"It appears that there are troubles at Omar, and we have had some trouble with, with Handover, and..."

Without seeming to move, Hoff was in front of the nearest holotable, tabbing the keys on the edge. The Omar and Handover systems sprang into being above the table's surface. After staring glassily at the images for a long moment, she said, "Trouble indeed."

"It appears that we have lost both systems," the Red Chinnick said nervously, "and in a very short time. Our staff is investigating why we haven't heard anything until now, and—"

Hoff gestured for silence, and the little lieutenant shut up immediately, still trembling and now sweating profusely.

"It secures Omar. It has conquered Handover, due to rebellion, most likely among our followers. No, not conquering; it calls it liberating, and the people accept that claim. Yes. Yes, it's spreading a virus among our forces, and now we must face it. But no; we will do something different...It's my brother, it must be. —Be silent! No; no I will *not* be silent, it's *my brother*. —Mine too! —No, it's not, it's mine, you're a monster, be GONE!"

Hoff continued to mumble to herself while pacing back and forth. "Only one thing left to do, or we lose, for the first time ever." She looked out into the universe, towards the yellow giant star in the far distance; an enormous planet, ten times the diameter of any normal habitable world but a tenth as dense, reflected back its glory, providing the illusion of two stars. Marengo. The image was marred by ships of both navies flashing past, hunting and killing each other, an occasional explosion dotting the ether as a ship died or was wounded. After a moment, she calmed down and smiled. "Ironic, my brother; shall you be my slayer? Do you even know, and do you remember? Or are you an illusion, perhaps a mirage or a flash from the past? —No, it's not your brother, you old fool; kill it, we must eat it we must, find its love and use it...or eat it too," said the monster. "Go, you. Tell them all to come."

The very confused Red Chinnick scrambled out of the bridge, feeling very fortunate—until it realized that a good two dozen senior officers stood in the corridor, waiting for a summary. The little man cleared his throat and then, a bit nonchalantly, pointed its thumbspur over its shoulder. "She wants to see you now. All of you."

There was some nervous shuffling and a few angry stares; clearly some thought the lieutenant had been a bit too cocky in front of the officers. The lieutenant didn't give a shit; it just left for its quarters, to change its soiled uniform before returning to its station many decks below.

FIFTEEN

THE cloudless blue sky would have been picture-perfect, had it not been for the many thousands of warships and private "cars" crowding the skylanes in long, glittering lines all across the capital city, all converging on the Nastasturus Federation's primary headquarters. To keep modern skyscrapers from ruining the view, they had been placed in a "second downtown" many miles away. The city itself, which was half the size of a continent, held over two hundred million citizens; including the suburbs, three times that number. At the center of the main square was an enormous statue standing in a fountain, hundreds of paces high. Waterfalls poured down in two streams into an octagonal pool below. The subject of the statue, crafted from white pearl, was a mythical K'Drak, its horn broken, standing on its hind legs as if it had been injured. On the creature's back clung a woman wearing ancient knight's armor, wielding a broken sword. The way she sat, it seemed she had lost control of the creature.

When a senior officer returned from a successful war campaign and proceeded towards the palace with the Army behind him, the base of the fountain would change its appearance. The octagon would raise a wide bridge for the officer to cross under the large statue, while several thousand select soldiers performed drills as they marched up in several squares alongside their leader. The military drill was more of a show to please the civilian crowd than anything else.

Despite the beautiful weather, the temperature was cold, and a strong eastern wind warned the onlookers that a storm was coming soon. The wind chilled the five million civilians gathered along both sides of the famous victory road, Nastas; normally there would have been well over four times as many onlookers, but this event was less popular than victory celebrations. The crowd was currently witnessing the inauguration of the many private fleets that would soon be deployed to assist the regular military in what was already being called the Third Universal war. Each fleet commander would receive a brevet rank of admiral, and his, her, or its second-in-command would be a full blown active Admiral from the Nastasturus military. These fleets had been invested in by civilians in an attempt to profit from the war. There were as many Intergalactic fleets as there were Galactic ones.

The white marble presidential palace had been erected on a hill, and its U-shape facade surrounded the main square, where up to one million onlookers could gather. At the building's center were several large levels with offices for important dignitaries, politicians, and high-ranking military officers. On each side of the levels were two mammoth staircases, accessing all the levels down towards the town square, where they combined into one staircase. At the bottom stood an honor guard made up of the Nastasturus Old Guard.

On the first and smallest level, at the very top of the structure, were the President, the Marshal, and the Speaker. The next level housed the various Vice Presidents and Governors, followed by the Senate and the Congress. Below the politicians were arrayed the various military branches. The military—demonstrating that there was no democracy in a military organization—had its own levels of organization. At the top were the Generals; on the second level, the

Admirals representing the InterGalactic fleets; and on the next level, the Galactic Fleet Admirals. Below them were the judges and advisors and, on the lowest level, were various VIPs, other politicians, high-ranking officers, ambassadors, diplomats, and others. Many civilian investors were allowed to stand near the Governors section. Altogether, the structure could hold over fifty thousand people.

As tradition had it, first came one thousand soldiers from the Old Guard's band, playing marching music in perfect harmony, followed by twenty thousand soldiers marching in unison, wearing their parade uniforms and bearing ornamental weapons. These soldiers had distinguished themselves with honor and bravery in battle, or in performing special services. With them came the Nastasturus battle flag, leading the rest of parade. Then came the representatives from the various private fleets, each numbering one thousand to five thousand representatives marching behind their many different banners and standards. Each unit had their own style and color of uniform, but the main colors, dark gray and dark blue, were the standard colors for all new units; the only differences between them were their insignia and unit patches. Between the various units hovered several open limousines bearing the highest-ranking officers with senior staff members; here the uniforms were a mix, depending on the position the officers held. A faint orange glow surrounded each open limousine: protective shields, erected in the event of any assassination attempts. After them followed more military hovercraft bearing various oversized flags and standards, the banners of the military groups that would participate in the war.

Bringing up the rear were the civilian police and a special crowd control unit: ten thousand androids, each of which was more than happy to zap a debilitating electrical charge into rowdy civilians as necessary. Hovering guard andies also moved among the crowd.

Thousands of news orbs hovered above and flew along the road, filming the festivities and reporting on their various channels throughout the Federation; the press was more or less free in Nastasturus. There were also many thousands of private civilian hovercrafts stationed above the procession route, intermingled with small to very large exclusive space and air yachts. The Nastasturians were a rich people, by and large, and didn't mind showing their wealth; indeed, they reveled in it. Meanwhile, less-wealthy people cheered from balconies and anywhere else they could get the best glimpses on the procession. Gigantic monitors filled the public spaces along the route, displaying the event, some of them with their own hover engines built in.

Even though the crowd was relatively small, the entire city and planet were in an uproar. After all, this day had been declared a Federal holiday.

When the units reached the end of their march they stopped, and the officers were met by high-ranking admirals and generals before escorted on hover-platforms to the top of the structure, where they were greeted by the President, Speaker, and Marshal. The Speaker announced each key member of each fleet group; their titles and names echoed over the entire region, and their live images flashed onto the monitors as they one-by-one saluted the three Seniors. The admiral or general in charge would then accept the commission for his or her fleet group. The commissions were printed on old-fashioned papers that had been rolled up into scrolls and decorated with ribbons bearing the relevant fleet logos.

"Was that all of them?" President Alexander Petrius III groaned, making it clear that he had more important things to do. Speaker of the Hall First Lady Móhatta glanced at an aide for the answer.

The aide looked up from her tablet nervously. "No, my lady, there *is* one more fleet, a Hornet group...sorry, that's the House of Hornet," and here she looked up at the Marshal. "Ahhhh, Section 21, it's called, and they should have been the third to last group introduced. They apparently did not return from their training run in time to participate...

She trailed off as both the President and the Speaker glared at the Marshal; Guss ignored them, remaining at his position, regarding the horizon. The aide whispered something into her wrist-comp, trying to find out if there would be any more units arriving or not.

The President knew that he could give his carefully crafted speech only after the last unit had arrived, and was clearly frustrated. The Speaker would give a short introduction, again, and then

Guss—his former friend and now chief adversary—would probably give a long speech of his own.

"Well, where is your son—"

The Speaker was interrupted as Guss nodded toward the Nastas Road. The crowd went dead silent, and the images on the screens started to blink, as if they were subject to some sort of strange interference. In the far distance could be heard the sound of drums and marching feet—many marching feet, but they weren't marching as a normal military unit would have. Instead, they marched to the beat of the drums. Alexander and Móhatta adjusted their eye zooms, and their eyes widened as they saw what was coming.

Two long lines of thousands of soldiers advanced toward them, marching—almost dancing—in unison, stomping hard on the pavement, all wearing different types of uniforms. Among them were dozens or more large drums on small hovercrafts; on the ground below each were hundreds of smaller drums carried by individuals, all being played with gusto. For a moment, the onlookers were taken aback by the strange new appearance, and didn't really know what to do; should they cheer or boo?

It took a while for the marchers to reach the end of the road and near the statue; but instead of forming up into a square like the rest had done, they lined up along the long road, facing each other, still marching in place, the drums still thundering; and now every other soldier lined-up bore long pikes that they struck on the ground in unison with the drumbeats.

Then there came the sound of a horn so horrible and loud that it sent chills down the spines of those who had them—and the crowd went ballistic. Several hundred riders on strange creatures very much like the white pearl statue advanced down the Nastas Road. First came Alec on his black K'Drak, followed by Bentor, who carried the ensign of Section 21, followed by Grimm, who held a standard displaying a holographic image of the planet Omar from space, with a word arcing above it: *Liberatio*—liberated. He was followed by Asturius, who held a similar standard bearing an image of Handover, with the same text above. It didn't take long for the news media to catch on that what had been a boring inauguration had turned suddenly into a victory parade.

The news spread like wildfire. The crowd stared in awe at the K'Draks, and then at the newscasters on the big screens shouting and screaming about Omar and Handover. Soon people rushed to the victory road, and chaos threatened to erupt.

Alec raised his hand, bringing his cavalry to a stop one-third of the way down the road; instantly, all drums and pikes stopped. The only sound that could be heard was the crowd, which eventually fell silent. Soon, the only sounds came from the snorting K'Draks as they impatiently waited, snaking their long necks back and forth, staring at the large crowd.

"Liberation of *what?* Omar? What the hell is an Omar...and our enemy Handover!" the president burst out angrily. "Has your son lost it, Guss?"

The Marshal ignored his former friend, and looked toward one of the aides standing behind them. The aide stepped forward and spoke in a stentorian voice: "Mr. President, my lady Speaker: when someone claims a liberation, then he or she must be honored with the same conditions as a victory parade. Furthermore, as Section 21 has not yet been commissioned, the fleet is free to liberate without breaking any rules of war. Thus—"

Alexander interrupted the aide, "Thus, my ass! Móhatta, *what is going on here?*"

"You heard the man. Apparently, Alec von Hornet and his Section 21 have liberated both the non-aligned system of Omar, as well as one of our enemy's capital world." She squinted towards Guss, who remained motionless. She got no help from him, and abruptly realized he wouldn't have anything to say until the civilians before them had become official military. For now, he was in charge of all the new inaugurated soldiers, but not Section 21; and per his remit, he therefore he held his peace.

For a brief moment, she could have sworn that the old bastard smiled. Now Móhatta smiled too.

"Mr. President, if you will excuse me, I must perform my office. I take it that these claims are accurate?" she asked Guss.

Still no response; yes, now he was definitely smiling. He'd probably known about this all along. She shook her head, rolled her eyes, and approached the center of the platform to turn on the speaker system. She cleared her throat, and it took a long while before there was complete silence.

"Honorable citizens, it appears that there has been a change of the day's venue. Not only have we had the honor of inaugurating 200 new fleets, we still have one more to commission. However, it appears that they have already seen action, and are reporting that the systems of Omar and Handover have been…liberated."

The crowd roared, and it was almost ten minutes before the Speaker could continue.

"Citizens! Let us show these victors how to be welcomed home after a successful campaign, and may it mark the beginning of the end of this war! For the first time, we have…"

Whatever the rest of the speech might have been, no one heard; because it was drowned out by the renewed rumble of drums and horns, and the screams of the crowd as the cavalry started to advance slowly toward the square. The infantry in the rear guard took up positions behind and followed until they reached the center of the square, where the other fleet formations stepped aside, allowing the victors the floor.

Alec, dressed in an Old Guard Admiral's uniform, guided his K'Drak forward and stopped, facing the Seniors and waiting for a long moment before he finally raised his left hand and arm in a stiff, straight-armed dictator's salute. There was a brief silence before his father slowly returned the greeting. Alec then raised his horn to his lips and played a horrible call, which was followed by many others— and then the crowd went nuts.

Instead of using a hover platform to reach the Seniors, Alec, Bentor, Grimm, and Asturius charged up the steps to the top of the hierarchy on their K'Draks, causing high-ranking people to spring aside, some cursing up a storm. Once they made eye contact with the beasts, though, they shut up. Now people started to realize what it was the men were riding: animals that had been mythical for ages.

When Alec reined in before the Seniors, all but his father stepped back. He dismounted and saluted everyone, and stopped facing his father. Guss was about to hand over his commission when he hesitated; he opened it and made a few changes with a small laser pen, then whispered to an aide, who made some changes in a protocol. He then handed his son the commission, and Alec could see that instead of "Fleet Group 199" he had changed the fleet's name to Fleet Group 21 Galactic. Guss nodded toward the document, and after a moment Móhatta signed it and looked at the President, who stared in disbelief at the monster next to Alec. Finally he smiled uncertainly, then he too signed the commission, without making a fuss about the alteration. He was just too taken back at the strange, beautiful creature—and already plotting about what this could do for him in the eyes of the populace. *I must have one of these creatures*, he thought, *no matter what.*

Alec and his colleagues did not attend the inauguration function afterward; instead, they had dinner at his parents' estate. Guss had to attend the official function, but left early to join with his family. He left his shuttle with several staff officers, and a military escort met with them at the landing site, where they entered several hovercraft and headed for the distant House Hornet.

"Tell the driver to stop," Guss ordered suddenly, when he noticed Alec sitting by his favorite tree. Next to him lay that mythical beast of his. The Marshal motioned for his followers and guard to remain in the background as he strode toward his son. It was a long walk up the hill, and Guss noticed that his wife and/or the gardeners had been up to something, because he didn't recognize some of the new purplish flowers that emitted a strange but pleasing scent. He saw that a few hills away, in their backyard, were several other K'Draks, apparently playing with their riders; and farther in the distance, hundreds of people enjoying themselves at an outdoor terrace set with a large dinner. For a moment, Guss considered leaving his son alone; but a gesture from Alec, who sat with his back turned towards him, encouraged him to join the boy.

As he came around the tree, he saw evidence that his son had wept, but what he normally thought about such things he kept to himself. A field commander should never display weak emotions unless alone; then again, his son *had* been alone, until he interrupted him. Guss did something he hadn't done in a long time: he actually sat himself on the ground, something his position normally did not allow. To his own surprise, he placed his left arm over Alec's shoulders.

"Death follows me, Father," Alec moaned.

Guss didn't have any response; he just held his son tighter.

"Wherever I go, people are hurt and die."

Guss held back for a while and then said, "It comes with the job, I'm afraid."

"That's not what I meant. I mean wherever I am, in battle or not, people die. But why?"

Guss removed his arm and gave his son a puzzled look.

"No matter what I do or where I am, people die—even before the war. When I was a cadet, a rebellion broke out and people died. My ship home was hijacked by pirates, and people died. At New Frontier-16, millions of people died. And then came all that followed... and now this."

With a friendly yet stern voice, Guss replied, "Those incidents were not your fault, merely circumstance—and you put an end to the killing each time. For someone in your position to feel guilt and blame is normal, and actually a good thing; it demonstrates that you do have empathy...feelings and worry about the consequences of your actions. For what it's worth, everyone in your position goes through the same emotional wringer. Trust me on this one."

"But..."

"There is never a 'but.' Things are what they are, son. Face them and never let anything get the better of you."

There was silence between father and son, and both looked straight ahead at the landscape. Far down the valley, a beautiful waterfall splashed its way down a rocky hillside. More of the K'Draks and people played and bathed in the pool below, while a few brave souls dived down the high cliff sides. Guss began to wonder if his son could lead his own force to action again, or if he was about to lose it—something Guss had seen many times, even in some of the best field commanders. Normally they would simply retire, but this was his son. By all means, after his recent feats, Alec ought to be able retire and focus on the House of Hornet, which he would one day lead; but Guss knew he need his son for the war effort. The entire federation needed him, but Guss would never say that to his son. Why place a greater burden on his young shoulders?

He decided to change the subject. "I have sent several fleets to Omar and Handover, and of course several battle stations," he announced, "the latter more to demonstrate our support than anything else. Smart move to place the captured Omega station at Fantaka…and do keep Fantaka's location a secret for now. I read your plan for Fantaka, and you have all my support—and your mother's, too."

Alec turned, facing his father. "Mother's? You let her read the report?"

Guss just raised his eyebrows and smiled. "When will your forces be ready for some new action?" he asked. "Perhaps at your convenience, you might want to share your plans with your old man. Figure that any orders from HQ—that's me, by the way—might be less favorable if you don't."

This time Alec smiled at his father's words. "The timing was not to our advantage, which was why I decided to advance—to buy more time. The results were very much to our benefit, I will admit. However, it will be a while before we can see more action. I'm still missing half my fleet, because more troops are undergoing training."

"Good! That will give you and your staff time to reorganize. Let me know as soon as you know you're ready."

"I'll do that, Father. Admiral Cook said something about another half-year, but I doubt we can wait that long, since the enemy won't wait to retaliate. By the way, who will be my SIC? I know HQ—that would be you—has to decide that. Let me guess: Cook?"

Guss removed his hat and placed it next on the ground next to him as he considered the question. Finally he replied, "Cook? Why, no. Let's keep him in charge at Fantaka with Lord Asturius. Let them keep doing what they're already doing; it seems effective. They're presiding over your reserve and training, and protecting Fantaka from idiots. The person I have in mind is a young, new, inspiring admiral—a woman."

There was a long silence, and Alec got a gut feeling that something was amiss. Suddenly, Guss got to his feet, leaving his hat on the ground. A long scimitar-tipped tail took the hat and lifted it up to him; Guss looked at the K'Drak, which still seemed asleep, then smiled and bowed as he took his hat and brushed it off. He looked down at the hat thoughtfully, then he turned his back to Alec, facing the valley ahead. He shook his head and continued, "This young woman was sent on an ultra-secret mission a while back, with a small fleet. It was so secret, in fact, that we couldn't tell you of it...despite the potential personal consequences." He looked back at Alec, eyes narrowed. "What have you heard about our new stealth scout?"

"The Grasshopper?"

Guss smiled at the ridiculous name the researchers had hung on the most advanced spacecraft ever built. "During a battle some time ago, scanners on several ships detected readings similar to those of our new...Grasshopper. As far as we know, only *our* ship could have generated those readings. And so...."

"So you sent this new admiral to investigate whether the enemy has the same technology, or has stolen ours?"

"Pretty much."

There was a long silence; then, suddenly, the K'Drak began to stir. It stayed on the ground, but its tail whipped back and forth and its eyes opened, glaring at the Marshal, who turned to face his son with a contrite expression. Alec glanced at the beast, then at his father; and then he felt chills rush down his spine.

Guss said, "I beg your forbearance. I was going to wait until later to present you with this information, but I fear that the K'Drak will soon be out of the bag, and you deserve to hear it from me first. Just promise me that you'll listen to everything I have to say, and won't do anything irrational."

With that said, alarms and whistles went off in Alec's head, and he leapt to his feet, standing next to his father. The K'Drak raised its long neck and moved its head closer, with a deceptively friendly and anticipatory expression.

"Was that little voice talking to you just now?" Guss inquired calmly.

"No, Father, that would be psychotic. It's not a voice. It's just within my mind, just like a thought, but not my own."

"Sounds equally disturbing to me, son, but what do I know? Seems to work for you."

Before Alec could respond, Guss gestured for silence and tabbed a few buttons on his wrist-comp, his eyes never leaving his son's. "I was going to introduce you to the lady Admiral during the supper we're holding for you and your senior officers tonight, but it's better to do so now."

A young woman in an admiral's dress uniform exited one of the hovercraft at the base of the hill and climbed the slope. When she reached the tree, she stood stiffly at attention. "Mi reporting as ordered, sir."

"At ease," the Marshal said in a friendly tone. "Alec, this is Admiral Eerized Mi, I believe you met each other onboard Crusher-5 a while back." She was a dark-skinned Oman with intelligent eyes, not conventionally beautiful but arresting nonetheless, and she seemed very young for her rank. Then again, he was very young for his own. She bore some striking features that somehow resembled Alexa, he realized suddenly, except that Mi was older than Alexa would have been—probably as old as Alec himself, perhaps even a year or two older.

"I heard something about your mission, Admiral," said Guss. "Any success?"

Mi looked first at Alec; and then, without moving her head, she looked at Guss, not sure how she should conduct herself. She preferred the old military style, where a younger officer stood at attention, reported, and then was dismissed. Clearly, this was not going to happen today. She cleared her throat and asked, "Sir, what can I say and what can I not say?" In other words, she wanted to know Alec's clearance level.

"Tell him everything. But for now, jump to the last part."

"Well, sir, we left for our mission, and…"

She hesitated as she noticed the expression on the face of her supreme commander. He gestured with his hands for her to move on more swiftly, and so she did.

"We managed to locate the abnormality that had caused the signal, and…"

More motioning.

Alec von Hornet just stared at her, in concert with the great awe-inspiring beast at his side. Mi did not feel comfortable at all.

Again she cleared her throat and continued, now speaking faster. "We located a survivor. We…" she looked directly at Alec and said firmly. "Fleet Admiral von Hornet, I believe Alexa, your fiancée, is still alive."

Alec took three fast steps and grasped Mi's shoulders. His grip was very firm, and the look in his beautiful dark blue eyes made Mi melt inside. Normally, if any man had handled her this way she would have kicked his ass, no matter his rank or status; but Mi had just felt the bottom drop out of her universe, plunging her into a river of lust. She would have gladly done things to him there in public, she realized, that should be confined to the privacy of a bedroom. He had but to ask…

After a moment, she realized that she was being shaken. "Tell me!" Alec shouted.

Mi shook her head and came to her senses. "Admiral, we have a survivor, and she's being treated as we speak—"

"WHO!"

"Nina! Her name is Nina! She was a member of the party of the *Beala-One*."

Alec let go of Mi, who started to brush the wrinkles out of her uniform. She also had to fix her hair a bit. Her hat was on the ground; a tail grabbed it and handed it to her. Mi smiled at the friendly gesture until she looked up into the eyes of the monster. It didn't look very welcoming, its eyes almost glowing.

"Sir, there's much more."

Alec stared at her, and then motioned for her to be silent. He looked at his father and then back at Mi.

"Sir, the little we know is that—" Mi began, but Guss cut her off.

"Alec, we believe that there are other survivors, and that Alexa is among them. However, they have been taken far into enemy territory."

"Nina has given us an account of what happened, and we're looking into it," Admiral Mi reported, "but she's badly injured, and had to be returned to the healers, and it will be a few days before she's in any condition to see anyone."

Alec stared at both and then at the K'Drak, who now sat waiting patiently. Suddenly that long tail moved towards the saddle and grabbed something from a bag. The tail then moved swiftly and handed Alec his horn. "Where was their last known location?" he demanded.

"Sir, we don't know exactly. It could be to one of two locations: either towards their capital onboard a cruiser belonging to a Zunzun or Zorzak, or something similar—"

Mi wanted to say much more, but she was interrupted by what had to be the most horrible sound in creation. She clapped her hand over her ears and then closed her eyes when a similar sound blasted away from the monster sitting behind her. Then there was an eerie silence; but it didn't last for very long. From the valley below and from the opposite side of the large estate more horns sounded as more of the monsters gathered; and moments later, six strange craft suddenly decloaked at scattered points all over the estate. There was a rumbling, as of great hooves, and suddenly there were hundreds, if not thousands, of people and K'Draks circling the base of the hill, keeping their distance.

And that's that, Guss thought looking sadly at what once had been beautiful new flowers imported from the Liberated World of Omar. *Beala will most definitely not approve of this. Glad I'm not Alec right now.*

SIXTEEN

THE opaqued duraplast windows had been cleared, so that onlookers could see inside the medical bay. It wasn't the largest bay on the med-station, but it was the most technologically advanced, and it lay near the center of the largest hospital station orbiting the military port of Inon-Luna. The station was part of a vast cluster of thousands of ships and stations, spacedocks for building and repairing ships, and research posts that orbited where Inon's one small moon had once been. The moon itself had long since been dismantled and converted into the stations and barracks that had replaced it.

Inon itself was under a blackout shield; even from orbit, it was difficult to make out with the naked eye the outlines of the continents and seas of what was a fecund, vibrant world. Inon was one of many military systems belonging to the Nastasturus Federation, and happened to be Admiral Mi's homeworld. She would not, however, be visiting on this trip.

Alec, Asturius, and Mi stood in the med-bay's gallery, observing the patient lying on the bed inside, wrapped up so tightly in diagnostic bandages that she looked like a mummy. A complicated mask covered her face, providing a mixture of gasses and medicines she needed to heal. Next to her stood an ursine physician, along with a pair of Omanoid nurses and a medical andy that might have been mistaken for Oman had it not been for its shiny white skin. The android and the physician were in a middle of a conversation.

"How much longer before we can talk to her?" an impatient Asturius asked through a communicator. The bearish physician glanced at the door and then waved his hand, irritated.

"You must tell me your story again, Admiral Mi," Asturius demanded.

Mi rolled her eyes, knowing that she wasn't observed, then took a deep breath and begun retelling a story she had not only told ten times before, but had also written a long report on. She knew the bastard next to her had read it and listened to the same thing from her mouth numerous times. She was just about to begin when Alec cleared his throat shook his head sharply.

"The story won't change the report or the facts, Asturius," Alec stated. "Let it be for now, and be thankful you're not my father."

"Your father?" Asturius sounded surprised.

"My old man thought that the research on this new stealth ship was so classified that we were the only ones to have it. He'll be in some hot water over that."

Admiral Mi broke in, "What my staff has learned is that the inventor first worked for Florencia, and that they have created a super cruiser that can make this kind of jump. But some of my scientists say that's impossible. Anyway, in order for the inventor to escape to Nastasturus, he or she sold some version of it to Gull knows who in order to finance his escape."

Asturius said quietly, "Must have been what saved them from the blast when Ogstafa blew up her ship."

"Who's to say that there aren't other survivors, in ships with similar capabilities?" Mi suggested.

"We can have Bentor's people look into it," Asturius suggested, looking at Alec for approval.

"Perhaps when we know more, but for now we sit tight. Let's see what our scouts have to say once they get back."

A beeping sound from Alec's wristcomp interrupted him. A small holographic image of Major Bax wearing his battle uniform sprang into being, reporting a commotion caused by the Vixens.

"Let the little troublemakers in," Alec ordered.

Moments later, the blast doors opened and Mohama, Miska, Kirra, and Zicci charged into the corridor, all still wearing their pilot gear. Just as they reached Alec and the others, the door to Nina's med-bay hissed open, and the ursine surgeon, Leppra, made his stand in the doorway, explaining that under no circumstances could his patient be disturbed. A million and one questions rained down on his head as the Vixens shouted at him all at once, as usual ignoring Asturius's demands that they settle down immediately. Alec rolled his eyes and cleared his throat, but no one seemed to care that he was everyone's Commander- in-Chief, except for the medical people. The cacophony ended when Bax arrived and let out a loud roar, shutting everyone up. "Our leader will speak," he said, once it was silent.

Alec moved slowly through the small crowd, facing Dr. Leppra. "How long, sir?"

"At least four more standard days."

"Why so long? Isn't she healed?" Asturius asked.

"Most of her physical injuries have been healed, yes. But she still needs to rest, as it was a very complicated surgery. Here is a list of what we think she had to endure—the torture, that is."

He handed Alec a computer pad; his eyes skimmed the list, from time to time looking up at the Vixens, who all had teary eyes as they waited. "They *scalped* her?"

"Partly—the side of her head. She had one of those tattoos that had been burnt into her flesh and then colored. They took it."

Asturius leaned over Alec's shoulder and glanced at the list. "Someone kept it as a souvenir?"

"We assume so. We must still test her for psychological damage from the torture and how it has affected her, considering the abuse she's been through." One of the Vixens muttered something about payback as Zicci stepped between Alec and Leppra. "Can she hear us?" she wanted to know.

"Yes, but I'd thank you not to bother her...wait, you little—!"

Zicci ducked under Leppra's arm and scrambled to the bed Nina was cocooned in. She began to weep when she saw Nina lying there, wrapped in diagnostic bandages, festooned with tubes, her face still hidden behind the horrible mask that regulated her breathing. The tired surgeon waved his hands in the air in frustration, shaking his head as the rest of the crowed entered the room. He threatened to call security and have them tossed into the brig, but they ignored him. Shaking his head, Leppra gestured for the medical andy to be still.

Mi couldn't hide her look of disapproval when all the pilots—officers they might be, but too young, she thought—disobeyed a direct order from the chief surgeon; and to top it all off, they treated a Lord of the Grisamm and their own supreme commander as if they were insignificant. There would be changes here—some very strict, very stern changes. Mi liked to run a tight ship. There was also this problem with all the different uniforms and outfits worn by the Section 21 troops; she had to address Admiral Lord von Hornet about that at the proper time.

"Can she really hear us?" Zicci whispered, standing right by the bed. From Nina there came a constant gurgling sound, spiced with the beeping of healing and diagnostic machines; but suddenly her wrappings moved, and a thumb popped up, disorganizing a carefully laid bandage. Doctor Leppra smacked his forehead with a palm, squinting in irritation, knowing he had to redo everything.

"Two minutes, no longer," he ordered, frustrated. "She must rest from her injuries, and a psychiatrist must interview her about the effects of the torture! *And* I must fix her wrappings."

All the girls leaned over Nina, whispering to her while giving comfort and support and making many different promises, especially about revenge. Soon, with the help of Bax and Asturius, the girls were shuffled outside, leaving only Alec and the medical crew. Just as Alec was about to leave, he turned, facing Nina.

"The others—Alexa and Tara. Do they live?"

The girls, who had been protesting against Bax's and Asturius's cruelty, heard Alec and were silent as they watched Nina's thumb move up and down.

"Does that mean you don't know?"

Thumb up.

"The last time you saw them, were they alive?

Thumb up.

A very upset Dr. Leppra interrupted when he noticed changes on the diagnostic monitor above his patient, and in no uncertain terms ordered everyone out. Everyone obeyed but Alec, who just stared at Nina; and when Leppra noticed, he calmed down and said, "Please sir, let her rest for now."

With that, Alec gave Nina a last glance and then joined the others in the gallery. All, especially the girls, were waiting impatiently; but when they saw Alec's expression, they made a path for him. When he reached a large port displaying a view of the chaos outside the station, he stopped and leaned on the railing below it, staring out into the Big Dark. "Admiral Mi," Alec said, still staring dead ahead, "ready the fleet. Lord Asturius here will help you become familiar with our forces."

For a moment the young Admiral looked hesitant, and sagged a little as if a very heavy weight had been laid on her shoulders. Then she straightened and said crisply, "Sir. Ready the fleet for what, if I may ask?"

Alec didn't answer.

Mi looked at Asturius for help, but could find none there, "Sir, I need time to get accustomed to this new fleet. Even though the Marshal of War has honored me by making me your SIC, my staff and I will need months before we're at 100%."

"The fleet must be ready for action by the day we can talk to our friend Nina."

"Sir..." she stepped up next to him and whispered, because she didn't want to obviously question her new commander in public. "Sir, that's only four days."

Alec just turned his head and stared at her, dark-blue eyes steady and emotionless. The goosebumps on Mi's arms and the cold chill on her back gave her all the answers she needed. This man was beautiful but frightening, and she would do anything for him. She took a step back and stood at attention, shouting, "Attention! *The* Admiral on deck!"

Her words were followed by everyone's boots banging smartly on the deck.

"Members of the 21ˢᵗ Galactic fleet! Prepare the fleet for action!"

Mi know that her order had only been a gesture, and a bit excessive at that; but it was the right thing to do. There would be time for her to learn more—or so she hoped.

With that, everyone left Alec alone, with the exception of Bax, who waited at the far end of the corridor with a pair of guards. The rest followed Mi as she marched away.

FOUR days later, Zicci, Mohama, Kirra, and Miska brought their fighters in hot on the med-station's landing platform, causing more than the normal amount of havoc among the ground crew as they landed. The ships normally landed in formation, lined up in perfect precision; but not today. After detaching themselves from their helmets and various telemetry probes, the dashed as a unit down to the nearest elevator. When they finally reached Nina's med-bay, they were stopped by a friendly Bax, who held up both his hands for them to slow down.

"Sorry, lassies, no one enters—including you. Have a seat over there."

His stare made sure none of the youngsters opened their mouths as he nodded his head to an adjacent waiting room. Inside sat Asturius, Grimm, and several others, including their new SIC. Her sharp glance towards the girls told all of them what she thought of them. Zicci poked her tongue out behind Mi's back, while Kirra muttered something obscene. That made the rest laugh, until Mi suddenly turned around, facing them. The girls halted, but instead of standing at attention, they only smiled and licked their lips.

Meanwhile, Grimm watched their antics, while Asturius read something from a pad, ignoring them.

The wait was long and terrible. Minutes turned into hours; hours into half a day. A few medical attendants and senior staff doctors of several species shuttled in and out of her room, all checked by Bax and the other guards, both coming and going. Finally, late in the day, everyone retired for the evening to Spartan living quarters, dining on field rations. They trooped back the second day…and they waited. As the second day threatened to turn into a third, there were many impatient people waiting. Admiral Cook had joined them, along with the Saurian Hawsatsche of Samari, along with some of their staff.

Mi had left after the first day but rejoined them again on the morning of the third. "Anything yet?" she wanted to know, addressing the entire room, but no one answered but for a few head shakes. Housekeeping androids buzzed around, offering much-needed refreshments, while another attempted to keep the place clean, constantly peeping and asking in its little girl voice for people to please move aside.

By noon, Mi was very upset; she had barely met with her commanding officer, and the last few days had been a trial like no other. The many new ships and their exceptionally advanced technology were mesmerizing, however; what should normally take years for engineers and scientists to develop were invented in a rush, new breakthroughs that would have been celebrated before treated almost casually, and there had been casualties as prototypes were rushed into service and the inevitable accidents occurred. Indeed, the new fleet group had suffered more casualties from their accelerated science program that they'd suffered in the Liberation of Omar. Still, she was extremely impressed with the little she had seen. But the uniforms—or more specifically, the lack of uniformity—seemed to be a serious problem, and more so, she didn't really know what she could or could not do, since *someone* had failed to issue her new orders.

Suddenly the doors to the waiting room slid opened and there was some commotion in the room as everyone leapt to their feet. In the doorway stood Guss von Hornet, the Marshal of War. He had stopped by the entrance and looked around thoughtfully. Everyone in the room moved slowly until Bax let out a roar: "Supreme Commander on deck!" and suddenly shot to attention.

"How did he get here so fast?" someone whispered in the background.

The Marshal smiled at the comment. "I have my ways," he announced. He looked over the crowed and his eyes stopped at Mi's. "Admiral Mi: report to Admiral von Hornet at once."

Mi saluted and marched inside the med-bay. The rest remained standing at attention. Guss nodded towards Bax. "At ease," he barked.

Before anyone could walk up to Guss, he held up his arms for them to stop. "Brother, a word. Follow me to my ship."

Admiral Cook left with the Marshal, while the rest had to wait, even more impatient than before. But no one dared rush after them and ask anything. After a short while, Mi reappeared; and before Bax could announce her presence, she motioned for him not to.

"There will be a written report available eventually," she announced. "However, all of you may see Nina now, and to make sure there will be no commotion, you will let her tell her story uninterrupted. What you are about to hear is classified, and our CO has allowed only for those of you present to hear the story. You may not repeat it to anyone."

Before she finished, she had to step aside to avoiding being rushed by the Vixens. The others followed a bit more slowly. The girls entered the gallery, and came to an immediate halt at the med-bay. Alec's K'Drak lay on the floor, taking up more or less all the space. Its neck and large head lay on the deck at the door's entrance, blocking the way.

"Crap," Mohama said aloud.

"Probably asleep, as usual," Miska whispered.

"Bloody lizard," Kirra complained.

The K'Drak raised an eyelid—actually, three eyelids—and stared at them with one eye.

"Yep, it's smiling," Mohama said.

At the sound of a faint whistle from inside the bay, the enormous beast raised its long neck and allowed everyone to enter. Once everyone had entered, it stuck its long neck inside and lay its head on a shelf on the wall, observing everyone.

When the girls saw their friend, all of them gasped in shock. Although Nina had been healed, the process was far from over, and she would have to undergo many more surgeries, especially cosmetic ones, to be brought back to normal. She was so bruised and patched up that they wouldn't have recognized her if it hadn't been for her voice, as she murmured something to Alec and laughed softly at what he whispered back. Her head was still bandaged, because her new eyes were still adjusting to her body; it remained to be seen whether her body would reject them or not. If rejected, new ones would be cloned, and they would try again. Her legs were propped up on another healing machine, and a medical android was working with Dr. Leppra on a vivid burn mark on the bottom of Nina's right foot.

It was a slave number, branded on the sole.

"Hey! That tickles," Nina complained softly.

"We can do this at a later time," Leppra suggested.

"No, please. I want to be normal again."

Leppra gave her a friendly smile and resumed his work. Meanwhile, the visitors gathered around Nina, but no one said much; they just stood there waiting patiently. When Admiral Mi entered the bay, Alec leaned over to Nina and whispered something into the metallic array where her new ear had been attached. He then began to leave the room, having already heard Nina's story.

"Alec, please wait," Nina whispered with a hoarse voice. "Have hope. Don't give up on her, please."

Alec turned back and said, "I won't," leaving puzzled expressions behind him as he left the room. Mi gave him a quick glance, and he only nodded while murmuring, "You know what to do. Meet me later, when you're finished here."

"But sir, I should be with you," Mi replied. It wasn't that she wasn't interested in listening to this young girl's story, but it was a waste of her time. She could always read the report later; and besides, she had more urgent matters to deal with.

"We'll have time to meet up later. This is a story you should hear; you'll learn much from it."

They were interrupted by a newcomer. "Admiral Vito reporting as ordered."

"Good. Vito, you should listen to this oral report from Nina. When you've finished, by all means look me up, and let's discuss the...'selection process' Handover is currently commencing."

"Excellent, sir, I really..."

Alec's stare told Vito to shut up, and he obeyed. Alec turned again towards Nina, smiled, then left. His K'Drak followed as new guards arrived; Bax and his escort followed Alec as he walked slowly away, thinking about Alexa.

He took a waiting shuttle to his new flagship, which was disguised as an enormous fuel tanker. When the shuttle docked inside at his personal docking bay, he couldn't help smiling when he saw the shuttle he had had stolen from Zuzack the pirate, stationed in a special location. His smile faded when he noticed his father's shuttle attached to the same wall.

After having cleared several hallways, corridors, and passages, he reached his office—and inside found his father, sitting in an armchair beside the ornately carved antique wooden desk his mother had given him. Leaning over his father's shoulder was his Uncle Cook.

"I'll be brief," the Marshal stated. "One: you will unify your troops with one main duty and dress uniform. Their respective mission uniforms I care little about. From the looks of it, you have one of the best, most sophisticated fleets in the Nastasturus Navy, but there is absolutely no unity among the troops, officers, NCOs, cadets, and enlisted. Remember your failure at your first command—the mutiny. Even though you weren't present, you were still the captain of the *Predator*." Guss paused and held up his left hand when he noticed Alec about to say something. "Secondly, you do realize that what Admiral Mi brought is a message to you—to us—and that Nina was that message."

After making sure his son followed and understood, he continued, "Thirdly, you will not advance yet with your fleet, despite your recent successes. Get your own act together, and perhaps so will your troops. Report to me in three days at our home with a plan of action."

There was a long silence, and then Alec nodded, thinking hard. That Nina had been a message he hadn't thought of, but now he realized that his father could be right. He had been blinded; and why the hell had he made such a scene days before at his home, blowing the horn and everything? He needed to take step back, and not throw himself head first into a black hole.

"Cook and Asturius will take care of Fantaka, the building of your fleet, and the training of the troops," the Marshal continued, "and don't worry: the Environmental people have the support of Senator Oranii and most of the Senate. Because they have the last word in this matter, it's a closed subject in the Congress. Our new dictator can scream as much as he like. Fantaka is a new world protected by several treaties, and you will be its Governor, Alec. You should have a plan of action for the system in the future—something to think about for now.

"Also, for your information, Cook here was shabbily treated after first being saluted as a hero, and later having his fleet taken away by shifty politicians who know nothing of war. The Military Board has decided to give him back his commission, and a new fleet group under the same fleet number: the 11th Galactic. His entire fleet will be a support fleet for your own, until your force is at 100%—and we all know that's not going to happen for a few more years."

His father had just delivered a lot of information, and Alec slowly motioned with his hand so that a comfortable chair raised from the floor, facing his father and Cook. He sat down, thinking hard.

"Fine. I'll do as you say," he said after a moment.

Both Cook and Guss raised their eyebrows at his quiet response. Alec noticed their expressions. "Would you like me to stand at attention and salute you, Father?"

Guss smiled. "No, not when we're with family, like now. But I'm surprised by your reaction."

"I can't believe I never thought that Nina could have been returned to us as a message, but now it's obvious. But a message from whom?"

"It's only a guess, Alec," Cook said slowly.

"If she's a message, then I guess it would be from the pirates—especially that damned cannibal," Alec said slowly.

He sat thinking for a while, then suddenly raised his head. "It doesn't matter who the message is from for now, because no matter who, they'll all be dead soon enough."

"That's the spirit, son. Kill them all and let Gull sort 'em out."

SEVENTEEN

NINA waited for Alec to leave before beginning her tale. She heard the door shut, and she could sense some commotion in the room. She thought about her story; she knew what she could say, what she had to say, and what Alec and his father had asked her to keep secret. *Oh well, here goes nothing,* she thought, and began speaking.

Major Bree was about to follow his troops when his last reserve shuttle, which had barely missed decapitating him earlier, opened up with sprint missiles and magma blasts. Not knowing what would happened to his reserve, he focused on the mission: rescue the hostages. The last thing he saw from space was dozens of destroyers heading towards the melee, all being launched from their respective Nastasturus Omega cruisers.

"Disarm this scum, and get everyone aboard the sloop," Bree ordered. He brought up a scanner to check the girls, but Nina misunderstood the gesture and kicked it out of his hands. The scanner fell over a railing into the void of the space dock. A soldier quickly subdued Nina and the other girls with a blaster set for stun. A medic brought up another scanner and scanned the Vixens.

"It's them, Major. We've found the primary targets."

"Excellent. Report back to base, and let's take cover inside the sloop—"

His order was interrupted by an enormous ringing sound, like a gong the size of a moon had been struck.

Major Bree looked around steadily and calmly, knowing full well what was about to happen, especially when he noticed the hull-wave. That sort of disruption could only mean one of two things: that the gigantic structure was about to breach or explode. He flipped his visor to a particular yellow filter, and that's when he saw the Anti-Materia fog filling the vacuum within the enormous hangar. Yes, dammit, the ship was about to explode, as soon as enough of the AM contacted ordinary matter an canceled it out. *Must hurry, no time.* He and what was left of his squad charged inside the sloop, a few pirates doing the same; no time to stop them. Time was of the essence. He shouted to his troops to hurry.

A large saurian female blocked his way, and he was just about to blow the ugly bitch's head off when she showed her large hands in a universal gesture of surrender, shouting, "My ship! I've just installed a program that can—oh, to hell with this!"

The big woman alien tossed Major Bree aside, slamming him into the wall as she charged down a short corridor and into the cockpit.

Myra raised her eyes and looked out the port, seeing several breaches in the distance. *Only seconds now at most,* she thought as she seated herself and buckled up, then immediate hit the button for the release clamps. As soon as they dropped away, she launched the *Titan,* which swayed back and forth as the entire ship they were inside trembled and range like a bell. As she aligned the ship, she began to accelerate as steadily as possible, aiming the shuttle towards the nearest open entrance, which was already clogged with fleeing ships and shuttles of all sizes. The explosions and fireballs surrounding them didn't help any. She checked the controls, and her eyes widened as she realized the outer airlock door was still open.

"Idiots, shut that lock or we'll be fried!" she shouted into a communicator, her finger on the override switch. She was about to press it when the telltales showed the door was shut, finally.

The soldier she had roughed up earlier, that Major Bree, tossed himself into the seat next to her and shouted, "Punch it!"

There was a strange tapping sound that could barely be heard above all of the commotion when Myra activated the new program she'd bought from the Florencian traitor and lay her hand over the button that would execute it. "Strap in, everyone, here goes nothing," she shouted as she hit the button hard. She'd never had the chance to use the program before; nor had she had the time to chart any route but forward.

Just as she hit the button to execute the program, Ogstafa's entire ship exploded—and everything went black. The ship slammed through its own self-created singularity, whipping them through tortured spacetime at a hundred times the speed of light, far outpacing the blast wave of the explosion. *Titan* wasn't built for such rough treatment, and some of the outer hull plates buckled, while others peeled off the ship like house shingles in a hurricane.

When the program completed its last subroutine, the ship was spat out into regular space at zero relative velocity. The sudden stop caused everything unattached to the ship, including people, to jerk forward, mostly into the nearest bulkhead. A few of the unprepared passengers lost consciousness, but were brought back to reality in seconds by a brief but intense drop in temperature, apparently a side effect of the new drive. Fortunately, Myra had been strapped into her seat; still, because the cold made the reptilian pirate sluggish, it took a precious few seconds for her to come to and see that they were drifting toward a sun, caught in its gravitational pull; they'd come out of the singularity too near a system's primary. She cursed as she tried to swing the ship around, but the controls refused to obey her.

"Do something, or we've just jumped from the frying pan into the fire, literally!" Bree shouted at her.

"Not working—won't make it," Myra shouted back, sweating and cursing profusely.

"Then try that jump thing again!"

She tapped the button, there was a frantic tapping, the universe blinked—and *Titan* found herself facing a battle cruiser, firing all weapons. "The fuck did that bastard come from!" Myra screamed as she jammed the accelerator down, zigzagging away from several laser and magma bolts.

Realizing that they were caught in the crossfire between several ships in battle, she glanced at her weapons console and saw that everything was down. Suddenly the tapping sound began again, sounding like it was counting down—and the ship made yet another sudden jump. This time everything went black again; but Myra and the fool next to her hadn't passed out. They could hear shouts and protests from the back, roundly cursing the pilot, letting her know that some or all of the other survivors were awake and aware. Myra had no time for them; she had to regain control of the *Titan* and figure out where the hell they were, or this might well be her very last trip in space.

Again the ship came to an abrupt halt as it popped into wide open real-space, undisturbed by looming suns and space battles. But where? The first thing Myra did was check the scanners for any indications of other ships in the vicinity. Nothing: in fact, they were far from any significant mass. Next, she ran a routine scan for engine and structural integrity; while it was executing, she unstrapped, rose from her chair, and headed aft. Sticking her head out the door, she roared, "Nina, Alexa, Tara! Report to the bridge!"

Myra still hoped that she would survive this situation and escape to safety, so her first plan of action was to get rid of everyone aboard, then try and make her way to some safe corner of local space. She knew she had to be careful; there many numerous bounties on her head. She also had a bunch of Nastasturian soldiers aboard, and none was likely to be lenient to an old pirate with her background. And then there was the problem with the girls, all of whom hated her for having killed that blithering captain onboard the *Predator*—Zlo, or whatever his name was.

Several alarms derailed Myra's chain of thought, and she decided to worry about the future at a later time. For now, she had to save her precious ship. Just as she returned to her seat, the odd tapping sound came again, and suddenly the ship blinked away, slamming her into the bulkhead. As she cursed, she realized this wasn't supposed to happen. Her little ship couldn't make this many jumps safely.

They flipped back into normal space, this time in the middle of a debris field—the remains of at least two demolished ships, if not more. Metal and composites pinged off the hull as Myra stumbled back to her seat and strapped herself down, checking the monitors and making almost instinctive evasive maneuvers to avoid the largest pieces of debris, including the shattered remains of what had once been sentient beings.

"Look there," Bree shouted, pointing at a large metal block the size of a small cruiser, tumbling in their direction like a lethal asteroid.

"Must be from a space station or a very large ship," Myra grunted as she maneuvered around it.

"Graveyard in space," Alexa said from behind, holding the side of her head, blood oozing from between her fingers.

"Alexa, take navigation, please, while I try to figure out happened to the engines."

"You've never used that program before, have you?"

"Nope."

"So was it supposed to make multiple jumps?" Bree wondered.

"No, only one. Not sure why it made more."

Nina stumbled into the cockpit, "Well, did you guys shut it off?"

Myra and Bree looked at each other in sudden realization and Myra said, embarrassed, "Um...no."

Just then the tapping countdown began, and the ship jumped again, slamming Nina up against the wall as it downshifted back to real space. "Alexa." Myra pointed at Nina, then began tapping at her console, trying to disable the grasshopper program.

Alexa unstrapped herself and pushed away, helping Nina into a seat a level down, at navigation, as Tara and several soldiers entered the bridge and strapped down.

"Secure the bridge entrance and strap in," Major Bree ordered into his wrist-comp. "How many survivors aboard, Lieutenant Gruene?"

There was no answer; all that could be heard was their breathing, and Myra's frantic tapping at her keyboard. After seeing to Nina, Alexa swiveled back to her own console and called up their location—or tried to. Nothing showed on the monitor, and when she looked up at the forward ports, there was nothing to be seen but pitch-black darkness: no stars.

"What now?" a groggy voice demanded.

"You're supposed to say, 'where am I?' Nina," Alexa said calmly.

"I'm aboard the *Titan,* duh. Now, maybe someone could shut down that damned program," Nina suggested.

"I'm trying, but I'm not sure I'm doing the right things," Myra complained bitterly. She had several holo screens up and running, peering at them all with stern disapproval. "While I work on this bloody program, see what you guys can do about the ship. We lost at least a dozen outer hull plates in the first jump, and someone needs to make sure the emergency foam system and structural integrity fields activated. Tara, look—would you *please* look into that?" Myra more or less begged.

"Got it." She called up the ship's blueprints on the operations console, overlaid a real-time image, and used the external cameras to zoom in on the damage. An orange glow surrounded all the damaged areas but for one. She reported, "The foam hasn't deployed, but the structural integrity fields are holding except for one location toward the aft, and I don't think that one's important."

"Where, what part?"

"By the engine in the back. Looks like an atmospheric wing sheared off...I'm not sure."

"Never mind that, but fix the rest."

Tara tapped a few keys, and a pale grayish foam deployed from the edges of the ruptured plates, filling in the missing areas like scabs cover wounds. Because of the structural integrity fields, the foam stayed in place as it hardened into what were essentially new hull-plates, as tough as the originals. "Finished," Tara said cheerfully a few minutes later.

"Good, now we can move around the ship," Bree said. "Gruene, report. How many onboard?"

A young man reported to the bridge, holding his helmet under his arm. "Sir! Eighteen are left from the strike force, but the LT and four enlisted are injured and out of action for now. Doc is checking on them. There are three original crew from the ship we attacked, who somehow managed to get on board during the confusion; the pirates have all been subdued but for her." He nodded his head towards Myra. "All the hostages we rescued are in here with you. All in all, 25 survivors, sir."

"Thank you, sergeant. Do a standard equipment and weapons check; make sure the prisoners are secured and guarded, then help the doctor with whatever she needs."

The sergeant stood still for a moment as he looked at his wrist-comp. "All kits intact, and we have two exoskeleton suits... wait. Two hand blasters are missing. They could have been lost in the fight, but I'm not sure. I'll look into it." He then nodded again towards Myra, who was busy overseeing the repairs and trying to restart the engines.

Major Bree just shook his head. "I'll take care of things here on the bridge." He looked at Myra, who suddenly realized they were talking about her.

"This is my ship. I'm the captain, and—"

The cold gun barrel resting on her neck reminded her that she might not be the captain of the ship after all. A quick glance, and she saw Tara standing behind her. She could have quickly subdued Tara, but someone cleared her throat, and Myra saw that Nina had swiveled 180 degrees in her chair, training a magma blaster on her. Alexa, still with her back turned, had raised her hand and waved one of her fingers sideways: *No no no.*

Where the hell did they get the weapons? she wondered. All of them had been frisked by the security force earlier.

Major Bree smiled as he realized that the two blasters had been found. There would be hell to pay for the poor bastards who had lost them, but that had to wait; there were much more important things to do now. They had to survive and find a way back to home space and report to his HQ.

"Is there an infirmary onboard the ship?" Bree asked Myra.

Myra grumpily tapped a few keys and jerked her head toward a screen beside him, which displayed the ship's schematics. "By the galley," she growled. She then realized that she had something to impress on the Major—and hopefully she might be able to escape in due time. "Your crew will be needed to run the ship. It's an old engine and computer system. I haven't had time to reconfigure everything yet, and the only upgrades have been here in the cockpit."

"We'll do our best," he replied. "but my crew are soldiers, not squids. The Navy ferries us places. We're typically qualified only for exosuits and shuttles."

Myra nodded her head, then turned to the girls. "Well, lassies, I guess we'll be the ones taking care of my little *Titan*."

"Is it shut off? The jump program?" Bree asked.

The tapping sound before she replied, and the ship launched itself through another micro-singularity. "Nope, didn't quite get it!" Nina shouted sarcastically.

The ship seemed to move slowly this time. Just after the viewports went black, there was a blinding white flash, and then another, as the ship abruptly decelerated. But in this space, deceleration was relative; they were still hustling along at many times the speed of light. When they popped out into reality this time, they were still moving at a fast clip—and a rather large blue-white world was coming at them, growing rapidly in the viewports. The *Titan* entered the atmosphere like a meteor, heading at an oblique angle toward the surface. Myra hit the retros frantically, but it wasn't enough to stop them. "Hold on!" she shouted. "We're going down fast! Brace for impact!"

The *Titan* punched through thick clouds, the entire ship shaking as weakened hull plates and exterior sensors sloughed off and burned, leaving a trail of gray-black smoke behind them. Klaxons sounded, and coolant burst from ruptures in the hull. Meanwhile, the occupants were shouting and screaming as they were tossed about the ship and the ground drew ever closer. The friction peeled through the hull until an inner plate buckled and tumbled away, letting in the shrieking wind.

"All hull integrity shields lost!" Nina shouted.

The four windows at the nose of the ship cracked, spider-webbed, and blew inward in a scatter of crumbs in less than a second. "Forward ports lost!" Alexa called into the com system. "Abandon ship, I repeat, abandon ship!"

Myra pounded the console and yelled, "Get to the escape pods—look for the blue lights. Get in and punch out. Those of you in the cockpit, stay strapped in! The cockpit will launch itself as a large escape pod! If that doesn't work, the seats eject!"

They were fast approaching a rawboned mountain range; it was now or never. They could hear the other escape pods ejecting as Myra punched a large green button, and the emergency fuel tanks dumped everything they had to the engines as she struggled to pull up, managing to lift the *Titan*'s nose slightly. The ship passed between two peaks, smashing through what seemed to be a colony of enormous birds the size of fighters, splattering them all with an orangish-yellow fluid that must have been egg yolk. Wiping the crap out of their eyes, Alexa and Myra cooperated in trying to level off the ship—in time to aim it straight at another craggy mountain. They brushed the peak, and the resulting thud and squeal made the entire structure tremble.

"Incoming!" Major Bree screamed. Before anyone could react, the ship was hit hard from above, causing them to go into a tumble.

"What was that, a missile?" Tara shouted as Myra managed to right the ship. They'd lost altitude and were headed back toward the surface.

Alexa shook her head and pointed upward, where a huge talon had pierced the skin of the *Titan*. Nina had noticed it too; she fired at the base with her magma blaster, severing it. Outside, a nightmarish dino-bird of truly epic proportions shrieked as it spun away from the monster that had ruined its nest. But it latched on again in time to keep the monster from escaping.

"Sending electric charges through the upper hull and firing off the braking boosters," Myra shouted.

The actions had little effect, only making the creature madder than ever. It lashed out with a toothy maw at a weak spot where the hull had already started coming apart, and was as surprised as the occupants when the monster split into two halves, the entire engine section tumbling away to smash into ruin in the mountains below. The rest of the ship tumbled and spun around, crashing into another mountainside as escape pods launched in all direction. As what was left of the *Titan* veered toward a sheer rock wall, the cockpit launched straight up toward the stars.

The escape pods frightened the dragonish creature; it had had enough of this hell-beast, which was beaten anyway, so it returned to the nest its mate was keening over and trying to repair.

For a moment, Myra and the survivors in the cockpit had a chance to breathe; in fact, they all grabbed for rebreathers from lockers under their seats, since the air this high in the mountains was a bit thin. Nina and Tara even found themselves helmets, which sealed to their shipsuits automatically.

"All systems down—sorry, folks," Myra called over the howling of the wind. "Brace for impact...We're going down hard."

The red-hot escape pod brushed the canopy of a forest, setting it on fire and worsening their tumble. Completely out of control, one stubby wind brushed a tor, which sent them straight down toward the surface. This actually saved their lives, because they splashed into a vast pool at the bottom of what had to be one of the largest waterfalls in the galaxy, sending up a massive cloud of steam as the water flashed into vapor. The pod hit the bottom of the river hard, and then strong currents caught the vessel and sent it through a series of rapids, each more powerful than the last. The ship slammed into rocks and the bottom repeatedly, swirling around in a ride from hell. Several more waterfalls and rapids later, the ship hit the bottom of a lake hard, splashing water for a kilometer in all directions. It sank like a rock, lights still flickering and orange fire emanating from the braking rockets, making it appear the water was on fire.

Major Bree was the first to react; in seconds, he was unstrapped and out of his seat, clutching his rebreather to his face as he checked on the rest of the crew. Everyone was alive, and he could have sworn that some of the crazy young women were actually smiling or laughing through their masks. Whatever; now that he knew they were fine, he was more concerned about the rest of the crew, especially his troops. He clicked on his communicator but got no carrier wave; no way to check in now. He figured at least some of them had made it, since so many escape pods had gotten away, but now they were scattered over half of creation.

Nina almost choked from laughter when she noticed Tara swimming around in a strange dance. Myra just rolled her eyes, and started rooting around for survival kits. A moment later, as she came up with one, the ship suddenly came to an abrupt stop, causing more commotion. Myra pointed at the first aid kit she'd found, and gestured at the prominently marked compartments where they could be found; Bree instantly swam over and started to unload them, tossing them through the nearest window, where they promptly sank to the bottom of the lake. No matter. After having tossed out the last one, he removed a handset from the wall where one of the emergency packs had been. He hit a red button, and the flotation devices on the packs filled with air, scrambling them to the surface.

When he noticed that no one but Myra was helping, he angrily turned around and tried to motion for the girls to help; and that's when he saw one of them suddenly being pulled through one of the shattered ports. Everyone froze but for Myra, who despite her ungainly size launched herself out the port after the girl. Bree looked out one of the broken windows realized that one of the former hostages had a sizable tentacle wrapped around her waist, and was being drawn toward the beak and single large eye of yet another monster this planet had vexed them with.

Bree looked around for his machine blaster, kicking the walls to jet back to his former seat. The rifle was still attached to the back of the seat—and just as he reached for it, something yanked on his leg. He turned to find one of those Gull-forsaken tentacles wrapped around his ankle. He lunged for the weapon, but the thing attached to his leg was too strong, and pulled him towards the window. Fortunately, one of the girls suddenly appeared with a large knife—no, a sword of some sort—which she sliced through the tentacle. The water boiled as the blade flashed red. It wasn't a knife or a sword; it was a hull cutter, normally used for repairs.

The girl grinned at him and held up a thumb. Bree realized she wanted to know if he was okay, and he raised his hand and gave her a thumb back. He then reached for his weapon and altered its setting for underwater combat, and when he looked up, the girl was gone. Move quickly, he swam towards the opening and looked down to find her slashing at a tentacle that had grabbed her when Bree had turned his attention to the weapon. Tapping a key that converted his tactical suit to underwater use, Bree spat out the rebreather as a spare helmet folded up from his back and sealed around his neck, purging the water inside in less than a second. He angled toward the water monster as flippers emerged from his boots and fins grew from wrist to elbows, then launched forward as the jet-pack emerged and activated. As he sighted down the length of his rifle, he noticed one of his soldiers, also with a reconfigured tactical suit, launch himself in the same direction. He kept the man's position in mind.

By now the water was murky from the silt kicked up by their impact and the subsequent struggle with what appeared to be a giant octopod, but he suddenly pushed through into a clear layer where he could see the thrashing of several large tentacles, each clutching a victim. It was a hellish melee, and he realized he had to be very careful; it would be easy to injure someone with friendly fire, because the magma blasts tended to spread underwater. He had to find the central body and make a precision strike to kill it. He glanced to each side, and saw that two more of his troopers had joined him. No time to check on his helmet comp who they were; he just ordered them to engage the hostile entity and rescue the priority targets. Nodding, they fired off their jet packs and charged into the muddy mess.

Tara didn't realize what had happened until the tentacle pulled her clear of the ship. Another wrapped around her waist, not hard but very firmly, and then she was pulled down. At first, she didn't see anything because of the murky water, but after a short, tense moment full of struggle it cleared up. She raised her head and saw that the ship had landed on an underwater cliff; and when she looked down, she saw the monster's single vast eye staring at her as it pulled her down toward its beak. Great, another sea monster like on the water world, and this time she had no weapons. Even biting the bloody thing was out of the question, given the helmet she wore.

Suddenly Nina appeared, holding onto a heavy supply crate that she'd used to pull herself toward the bottom with its weight. She sank fast toward the staring eye, going for the kill. In her belt she carried the handset for the inflation device. Nope, not for the kill; instead she gestured for Tara to grab hold of the box. Tara reached out and wrapped one rope handle around her wrist, then looked at Nina and nodded her head; she then dared look down, and to her horror found herself just a few feet from a wide, gaping maw lined with hundreds of fangs. Then, with a strong jerk, she was pulled clear as Nina used the handset to inflate the supply box. Both shot toward the surface, only to see Myra in the clutches of several long tentacles. Suddenly, Alexa passed by, tangled in the beast's limbs, pulled implacably toward the thing's mouth.

Tara looked at Nina, and both smiled through their helmets. Simultaneously, they let go of the buoyant crate and started swimming strongly toward their friend. But Alexa was hardly helpless; she swung the hull cutter at the tentacle that had lashed onto her ankle, slicing it off cleanly, which only pissed off the beast more. In response, three more tentacles grabbed her waist, leg, and the arm with the cutter, and jerked her downward. Unable to swing her arm now, she was pulled towards the thing's sharp maw.

Myra was already there, her thick legs braced against the thing's bottom jaw and her arms pushing up the top half of the beak, keeping the jaws open with her enormous strength; but as big as she was, she was only one woman, and she was losing the battle. She gave Alexa a wry smile as Alexa was pulled closer and into the opening. Alexa, clear of the jagged teeth, started to panic, and struggled against the creature; but even her best efforts only made the tentacles tighten. She was beginning to think the thing would snip off the end of its own tentacles if it meant it got a chance to taste delectable Oman-flesh.

Suddenly bright lights strobed above, and there came several loud *whumps* so close together they almost blurred into one long staccato sound. The tentacles went slack, so she kicked them off and started to swim upward through the open maw, keeping her limbs close to her body to avoid the teeth, and gave Myra a thumbs-up. But Myra didn't move; she was stuck in the beak of what now appeared to be a very dead creature, if the lack of the top of its "head" meant anything, impaled on razor sharp teeth; had she sacrificed herself for Alexa? She certainly wasn't moving, and strings of blood were whisping out of her helmet.

A pair of strong arms pulled Alexa clear, and Major Bree attached a life preserver pack the size of a fingernail to the breast of Alexa's flight suit; before she could do anything, he had activated it, and it jerked her toward the surface as it inflated. Alexa looked down as she spiraled upward, and saw that at least two of the troopers were working on getting Myra free; but it was hard to tell how, as there was so much blood in the water. A third soldier was helping Myra with a rebreather, it seemed.

Alexa broke the surface and looked around. The indicator on the rebreather went to zero, which told her that the planet's atmosphere had plenty of free oxygen and no trace gases or toxins that would immediately damage her. Not surprising; most known life depended on oxygen, given its ability to react with other chemicals in an energetic fashion. Few other liquids or gases were as effective, and none were as common. Several large crates floated in the water around her, and in the distance she saw the terminus of a high waterfall. They'd gotten lucky, she mused; there didn't seem to be any rapids in this section of the river. Then she thought, *Lucky? I just fought another fucking sea monster, and almost lost this time!* With that thought, goosebumps erupted on her flesh. Maybe there were other monsters lurking below...

When she plunged her head under the water, she saw that the others were on their way up to the surface, and, relieved, she started to swim towards the shore. A few moments later, she crawled on all fours onto the beach side of the lake. It was muddy and filthy, but Alexa didn't care; it was *terra firma.* Breathing deeply, knowing she would probably go into shock soon from the trauma, she lay back but jerked upright when Tara shouted, "Look! The rest are okay!"

"Wait, two more," another voice muttered. "Did some of the other troops make it? I thought they were at the back of the ship?"

"No, Nina, most were in the middle of the ship by the galley, and a few below the cockpit, I think. We never had much time to check out Myra's ship."

"And look, there's our princess!" Tara squealed, pointing at a bruised Alexa, who was now crouched on all fours, coughing.

"You're right, Tara, our own Princess...of MUD, that is."

"I'll take it."

Alexa, having water in her ears, ignored the two fools until she was rising to her feet and something soft and oozy hit her in the face: mud. Laughing like children, Nina and Tara bombarded her with mud pies, and it wasn't long before Alexa did the same to her friends. The melee was brief, though; soon the girls were helping an exhausted Myra onto dry land, where she collapsed and began snoring.

Major Bree immediately took charge. The girls didn't mind; they were used to it by now, and besides, he was a friendly. Bree ordered his sergeant to aid Myra and a private to return to the ship and look for survivors and more equipment; he then turned to Tara and told her to collect the many crates floating around the pond. Some of them lay on the opposite side of the lake, while some bobbed back by the waterfall. Meanwhile, Nina was to help him with Myra.

He nodded towards a medical kit floating a few meters offshore and pushed Tara gently toward it. "Oh, no, I ain't going in that Gull-forsaken water," she protested. "Don't feel like getting eaten."

He lifted an eyebrow. "Get real. A creature that size in this little pool, I doubt it had any competitors. But if it makes you feel better, take this." Bree tossed her something that looked like a weapon.

Tara looked it over and realized it was a collector tool. You aimed at something and fired, and a long, thin tongue of adhesive material shot out and stuck to your target. The adhesive would cohere to just about anything, and released only when a brief electrical charge was passed through the cord. It could be used over and over, as long as the filter was cleaned and the fuel cell changed once in a while. Actually, it was even more robust than that; if the charge pack ran out of juice, you could pump the handle for more energy. She walked the shore line, making sure she didn't touch the water, and started firing away at the crates she could reach, making a game of it. Major Bree could swim out and get the others, she figured.

"What about her?" Nina complained, pointing at Alexa.

"An Elite citizen of her rank doesn't have to work; she should be served. She's a member of the House of Hornet," Bree said stiffly.

"Say again? She's what? That slut?"

Bree shot Nina a surprisingly outraged expression, while Alexa smiled and stuck out her tongue, looking like nothing more than a muddy young brat. She then went over to Major Bree, murmured to him, then started helping the other survivor drag the comatose Myra ashore. Once she was far enough up on the bank, Alexa and the sergeant got to work with the medkit Tara had already retrieved, while Bree and the others begun setting up camp beyond the high-water mark. When Alexa had done all she could, she finally leaned back and sighed, taking notice of the dense jungle a few meters away for the first time. By then, birds and beasts had gotten over their shock at the sounds of battle an hour before, and were filling the air with their calls; there was also a sweet aroma rising from the many colorful flowers dotting the climax vegetation. She turned her interest to the waterfall, and saw Tara jumping from one rock to another, doing everything she could to avoid falling into the pool as she snared their supply crates. It wasn't long before Tara slid off a rock and fell into the beautiful and now-clear water. At first, Alexa was concerned; but when she saw Tara more or less fly up onto the rock, coughing and cursing, she smiled.

They were alive and that was what mattered. Their predicament wasn't a great one, but as long as there was life, there was hope. Thus far, they had located only seven survivors, including all the Vixens onboard, but maybe some had made it to the other escape pods. If so, they might be as much as hundreds of kilometers away.

As if Bree could read her mind, he walked up next to Alexa, observing the pool and Tara's dance among the stones as she fired her collecting tool at another trunk near the waterfall. "We need to find the others, see if they're alive, and try to fix what remains of the ship."

"Doubt it's spaceworthy," Alexa answered, eyeing the major. "And I doubt there would be enough left to fly, even if it were. Who are you, by the way?"

Major Bree removed his helmet and introduced himself. He was in his early thirties and very handsome, Alexa thought, even with that long scar on the left side of his face. "We have to make the best of the situation, and somehow contact our people up there." Bree nodded towards the sky.

A coughing Myra interrupted, "*And* look for survivors." She retched up blood, and the medic did his best to calm her. Bree nodded, even as he gave the big woman a suspicious look.

Tara hurried towards them, looking very concerned, and immediately Alexa knew that something was wrong. "Guys, I found some strange markings on a rock behind the waterfall. I don't think we're alone here."

EIGHTEEN

TARA led Major Bree and Alexa around to the back of the waterfall, where she'd found the petroglyphs. Most of the images were pecked into a single large, flat stone; and as they investigated, they found more of the pictographs on the wall behind the fall. The water splatter forced them to be very careful about where they planted their feet; no one wanted to fall back into the pool, despite Bree's theory that the murderous cephalopod was solitary.

"What makes you think we're not alone?" Bree wondered, looking over the image. They seemed ancient.

"Look over there behind the fall," Tara pointed.

"Fresh carvings," Alexa said, as she ran her hand over some of the strange markings. "Looks like some type of words, not just pictures."

"Usually, old carvings like these represent people and animals, especially hunts," Bree suggested.

"They're not all old," Tara pointed out. "We have to find out what planet we're on."

"Gull only knows," Bree muttered as he ran a hand over some newly-chipped carvings. "I think we'd better get back to the others."

"Look! More survivors, it seems." Alexa stood by the edge of the cliff, far above the pool, and pointed at two more armored soldiers emerging from the water below, one being supported by the other.

"That makes us eight for now. You three, the criminal…"

"Criminal?" Tara asked.

"The big Saurian? I assume the captain of the ship belongs with the people who captured you?"

Tara and Alexa nodded.

"We need to keep an eye on her."

"That's for sure," Alexa muttered.

"I assume you know her from the past?"

Their body language confirmed his initial suspicions, so he went on. "Then we have Sergeant Roni, Corporal Dora, and let me see," he tapped into his wristcomp, and names appeared as the system polled the remaining troops, who all came up as out of range or dead except for one: "Private Elaan."

They moved away from the cliff and down toward the beach, following what appeared to be a game trail. Soon they came upon a small bluff that was elevated, but not too much so, and provided easy access to the water and the recovered flotsam and any that might yet appear; Bree decided that it would make a good place for a camp. All of them had to help move Myra, however, due to her large frame. They laid her under the shelter of a large tree, and Bree attached some zap-cuffs and an ankle bracelet. The later was controlled by a small device that could stun the wearer if the controller found it necessary. Myra remained unconscious the entire time and probably would for some time yet, given the number of medical patches attached to her shoulders and back. Nina also placed a healing mantle on her; the mantle changed color to match the surroundings, typical of mil-spec med supplies.

They had to go back to move the recovered crates and other supplies up the hill and into the camp. When they were done, Major Bree unpacked a blaze-orange case, revealing a series of bird-sized drones lying sleekly in their charging cocoons, close to 20 in number. After tapping a series of commands into his wrist-comp, the case's telltales lit up, and he was able to launch an experimental drone from the pack. It performed flawlessly, buzzing straight up and out over the lake and then up and over the opposite side of the waterfall, seeking higher ground.

Bree walked toward the edge of the bluff, keeping an eye on the feed from the drone, and scowled as the sensors in his uniform warned him that someone was following him. "What're you doing?" Nina asked, interested as always in high-tech toys.

"Making sure we're alone for now, and that nothing can surprise us," Bree growled. "This drone will scan the nearby region and warn us if anything or anyone approaches. It'll also let us know if it finds any lost equipment or personnel."

Together, they began exploring the area near the pool, Bree keeping his eyes on the wrist-comp display while Nina leaned over him, trying to get a glimpse. Frustrated, Bree let out a sigh and moved his arm a bit so the girl could watch. She'd proven useful before.

A few moments later, Sergeant Roni cleared his throat. Bree waved his hand for him to wait, then looked at Nina. "Would you like to scan the area for us?"

"Sure, just show me how it works."

Bree detached part of his wrist-comp and demonstrated for Nina how the drone worked, then turned to the waiting Sergeant Roni, nodding for him to continue. "Sir, we found several weapons in one of the crates, along with some demo charges, but they're only light weapons. Sidearms and breaching charges."

"Let's hope we won't need anything more. Distribute the sidearms amongst all the survivors except the saurian woman under sedation. We'll take turns guarding the camp, but for now we need to get something to eat and then rest."

"What about the others, sir? Possible survivors?"

"I'm sure there are some, but they're out of range of my C-and-C app. We'll make a plan later on for a Search and Rescue, and in the morning some of us will go looking for them, or at least for a high place where we can detect them and communicate with them. For now, let's get some chow and rack time, and set a guard rotation for tonight. Have you finished scanning the surface with the environmental scanner?"

"Yessir. It's looking like a standard W-4 planet, but of an unusual high grade. We'll have to wait until tonight to get some stellar positioning information. But there are several readings that are unclear, sir. The scanner can only do so much. I'd say we're on an uncharted and uncolonized world, but where it is I have no idea yet. We can drink the water after we've filtered it, but I don't recommend consuming any of the native life for now; there are some amino acids we may not be able to metabolize."

"What about our food supply?"

"For the eight of us, we have enough food for at least a month. But if we find more survivors, then of course that figure will change, depending on what they can add to the pot—or not."

They were on the opposite side of the camp now, and far enough into the jungle they could barely see what little they had left to represent civilization. After climbing a few rocks, they reached the top of the local upland and could look over the area. By that point, the thundering of the rapids dominated the local soundscape, so Bree signaled a halt. He used his communicator to contact camp, reaching Corporal Dora, who reported all was well. They moved on; the closer they moved to the river, the more deafening the roar became. When they had been below, the side walls had shielded them from the sound.

"Wow, what the hell just happened?" a loud voice said in their earbugs.

Bree and Roni turned their heads towards Nina, who stood there shaking the remote control for the drone.

"What's wrong?"

"This thing no longer works. Look," Nina held up the display, showing only a blank image.

"Use the holo screen," Roni suggested.

"Yeah, well, that don't work either."

"Let me look at it."

"Rewind the last recording," Bree ordered calmly.

An image popped up on the holo display, showing an overview of the waterfall area, before something seemed to streak in from the left and the image vanished.

"Could that have been a predator, some sort of bird?" Nina suggested.

"Possible, but unlikely. It would have been jolted by an electric charge. Those little suckers can take a hell of a beating," Sergeant Roni said.

After examining the last images a few more times, Bree pointed and said, "It should be right over that ridge."

Carefully, they moved up and over the ridge, to find themselves on a small plateau facing the waterfall. When they'd crested the ridge, Nina let out a shout. "There it is!" She hurried towards the pathetic little bundle of composites, and lifted it so the others could see what had taken it down. At first they didn't realize what they were seeing; it looked like twig with bright orange leaves clustered on one end. It took a moment for them to reinterpret the "leaves" as what they really were—fletching—and realize that the twig was actually an arrow. Eyes wide, Nina pulled it out of the drone; the arrowhead was knapped from white stone or dense bone.

"Don't touch the tip—could be poisoned," Roni warned, from where he and Major Bree had ducked for cover as soon as they recognized the weapon for what it was. Still clutching the arrow, Nina hit the ground fast next to the others.

"Well, at least that answers one question."

"What's that, Major?"

"We aren't marooned on an uninhabited world."

"We knew that from the pictogra—" Nina began, but was interrupted by the short barks of a projectile gun firing, followed by the angry *hiss-chun* of a magma blaster.

They looked at each other, then the soldiers crawled quickly toward the edge of the plateau. Bree flipped down the visor on his helmet and upped the magnification, zooming in towards the camp below; then, suddenly, his view was blocked, just as Nina shouted out a warning and Roni fired his own magma blaster, drilling a large, hairy omanoid between the eyes. Everything moved very fast after that; the natives scrambled up over the edge of the plateau as Roni shot amongst them, and Bree scrambled for his own sidearm. More of the apish natives entered the camp below from the water, while others converged on the camp from the trees. Nina, Bree, and Roni were too worried about the dozen or so they were dealing with, who mostly clutched spears or stone axes. Others stood at a distance, bows drawn; but there were too many of their tribesmen in the way to fire. Roni hit a native menacing his Major in the chest with a well-placed shot, and it fell away with a strange scream as maroon blood splattered all over them, its fur burning from the clinging magma.

Nina rolled to the side, only to face two large hairy feet; without thinking twice, she raised her right hand and slammed the arrow she still held down hard into one of the feet, raising a loud scream of pain. She looked up and realized that something huge was coming her way, so she again rolled to the side, just in time to avoid a club studded with the fangs of some large animal they hadn't encountered yet. With a gymnastic twist, Nina was on her feet, her hand now filled with the comfortable butt of her pistol. She fired several rounds into the club-wielding native, sending it crashing back on another attacker in a tangle of singed and bloody limbs as the deep *booms* echoed through the forest. Bree's machine pistol, meanwhile, was almost silent compared to the hissing roar of Sergeant Roni's magma blaster, which seemed to cause the creatures to collectively cringe whenever it went off. "Turn off your silencer!" Nina shouted to Bree, hoping he would hear her.

He did; the machine-pistol began chattering loudly in short, controlled bursts—and suddenly the fight was over, almost as soon as it had started. Seven natives lay dead around them; the others had taken cover below the rock formation, making strange and frightened moans that the visitors doubted were war cries. A sound from a horn in the far distance came, though, and suddenly they began attacking again.

"Switch to laser, Sergeant," Bree ordered, "and try and conserve your charge batteries and ammo. Don't use the bloody magma, it takes too much energy." He took his own advice, switching his sidearm to laser operation.

A moment later, a hail of arrows rained down on Bree and Roni, only to bounce off their armor; then they were struck by several deftly hurled spears. The spears didn't penetrate, but did knock the men off balance, providing the attackers the time they needed to attack again. Under covering fire from arrows and spears, a few of the larger natives charged; one swung at Bree's head with an enormous wooden club. He ducked, but the club glanced off the side of his helmet, sending him crashing to the side. Roni shot the creature with his weapon, but it was too close for effective use, so he popped the bayonet out and gutted the native. When it fell back, he shot it in the face.

Bree regained his feet and started to fire again, picking each target carefully. The problem was that this was the classic target-rich environment. There were hundreds of natives pouring onto their plateau from all sides, and whoever was sending them didn't give a damn about casualties; they were already building up a rampart of dead enemies before them. The first wave had overcome their fear of the strange weapons, and now they also began attacking again, the larger natives leading the way. Standing back-to-back far above the pool where they'd splashed down on this murderous world, Nina, Bree, and Roni fired until the barrels of their weapons turned red-hot, killing the natives by the dozen; but they just kept coming, howling, to their deaths.

An arrow hit Bree's shoulder, bouncing off his armor; but Nina wasn't armored, and she was hit by two arrows. She dropped her weapon in shock, and fell to her side, screaming in pain. Major Bree shouted, "Sergeant, take the girl and jump; I'll hold them off."

Sergeant Roni shouldered his weapon and tossed Nina over his shoulder as more arrows came flying in; one hit her in the left buttock, and she yelped loudly at the indignity. "Gull, that one really *hurt*," she bit out. "What are you waiting for? Now is a good time to jump!"

Roni jumped, and almost a second later they both hit the water hard. The armored Roni took the brunt of the blow, but the thrice-impaled Nina was none too happy about it.

Meanwhile, Bree grabbed a grenade off his munitions bandolier, set it to high yield, and tossed it into the massed attackers before he, too, jumped over the cliff. A massive explosion bloomed on the plateau behind him; then he also hit the water, debris and bits of hostile native peppering the surface as he sank deep. When he was below the surface, he altered his combat suit for water warfare and turned on his cloaking device. The sergeant had clearly done the same, because Nina was floating immobile about two meters below the surface, sucking on a spare breather apparently attached to nothing.

Bree tapped a key on his wristcomp to access infrared, and now he could see both of them. Nina was fine when it came to oxygen, but she was losing a lot of blood and was starting to look a little blue. This cool water was no good for her in her injured condition. Assuming Roni had the IR mod up and running, Bree motioned for them to break the surface, which they did very cautiously. When they reached the surface, he looked towards the plateau; there were still hundreds of the natives standing there at the edge, waving their weapons in the air. Something was burning still, because there was a lot of black smoke rising behind them, and the charred-meat stink suggested it was mostly bodies.

Bree made a couple of hand gestures, and they used their jet packs to move swiftly towards the muddy beach near the camp. Suddenly, the background shouts and screams from the natives ceased—and Bree realized that they were totally surrounded. The apelike natives were everywhere, but they only stood there, looking flabbergasted. Now that they were quiet, he could hear a fierce firefight raging from the camp.

"Healer pen," gasped Nina.

"You still have the arrows in you," Roni protested.

Nina, too weak to argue, gave Bree a pleading look. After assessing the situation, he pulled a healer pen from leg pouch and injected Nina with the medical nanos it contained. She almost immediately perked up, and the bleeding slowed precipitously.

"It'll be hell getting those damn arrows out now," Sergeant Roni growled.

"Don't care, jarhead. Weapon?" She raised her left hand expectantly.

Rolling his eyes, Roni handed her his sidearm. "Hang onto me. Once we reach the beach, stay low and maintain a constant rate of fire. There's an extra battery in the gun butt. Use the laser—it doesn't require nearly as much power. I'll carry you to the others."

"Great! So can I blow you when we're done?"

"Say *what*?"

Bree and Roni looked at each other. "Yep, the arrows must be poisoned," Bree grunted. "Now, by the numbers," he ordered, leading them towards the shore.

With the help of the propulsion jets in their uniforms, they moved swiftly; and to the omanoid onlookers, who had only the standard Mark One eyeball to see by, it seemed as if Nina were gliding through the water with no effort on her part. She took advantage of their confusion to start placing shots among their midst, generally skill-shots in the forehead and center mass. Every native she hit dropped dead, and they were staring at her wide-eyed, but still, there were so many...

When they reached the shore, Nina had cleaned a path through the locals, and hadn't stopped shooting yet. Major Bree joined her as they crawled out onto the mud, firing his laser with pinpoint precision. The onlookers stared in awe at the blue-green lightning that leaped from midair over and over to land among them, leaving members of their army dead, with smoking holes in their bodies. And then there was the very pissed-off little female demon with several of their clan arrows in her, firing her own lightning weapon, screaming like a monster. She seemed to be assisted by spirits, sitting in midair, flying without wings as strange lights flickered around her.

This was too much for the attackers, who threw down their weapons and fled in panic, trampling each other in their fear, scrambling back into the mother jungle despite the exhortations of the horn in the far distance.

When the last of the living natives were gone, Bree and Roni turned off their cloaking devices; they were energy-hogs, and the combat suits were already down to half-power. Nina still sat on Roni's back, straddling him with her legs wrapped around his waist and her injured arm around his neck; in the other hand she aimed and fired into the jungle where the natives had fled, still shouting. Roni reached up and tapped her wrist, saying, "We won, kiddo," and she stopped.

They hurried towards the camp, and when they got there, they found windrows of dead natives. Many of the supply boxes were either opened, emptied, or missing, but there were several lying around unharmed. Myra still lay rapped in her healing mantle under the tree, snoring.

"Where are the others?" Nina blurted.

"Hail them, Sergeant."

Roni called both Corporal Dora and Private Elaan each several times, but when they finally got a response it didn't come over the commlink. "Over here," Alexa shouted from deep in the brush. "We're over here."

"Sergeant, stay here and help Nina—and see if you can wake that blob over there." He nodded towards Myra, whose healing mantle had apparently camouflaged her from the attackers.

Bree was just about to head in the direction of Alexa's voice when she and the others came into sight, stepping out of the jungle a few dozen meters away. "We were going to help you guys, but we were cut off," Alexa called.

Bree nodded towards Alexa, then glared at his troops, who snapped to attention. "Why did both of you leave camp?" he barked.

"Sir!" Corporal Dora responded, standing at rigid attention. "We saw them climbing the rocks behind you, clearly intending to ambush you, sir! We tried to hail you on the comm but you didn't answer, sir, so something must be interfering with our signals, sir! We thought it best to try to help, sir!"

"As you were." Bree nodded as he accepted the corporal's explanation; for now, everyone was all right except for relatively minor injuries.

Corporal Dora continued, "We fired off a few rounds, sir, hoping you would hear them, but we were cut off during our advance. These natives were everywhere, and they attacked from the trees, sir. We held our ground and fought our way back to camp, and suddenly all of them more or less vanished, sir."

"Still, corporal, you should have left someone at the camp."

"I did." Corporal Dora nodded towards Alexa and Tara.

"We weren't going to sit on our asses when Nina needed us!" Alexa protested before Bree could comment.

Both Alexa and Tara had bruises and were bleeding from several minor injuries. The stump of one arrow stuck out of Tara's thigh, and Alexa supported her as she limped back to camp. They patched each other up with the first aid kits—removing the barbed point in Tara's leg was a painful and difficult procedure—and then lay down next to Nina, who lay on her stomach complaining about the pain in her ass.

"Funny, Nina, I never heard you complain getting it in the ass before," Tara mused.

"Oh, ha ha ha. May an asteroid smite thee upon thy head, slut," Nina responded.

A loud yawn made everyone turn their heads towards the large bulk under the healing mantle, and suddenly Myra's head popped up, blinking woozily. Her handcuffs hindered her from stretching her large arms, and she gave them all an irritated look. "Anyone got any food...NINA!"

The large woman crawled over to Nina and showed both Tara and Alexa to the side, leaving them cursing. "Watch it, you big ogre," Alexa hissed angrily towards her.

"My dear, dear little Nina, what happened to you?"

"She got butt-plugged," Tara laughed.

Myra shot Tara a baffled expression, and then noticed the many bodies of the large, hairy natives lying around the camp. "You had a party without inviting *me*? You selfish little bitch, you," she said, then embraced Nina in a giant hug as Nina proceeded to complain and protest.

Myra carefully inspected every inch of "poor Nina's" body for injuries, despite Nina moaning and begging for her to stop. Myra looked around, and then noticed a crate a little bit away, still closed. "Alexa, grab me that one, will you?"

Alexa went to get the crate, but Bree stopped her. "Don't you dare treat a Nastasturian Elite like a bloody servant, woman!" he told Myra.

Myra just ignored Bree, as well as Nina's complaints, and gave Alexa a sweet smile while rolling her eyes. Alexa got the crate. Inside were more advanced healing kits than they'd used before. Myra looked at Bree and cleared her throat, nodding towards her cuffs. "We're all in this together, soldier, and from the looks of it, you could use another shooter."

Bree gave it some thought, then removed her cuffs—but not the ankle bracelet. Warnings and threats were superfluous, so instead of telling Myra what would happen if she tried to betray them, he only gave her a long, hard stare. No words were necessary; both were seasoned professionals. Myra stared at the major's back as he walked to help his troops fix the camp, and she knew that he wouldn't hesitate to kill her; and with that, Myra decided to like Major Bree. *Must make an impression on him,* she thought, hoping that she could still get away when a chance presented itself.

When Myra was done with Nina she brushed off her forehead with her forearm, and when she noticed that Tara and Alexa had lined up, she tossed them a healing kit each. She then walked over to one of the dead bodies carried in by Dora and Elaan.

"Hold it for a moment," she ordered.

Myra grabbed a necklace from the native's neck and tore it off. It was made of rope and wood, with a wooden pendant bearing a carving on it: that of a bulbous-headed thing with one eye and many arms. "Looks like we killed their god," Myra muttered.

"Say again?" asked Major Bree, who had just walked up to them.

She tossed the neckless to Bree. After he examined it, he muttered, "No wonder they were so pissed. And so many."

"If it's their god, they'll be back. What are your plans, Major?"

"I'll take Corporal Dora with me, and see if we can locate any more survivors while the rest of you hold up here."

"Despite your high-tech uniforms and fancy weapons, you might want to rethink that."

"Do you have any better suggestion?"

"If we can salvage the cockpit, we might be able to fix it."

"You're forgetting that the ports shattered, and the ship is flooded."

"True, but the emergency system will have automatically covered all the instruments with a protective shield—though bear in mind that the shield will only be maintained for a few more days, so we need to hurry. What's left of the ship is still our best way off this planet."

Bree thought about it and started to shake his head. Alexa stepped up and said, "Major, she could be right. After all, how far will we get in this jungle?"

"I was planning on staying by the river."

"Still, it might be a very long way before you reach the first escape pod. It could take days."

"Probably the same amount of time as it'll take for us to fix the ship. Major, I'm well aware of the importance of not leaving anyone behind, and we won't if we can—but look around you. Half of us are injured, and even if you leave some of us here, splitting our force is not the thing to do right now."

"Spare us the lecture. You really think you can get that ship back into space?" Sergeant Roni joined in on the conversation, not liking the fact that his officer had been questioned.

"No guaranties; it all depends on how much *Anti-Materia* is left in the tanks. The spare boosters are emptied—did that to avoid a mountain peak. And if we can't get it to space, at least we'll have it as a hover transport—and I'm sure all of us would prefer that much more than walking."

"So we should dig in, maybe find a better position to defend ourselves?" Alexa asked.

"We'll dig in, all right," the Major said, "but as for changing our position—no, this looks like a good one to hold for now. We might want to rig a few more warning devices, though."

Roni nodded, and gave a few quick orders to his few remaining troops as Bree and Myra headed to the muddy shoreline. On the way, Myra went by the weapons crate and grabbed a laser rifle, a side blaster, and a long knife. When they reached the water, she dropped all the weapons on the shore except the knife. Without hesitation, she dove in the water as Bree kept watch. Just after Myra had vanished under the water, Bree saw some of the natives returning on the cliff near the waterfall. He sent a warning to the rest in the camp, and took up a defensive position between a large rock and a tree with its roots hanging in the water. At camp, the others took up their own defensive positions behind whatever cover they could find. In the distance, they heard the sound of a horn, and soon the brush around them was moving. But none of the locals advanced; they kept a careful distance from the troops.

After what seemed like forever, Myra finally broke surface, her teeth clamped onto a section of tentacle a meter long. She swam like a fish to the muddy shore and stood, tossing her newly acquired souvenir over a shoulder, and looked down at Bree, who was crouched nearby, surveying the bluff.

"What ya doing down there, Major?"

"They're back." He nodded towards the waterfall.

Myra turned her head, and now she too could see hundreds of natives lined up along the ridge. She grabbed the tentacle, bit off a chunk, and stood there chewing it while assessing the situation. She made a disgusting grimace and spat out the meat in her mouth. "Tastes like ass. So much for breakfast."

Suddenly a large native clambered down from a tree nearby. When he reached the ground, he dropped his toothy club and immediately lay prostrate on the ground, muttering in a strange language. Myra reached for her blaster, and gave the hairy man a suspicious look. Bree was nowhere near, she noticed; but then a small movement next to the native gave him away. His cloaked uniform really impressed her, though there were some electrical issues whenever the uniform came in contact with water. Suddenly the native noticed that something strange stood near him, and it gave a strange warbling cry before it knelt and bowed its head over and over again. When Bree suddenly showed himself, it startled the native so much he fell on his back and tried to crab backwards away from Bree and Myra, absolutely terrified.

Myra took two giant steps forward and tossed what remained of the tentacle onto the head of the native. He stared in disbelief, and then slowly touched the tentacle. He grabbed it careful, then emitted a cry of agony. Bree immediately readied his weapon, but the native shot to his feet and scrambled back up the tree trunk, the claws on his fingers and toes leaving noticeable divots on the trunk. "Well, that's that, I guess," Myra said, showing no signs of fear at all. A moment later, the hundreds of natives on the bluff vanished again.

"Now let's get my little *Titanette* back on dry land, shall we, Major? We're good on *Anti-Materia*." Myra gave Bree the friendliest smile she could muster, and Bree returned one, despite thinking she was one hellishly ugly woman.

NINETEEN

"**KEEP** jumping and humping, you lowlifes...she's coming soon!" Myra shouted across the lake, staring at the water.

They'd removed the airbags from the many crates they had rescued, emptied them, and then Myra and Bree had attached them to the hull of what remained of Myra's ship. Myra and Nina had then constructed an air pump from one of the inflator bellows on the copilot's seat cushions. Otherwise the seat was damaged and useless, and they all agreed that sacrificing it would be acceptable. Across the lake on a small rocky shelf Alexa and Tara, dressed in their undergarments, jumped and danced up and down on the bellows, laughing and screaming in glee. Nina, still injured, lay under a tree in the shade, looking on enviously, still too injured to join in on the fun. Once in a while, Alexa or Tara would slip on the pumping device and fall into the water, screaming and shouting even louder. Every time that happened, Myra would scream and curse them, because the air pump had to be worked constantly until the ship had been raised. All the airbags had been filled with air; now they had to fill the ship with air, forcing out the water so it would finally stir from its silty bed and rise to the surface.

"You sure you sealed her up tightly?" Myra muttered while staring at the water.

Bree replied irritably, "of course I did. Private, get out of your battle suit and help those two," he ordered through his communicator.

Private Elaan saluted from his position above the girls, and then removed his uniform and joined the girls on their "jumping" task. Tara and Alexa enjoyed having a male companion, and it didn't take long before they were fighting each other for dominance on the inflator. Bree groaned and shook his head in frustration when Elaan was pushed into the water.

"You're sure there aren't any more of those creepy tentacle monsters in the water?" Nina asked from her spot beneath the tree.

"I told you before—a predator that large in a small lake like this won't have any competitors," Myra replied. "Neither I nor the Major found anything else dangerous in the lake."

"Yeah, that's all well and good, but what if there's an underwater cave or stream and another one pops up?"

"Then I'll kill it, rest assured of that," Myra vowed.

"Here she comes." Bree pointed at the water as it began to roil and the cockpit capsule of the *Titan* broke the surface. Sergeant Roni rose into view next to it, his battle suit in diving mode, and shot them an "OK" sign.

Myra dove into the water like a big, scaly fish as Major Bree checked with Corporal Dora, who stood guard on a small hill near the camp, keeping an eye out for more natives. Quietly, he ordered her to remain there; Nina could keep a close watch over the lake. There hadn't been any more problems with the locals for the last few days, but he knew the natives were observing them from the jungle. "If anything appears on the sensors, alert us immediately," he ordered Nina, who was watching a monitor tied into the sensors scattered around the lake.

He slapped down the visor of his helmet and dove into the water after Myra. He felt anxious about getting underway and locating more survivors, but he held his calm. The jungle was too dense to travel through here, and there were too many risks, known and unknown, in trying to enter it. Remaining at the lake had been the best course of action, but it didn't change his mood and his determination to find the other survivors and get off this rock. Gull only knew how many regulations against noninterference alone they'd broken when landing on this planet. Despite the fact that it had been an emergency, he knew the Universal Courts wouldn't take their actions lightly, because interfering with the cultural evolution of a non-spacefaring world was strictly forbidden.

He shoved those worries out of his mind and swam jetted to the ship, where he helped Myra and Roni steer it towards the shoreline. It took the rest of the day to get the ship secured on the muddy bank, and in a position where they could inspect the damage. Aside from the broken ports, the damage wasn't as bad as they'd thought; and repair nanos were already scavenging silicon from the sand on the shore to repair the ports. They were having a harder time finding titanium for the hull, but were able to find enough iron and aluminum to start slowly healing the gashes and holes. Fortunately, it wasn't as badly damaged as they'd feared.

There were some things that the nanobots couldn't repair. Myra had given Nina a diagnostic tablet hooked to a series of small crawler bots, and while Nina went over the internal damage on the screen, she reported it to Myra, who had crawled halfway into a large hatch next to the emergency engine compartment. Bree handed her the tools she needed to make repairs to the delicate machinery inside.

"That hunk of junk will never get us into space. Engine's too small," Alexa growled as she looked at the crappy little escape capsule and former cockpit.

"True, but hopefully it will at least hover, and then we can go and look for other survivors," Nina replied, her eyes fixed on the screen as her fingers tapped on the keyboard.

That night, after having secured the ship on the shoreline, everyone sat around a small fire, eating light rations. The last surviving hover orb guarded the camp, and Sergeant Roni glanced at his wrist monitor from time to time. Normally he would have used the monitor on his helmet, but the helmet lay next to him. Tara also sat next to him, viewing monitors displaying the sensors they'd placed around the camp and along the edge of the jungle to warn them of any more attacks or intrusions.

"So all of you were pirates, you say," a curious Elaan asked.

"We were, except for her," Tara said, not looking up from her monitors but nodding her head towards Myra. "She still is."

"Me, a pirate? Come on. And you're not?" Myra defended herself.

"You murdered Captain Zlo," Alexa said coldly.

"You should talk, Your Highness. How many people have you murdered or had killed?"

Alexa ignored Myra's remark, turning her head away.

"No, dear, look at me. Weren't you the famous drifter who got so good at your work that your Captain, a notoriously brutal pirate, adopted you as his daughter?"

Alexa froze for a long moment before turning her head to glare at Myra with a look that could have cut steel. When she spoke, her voice was dead of emotion. "His 'adoptions' were his way of tying us to him so that he could abuse us whenever he wanted, and share us with his friends. Mention it again, and *I will end you.*" She turned and climbed up on a large, round rock, where she sat down at looked up into a calming sky filled with stars and three small moons.

"You had to bring that up, didn't you?" Nina snarled at Myra.

"Why are you defending her? Weren't you her pet, a *gift* from her so-called father?"

"Um, what's a drifter?" Corporal Dora wisely interrupted.

Nina glanced at him. "Drifters are the youngest of pirates, kids who don't really understand that they *are* pirates."

"Makes no sense, what you just said," Bree said.

Nina sighed. "It does if you understand how pirate culture works. You probably think that most pirates become pirates as adults, and you're not wrong. But a surprising number of us are either born into the culture, sold by their families—like Alexa was— or captured in raids, like I was. Kids have their uses. With me so far?"

Bree nodded.

Tara said loudly, without looking up from the monitor, "A drifter is a child used for psychological warfare. Sometimes they're 'rescued' from disabled ships by ships the pirates want to capture. Sometimes they're slipped aboard as stowaways, or accompany an adult on a passenger liner as their child. They then work from the inside, sabotaging the ship and causing terror among the crew until the ship's helpless enough to be taken with little or no fight. When she was little, Alexa was the best, but eventually she grew too old and...went on to other things."

"Were you ever a drifter, Tara?" Elaan asked.

"No, I was trained to be a hacker."

"Stick to the drifter part," Bree insisted.

"Whenever a prize is taken and there are a lot of crew or passengers aboard, it's important to strike fear into them—and to do that, pirates use drifters. For example, after the fighting is over, or mostly over, the drifter hides among the passengers, preferably next to a couple. It only works on ships with a lot of people, though."

"Do they all have to be the same species?"

"Stop interrupting, Private," Roni barked. "Go on, miss."

"No, that doesn't matter. Anyway, when the right time comes, the captain or another high-ranking pirate will grab the drifter, and take him or her out of sight but still near enough so that everyone can hear. The drifter will then scream or beg, or do something else to make everyone think that he or she is being harmed or raped."

"And that works?" Bree sounded doubtful.

"Every single time," Myra assured him mockingly, "especially if there are a few fighters left who have locked themselves away and still control part of the prize.

So the crew and/or passengers think that the pirates harm the youngling, and then they surrender very quickly."

"But don't they harm children?"

Myra shot Bree a strange expression. "No. Never. And don't go thinking there's any noble reason for it. Children, no matter the species, are as precious as any treasure. Children are the future for any pirate clan. They're held separately from the rest of the crew and never harmed. They receive a normal education, and as they grow older, they're introduced to weapons and trained to fight. I've have never heard of any pirate clan that actually harms children, but then again, the rumors are that we *do* harm them. And those rumors come from the drifters."

While they were talking about the past, and the pirate life that fascinated the Nastasturian soldiers, Alexa sat looking towards the nearest moon. It was full and beautiful, reflecting bright light onto the dark jungle. Here and there, phosphorescent lights glimmered from plants and trees, only enhancing the beauty of the dark landscape. Every now and then, faint shrieks arose from the dense jungle as prey was taken down by from some hunting beast. The aroma from the many flowering plants was pleasant, but the humidity rising from the swamp to the south was like a heavy, oppressive blanket.

When she looked at the moon, Alexa could almost see a smiling Alec, and the thought made her smile back, even as a tear ran down her cheek. *Will we ever meet again, love? Do you still live? Are you looking for me?* She lost herself in thoughts of the good times they'd had.

Her thoughts were interrupted by a horrible scream in the distance. Alexa looked up, and saw that everyone in the camp stood in a half circle with their weapons drawn, peering into the jungle.

"Someone probably became dinner just now," Myra joked, then took her seat again. The others soon followed, and went back to talking about the pirate life. Alexa ignored their voices in the background as she kept thinking of Alec, but this time she didn't think about the good times. The shriek from the jungle had sounded almost like Alec had when he'd been raped in the basement of that wealthy pervert. She, too, had been raped, but that hadn't hurt her as much as that awful sound from Alec.

Dark clouds scudded in to cover the moon, and Alexa's thoughts. "You'll never be the same..." she said softly, thinking about Alec.

"You what?" Tara said from behind her.

"Nothing," Alexa said quickly, and turned around to see a nervous Elaan looking at his own feet behind Tara.

"Oh, sorry, I'll move," Alexa said, when she realized that they probably wanted some privacy.

"Don't bother—I was going to ask you something. I would have asked the horny one, but Nina is still a bit injured, and Myra is watching over her like a crazy bitch."

"What do you want?" Alexa said suspiciously.

"The young private here has probably never had a threesome, and I was thinking we could do him, and you can do that nerve thing you know."

Private Elaan looked back and forth between the girls, his expression a mixture of surprise and excitement.

"Thanks for the offer, but I'm gonna rest."

"Wait," Tara said, and then climbed up on the rock, whispering to Alexa, "Please, he'll probably explode before I even get going, and I'm *really* horny!"

Alexa stroked Tara's cheek and said, "Be quick about it, and I'll do it."

Before a very confused Private Elaan could say anything more, Tara had grabbed his hand and hurried away down the shoreline; before he knew it, she had unbuckled his battle gear and tossed it aside. She knelt, grabbed some water from a puddle, and cleaned him quickly; and then before he knew it, she closed her lips around his penis. A moment later, he climaxed all over Tara's face; she only gulped and laughed at the same time, very excitedly, and hissed to her friend, "Come on, bitch, do your thing so I can ride this stallion till dawn!"

Alexa jumped down off the rock and walked over to them. "Stand straight and spread your legs," she ordered the young soldier; and before he knew it, her right hand was working his perineum, the region between his scrotum and anus, as she faced him and stared into his eyes confidently, her left hand softly massaging his testicles. Alexa suddenly leaned over and slid her lips around his manhood. What Alexa was doing to him Elaan would never know, but suddenly he let out a lustful, half-agonized cry, and Tara emitted a happy shriek while clapping her hands and jumping like a silly kid.

Alexa looked up at the stud, and when she felt him harden in her mouth, she stopped. She cleaned her hands and walked away. She didn't watch, but she heard when Tara tackled the poor fellow and gave him the ride of his life. If she hadn't just thought of Alec and the horrible scream from the jungle, she would have joined Tara. The guy was well-endowed and attractive…but he paled in comparison to her Alec.

What she had done just now she didn't consider cheating; she was just helping her friend, that was all. Besides, cheating didn't exist in Alexa's mind. Only people with hang-ups bitched about that shit. Sex was a natural thing to her and her best friends, nothing more, like running or walking; or better yet, breathing, since it was essential. *Will Alec and I ever be able to function like a normal couple?* she wondered.

THE next morning, they worked on the ship. Halfway through the morning, they were interrupted unexpectedly as the world begun to tremble, tossing them all to the ground. They heard a sudden explosion from far in the distance, and felt the weak remnants of an over-pressure wave wash over them. This was followed by more tremblors, even worse than the ones that had preceded the explosion.

"Sergeant, what's going on? Can you see anything?" Bree talked into his communicator.

Roni, standing watch on the high ground on the opposite side of the lake, replied, "Volcanic eruption, sir—looks like about 80, 100 kilometers or so distant. It's from the same range we hit coming this way, but much further to the south. I can see a huge ash cloud, and it's drifting this way; we may have some fallout in a day or two. Hold one; just caught another flash through the smoke. Another eruption. Same range, but closer. Hold on tight, sir!"

There was another, more terrifying earthquake a moment later, followed by another explosion and subsequent tremors.

"We need to hurry," Bree said calmly to Myra, whom ignored him while shouting for another tool from Elaan.

Roni peered at his monitor and sent new instructions to the orb hovering over his shoulder, sending it in the direction of the misbehaving mountain range. It was the only orb they had left and usually served in a sentry function, so he hated to risk it, but they needed to know what the hell was going on. It was his own personal orb, slaved to his battle suit sensors, and he hadn't liked when his Major had ordered him to surrender it for general use. But the others had lost their orbs fighting the pirates, and it was a legit order, so he surrendered it without complaint. The box with the spare orbs had been lost during the first attack.

Sergeant Roni followed the orb's flight on his helmet monitor, watching several different views at once, and saw another wave passing through the jungle, causing the trees to stir wildly and some of them to come crashing down. Shit, there was a hell of a quake coming their way—the geological shockwave of another damned blast, moving faster than sound. "Incoming quake, incoming from the ridge and the jungle," he warned over his communicator to the others. "Brace yourselves!"

Thousands of birds exploded out of the swaying trees, and the native animals went nuts. An enormous saurian with six legs and a long neck crashed through the camp, tripping and falling and damaging their gear, ignoring the personnel as it wreaked havoc. After a few attempts, it got back on its feet and let out a roar of either anger or desperation as it launched itself back into the jungle. It left the camp in chaos, and many of the crates ruined.

More animals followed, many small, with a few as big as a house. The ground trembled. Several of the hairy locals that had attacked them many days before also passed through, running for cover. Dark clouds covered the landscape, and ash began to fall.

Myra continued to work on her ship like nothing was happening, even as the rest looked on nervously.

"Here goes nothing," Myra shouted, and suddenly the ship jumped up a few feet, hovering above the shoreline and lake. "Ha, got it on the first try! Not bad for an old hag like me," she laughed, while struggling to close the engine hatch.

"Well, what are you waiting for...what the heck happened here?" she demanded. Myra looked over what was left of the camp site, then just shook her head and climbed through the hatch. The ship's nanos had finished repairing what they could, and the rest of the holes were patched with spare welded plates. The *Titanette* looked terrible, but at least it could hover.

Quickly, Bree carried Nina inside and handed her to a waiting Myra, who took her gently and carried her to the tiny temporary medbay. The rest scrambled around the camp, trying to save what they could. Last to leave was Major Bree, who looked over the camp, making sure they hadn't forgotten anything of value or anything that could affect the social evolution of the people on the planet. In frustration, he realized that many tools and equipment still lay scattered around, and there was no time to do anything about it. Alexa noticed the Major's concern and shouted from the hatch for him to hurry. He climbed inside.

"We might be able to come back and recover the rest once it's calmed down," Alexa assured the Major, who realized she had read his mind. He gave her a friendly smile and nodded.

Myra began flying slowly over the lake and up toward the high cliff on the opposite side to pick up Sergeant Roni, who used his jet pack to meet the ship. He entered the open hatch as thicker ash began to fall, then sealed it shut as Myra began maneuvering along the wild river, which that had turned black from the sediment load of the storm and earthquake. The ash began to fall more thickly, laying a grayish blanket across the landscape. Nina joined Myra at the helm as copilot, her hands on the secondary steering yoke and ready to take over as they moved along at about half-speed, while the rest looked out the ports, now repaired by the nanos.

"Myra. Where are you heading?" Bree asked as he entered the cockpit.

Myra pointed at a display screen. "I'm following our incoming path before we crashed. It's the best chance to find survivors, and maybe lost parts of the ship we can use for more repairs—or for survival if we're stuck on this planet for any length of time."

Her last words sent chills down the spines of everyone onboard. They'd been too busy fighting and repairing the ship to put much thought into the possibility they were actually stranded on an unknown world, and might end up here for the rest of their lives.

"What about the volcanoes?" Elaan demanded. "We're heading toward them, not away!"

"We should be all right as long as we keep to the air. The eruptions are still very far away," Myra called back.

Alexa peered out a port and saw that they were surrounded by thousands of birds and near-birds flying frantically away from the eruptions; further below, on the ground, creatures of all sizes were visible, running for safety. As they passed one of the lakes, she even saw one of the tentacle monsters clambering out of its ash-choked home onto a nearby cliff. Soon they cleared the jungle, soaring over rough, mountainous where the ash, both in the air and on the ground, was very thick. Most of the instruments weren't working on the ship, which made their job more difficult, but Nina focused on those that were and the others kept their eyes on the surface below, looking for evidence of survivors and debris from their initial impact. Their job was made more difficult by the fact that another volcano in the chain had erupted shortly after take-off, choking the air with more ash and smoke.

"Check the air intake filters, will you, dear?" Myra said calmly to Nina.

Nina gave her a puzzled look and then checked one of the few working instruments, which showed a decrease in the efficiency of the atmospheric turbines. A quick steam purge cleared them as Myra made a noticeable alteration to their heading. Nine jerked her head toward Myra while giving Alexa a glance.

"You're altering our course, Myra. Why?" Alexa wondered.

"North of the mountain range, yes, because that's where we came from. I recognize the pattern of that ridge," Myra pointed towards the far distance.

"Good, there's much less volcano activity there," Bree said, still peering out a port, looking for any sign of survivors—though that seemed more and more like a lost cause.

"If there's any debris left from the earlier impacts, or any surviving escape pods, they should be on this side and on the other side of that ridge, I think." Myra sounded doubtful.

"Look for any signs or markings survivors might have made on the ground," Bree barked—harsher, perhaps, than he had intended.

They advanced very slowly towards the northern part of the range, away from the ash cloud; as the air cleared somewhat, they found another type of forest spread like a green carpet on the foothills of the mountains.

"There, over there!" Tara shouted, pointing to the northwest. "There's something reflecting in the sun, and I think it might be manmade!"

Myra altered course, following Tara's instructions. When they got closer, they saw what looked like fragments of Myra's ship spread out across a fresh scar in the forest. Myra circled the clearing a few times before she brought the pod down gently just above the ground, still hovering on ground-effect engines. "I'd rather not land for now," she noted. "Not sure we have enough energy to get it started again."

"We can always charge the emergency reserve engine with some of the smaller solar panels," Alexa suggested.

"Not if that cloud spreads this way." Myra grimaced, gesturing towards the dark cloud south of them, which had cast the land beneath it into gloom.

"Corporal, you're with me. The rest of you, remain here." Bree sounded a bit too excited when he gave his order, having little patience left in his eagerness to search for the remainder of his force.

Bree hopped from the hatch to the surface, followed by Corporal Dora. As Bree headed toward the debris, Myra joined them. "Who the hell's driving?" Bree demanded.

"The little princess," Myra answered, jerking a thumb over her shoulder. "Nina's just as good a pilot as me, and I need to check this shit out."

She clumped forward and inspected the first cluster of debris. "Yep, it's from the *Titan*," she concluded. "That there's part of a starboard ventral controller."

"Look, tracks," Corporal Dora's voice came through their helmets. She was pointing toward the ground with her rifle. Myra and Bree joined her. "Looks like Nastasturian military issue boot prints," Dora said, looking in the direction they led—into the forest below the mountain range. The trees were giants here, a mix of both broadleaves and needled conifers approaching a hundred ems high in places.

"Looks like one person walking with a heavy load," Myra said, examining the tracks with experienced eyes. "Either they were carrying a lot of gear, or likely one of their buddies."

"Let's get back to the ship and try and follow them," Bree ordered.

"Yeah, we can, but eventually someone's gonna have to get back to the ground and follow them that way, Major," Myra said drily. "We won't be able to see any tracks through those damn trees, and my infrared scanner's ruined."

They returned to the ship and very slowly followed the tracks, but even with high magnification detectors, they soon faded out into the underbrush. After a depressingly short flight, Bree and Dora used their jetpacks to head back to the surface, while the rest remained on the ship, following above the tree line. They couldn't see Bree or Dora, but their communicators worked fine.

"Look over there," Nina said, while pointing towards a huge opening in the forested mountain ridge.

"Didn't notice that before," Alexa said.

"Right, the big rock in front of the fracture concealed it nicely from our original orientation. Tell Bree what we're looking at, and try and get a fix on them and see if maybe the tracks are heading in that direction. Looks like a good place to take shelter. Also, look for a clearing so we can pick 'em up," Myra said.

"Might have to use the crank to get them up from the surface if we can't find one."

"They have grappling hooks on their uniforms," Roni pointed out.

"Yeah, well, will they reach above the tree line?" Myra wanted to know.

Alexa interrupted, "There, over there on a ledge below the opening! It looks like someone planted a flag or something. And wait...there's smoke!"

"And where there's smoke, there's fire," Nina said tiredly.

"Roni, can you use your zoom on your helmet?" Alexa asked.

"Major, I think we have visual confirmation of survivors near that gash in the ridge," Roni reported.

"We're coming up." Moments later, there were two thuds on the hull.

"Guess that answers my question," Myra said in a bemused tone. She released the hatch, and the two soldiers entered the ship as Myra turned toward the smoke. Soon she was hovering about the ledge where Alexa had seen the flag. This time, Bree descended alone and checked on the ground.

"Looks like one or two of my people were here, and that they headed into the valley next to that opening on the ridge," he reported.

"They were probably headed back to the other part of the rear of the ship," Tara guessed.

"Well, some of the debris we found at the first site looked like it came from an emergency escape pod, or at least the door."

"What happened to the escape pod, then?" Alexa wondered commenting on Myra's words.

"We must have missed it. Too bad most of the instruments and scanners are out of order. Maybe you can fix 'em, dear," Myra said, blowing a kiss towards Nina, who just rolled her eyes.

Myra increased her speed, zigzagged though the narrow mountain fissure. Suddenly the ship emerged into a large clearing within the mountain, and from their position they could see several cracks in the extinct caldera, all leading in different directions.

"We have to land and make camp," Bree suggested, his words sounding more like an order than a suggestion.

"I'd rather land where there will be sun tomorrow, so we can charge the engines." Myra replied.

"Look, a settlement!" Alexa shouted.

Alexa pointed towards a large cliff, where there were over a dozen caves surrounded by debris from the ship. There were no fires, but in the far distance, in front of one of the caves, stood one person, waving their arms, apparently dressed in the same uniform as the rest of the Nastasturian soldiers. They landed, and the first person out of the ship was Bree, who raced towards the lone survivor, whom stood at attention.

"Private Echlon reporting for duty, sir!" the man said in a shaky voice.

Next to the soldier lay a large package bristling with electronics. Echlon told them he had been one of three people in the escape pod. The other two hadn't made it, and he'd used the destruct feature on their uniforms to disintegrate them, as he didn't want their presence to damage the future of this world. "Saw these caves and decided to make a camp for the night. Actually, I just got here."

"Why did you head in this direction?" Alexa asked.

"I saw your ship a day ago and started to follow. You didn't see my signal flare, so I…"

Myra interrupted, "Where did you see this ship? What direction was it going?"

"It wasn't ours," Bree also interrupted.

Echlon looked puzzled, then he pointed towards one of cracks leading through the mountain. Echlon and Bree entered the ship with Echlon's package, and they followed in the direction Echlon had pointed out. By the time they had reached the other side of the mountain range, they'd used up most of the engine's energy.

Just as they began landing, the little ship jolted in midair and went crashing to the ground. Everything went black.

Nina had no idea how long she'd been out when she came to. "What happened?" she muttered.

"Hush, Nina," whispered Alexa.

"My head hurts like h*ummmph*."

Alexa laid her hand over Nina's mouth and whispered harshly, "Shut the hell up. We're under attack."

She was outside the ship in the forest again, in a place where a handful of conifers were mixed with the jungle hardwoods. As before, the many colorful flowers emitted a strong, intoxicating aroma. She had no idea when she'd been dragged out of the ship. Nina shook her head to clear it, then rolled from her back onto her stomach. To her right lay Alexa, glaring straight forward into the woods with a laser blaster in hands; to her left lay Tara with an older magma rifle with a scope, aiming at something.

Nina blinked a few times, trying to focus, and heard several people speaking in an unfamiliar language. They seemed to be hiding under the cover of a stretch of bushes along one arm of a small river. Tara cleared her throat quietly and nodded towards another weapon next to Nina: a laser blaster similar to Alexa's, but with a much shorter barrel. It smelled burnt, souring the scent of the flowers; but then, they weren't here as tourists. Nina took the weapon and checked it; when she looked around, she could see no spare charge magazines, but Alexa wore a belt with several that would fit her weapon. Alexa quietly handed her a spare as if she knew Nina's thoughts; then again, she probably did, as their shared battle experience exceeded that of most career soldiers.

Nina blinked and focused towards the sound of the voices, then crept forward silently through the thick grass, searching for a better position. There was a small clearing facing them; behind them was the mountain caldera with the fracture they had flown through. It seemed very far away now. She pushed aside a clump of grass as saw some twenty locals lounging on fallen tree trunks and rocks. These natives were somewhat different from those they seen before, very omanoid except with larger heads. They had less hair than the people by the lake, but were still very hairy on their backs; all also wore very long hair and bushy beards, even those who appeared to be female. They wore leather clothing like the other natives she'd seen, but this group also wore moccasins. All were weighed down with clubs, axes, spears, and what looked like blow guns. They were muscular and had large canines, almost fangs.

The aliens spoke in a strange gurgling language that fit their long tongues, but the dialog was suddenly interrupted by a high-pitched shout in Nadjarish, the universal language spoken by most people in the modern universe. The accent was unfamiliar, but the girls did understand some of the words as a small non-Oman ran around the clearing, issuing orders. It wore a large hat woven from grass, and its clothes were torn and ragged. It also had what looked like a large knife or a small sword hanging from a belt decorated with gems that was cinched around its waist, and it carried an old long-barreled magma rifle. Two bandoliers of charge magazines were slung across its narrow chest.

From the looks and sound of the ferret-like creature, it was male, but Nina wasn't sure. She noticed that there were several small brushfires burning, apparently caused by the fall of Myra's ship, and Myra's ship lay on the ground with smoke pouring out of it. The bodies of many of the locals lay spread about the clearing, but it didn't seem that anyone cared about them—not even those that were noticeably injured. The little alien-in-charge ordered the locals around with the help of a laser whip, screaming and shouting, and once in a while it went inside the ship, apparently in an attempt to salvage gear, but frequently it had to get out in the open for fresh air. It also sounded like it cursed a lot in a different language from time to time. Next to a large tree lay all the Nastasturian soldiers, tied together with carbon nanofiber rope. They'd been stripped of their uniforms, and all of them seemed smaller now in their undergarments. There were no signs of Myra.

"Should we take them?" Tara whispered.

Alexa whispered back, "There's only one modern weapon among them."

"Too many of them...if I weren't injured I'd gladly help wipe them out, but I'm not sure I'm up for it," Nina admitted, embarrassed.

"We can't leave the others behind," Tara insisted.

"Then we'll follow them and wait for an opportunity to release the soldiers. Can you walk, Nina?"

"Yes, Alexa, as long as I'm careful. My injuries are healing well. Give me a day and two with the healing patches, and I should be all right."

One of the locals rose from his log and started to walk towards the girls' hiding place, stopping a few paces away. They were apprehensive for a moment, fingers tightening on triggers, until he moved aside the hide he wore for clothing and relieved himself. The wind was blowing from his back, but still he raised his large, flat nose in the air, sniffing. The girls lowered themselves further down in the high grass. It was then that Nina noticed she had mud smeared on her arms and face, just as Bentor had taught them. Hopefully, the mud would cover their scents.

It did. The alien left and headed back to the others. The five prisoners, all injured it seemed, were jessed by hands and feet and then strung up on long pole, each carried by two aliens. The little alien-in-charge took the lead, screaming and shouting, while the natives followed, carrying the prisoners and all kinds of spoil. They headed towards the river behind the girls, but further upstream towards a path on the opposite side. Once they had left the clearing, Tara and Alexa crawled towards their camp. Nina remained where she was, but changed her position, facing the small jungle path across the river. "Here, take this instead," Tara said before she left, handing Nina her magma rifle as Nina handed her the smaller blaster.

Tara and Alexa were back after a while, empty-handed. "Nothing! They left nothing, and it wouldn't surprise me if they returned for more stuff from the ship," Alexa complained.

"We need food and water, or we'll never make it." Tara was angry.

"Let's go after the bastards and do them all in," Alexa ordered. Then, realizing that she didn't want to order her friends around, she started to apologize.

"Shut the hell up, Alexa, you've always been in charge," Nina hissed, "so just be normal and do your thing and Tara and I will do ours."

Tara nodded in agreement. "You sure you can fight, Nina?"

"Don't worry about me, I'll take cover and put the fear of Gull into them with this beauty," she patted her long magma rifle, "while the two of you have yourself an orgy on the bastards."

The three girls provided each other cover as they camouflaged themselves further with mud, leaves, branches and anything else that made them stealthier. They used ashes from a fire to paint their faces; all their clothing was already torn and ragged. They split the spare ammo between them, and when they were finished gave each other grim looks. Alexa said calmly, "Lassies, let's hunt."

They headed after their prey.

TWENTY

AT the river's edge, Alexa handed them each short lengths of zip cord, and they created shoulder loops for their weapons so they wouldn't lose them. Tara took the lead crossing the river, which turned out to be only waist-deep. She took cover on the opposite side, and then Nina hobbled over while Alexa kept cover, and finally Alexa followed. By the time she was over, Tara was already moving swiftly down the path; Alexa made a loud bird-whistle, causing Tara to stop. Nina and Alexa hurried to Tara.

"What's your hurry?" Nina asked.

"Probably that Elaan boy," Alexa teased.

Nina looked at both Tara and Alexa a bit suspiciously. "What's so special about him?"

Tara just smiled, while Alexa rolled her eyes.

"You did him, didn't you, you slut! Nice?"

Tara nodded towards Alexa. "What did you think, Your Highness?"

Alexa said, "He's no Alec, but he's well-endowed and seemed to have plenty of stamina."

"You too!" Nina almost shouted.

"Relax, she only blew him...and then I rode him like a demon from hell," Tara laughed.

"Shit, not fair at all! I was injured, you sluts. And you, Alexa, weren't you saving your dry ass for that knight of yours?"

"I only blew him a little bit for Tara."

"Tara, what, you don't blow anymore, you hideous little wench, you?"

"Yeah, I do, but I needed help to get him up again."

"Quiet, you horndogs," Alexa warned, "Shit. Lesson Number One out of many, lassies, and we've already broken several."

"What's she going on about now?" Nina demanded.

"Never follow a path when you're following an enemy, and never make this much noise."

"Yeah, well, the brush is awful thick here, and we don't know the terrain," Tara grumbled in a low voice.

"We'll just have to take it easy now. Let's get out of here."

"You think those beasts are cannibals?"

"No, Tara, I don't think so; then again, they might be."

"You might be right. I think I saw a few shrunken heads among their decorations. And by the way, since they're a different species, we couldn't call them cannibals if they eat Omans," Nina whispered.

Alexa shook her head. "Any sentient being is a cannibal if it eats other sentient beings. Universal law." The girls left the train and ghosted through the thick brush, trying to keep the path visible to their left. Once in a while, one of them had to edge closer to the path to make sure they were still following it. After a long, stealthy walk, they noticed the first trap on the path. They inspected it carefully: it was a large hole in the middle of the path that had been dug quite a while ago. From within came the stench of dead meat. The bottom was lined with dozens of sharp sticks coated with dried blood, suggesting it was an old trap, but the cover on top was newly-made.

When they reached another narrow river, they paused and rested. The tracks on the opposite side were easy to follow. Tara tried some of the water, and drank slowly from her hands. Alexa followed.

"Guess we're braking another rule now, huh?"

"Guess so, Nina," Alexa answered.

"So, what did it taste like?"

Tara and Alexa looked at each other and said in unison, "Like fresh water."

"No, not the bloody water! Elaan's nectar! Did he taste good?"

Tara tossed her arms up as she started to cross the river, while Alexa just shook her head before helping Nina with some water. "Not gonna let this one go, are you?"

"Nope!"

"Fine. He was sweeter than normal."

Nina leaned on Alexa as they crossed the river, and when they got to the other side Tara was nowhere to be seen. "Great, Tara's lost," Nina complained, and whistled a quiet birdsong.

There came a brief response from Tara further ahead, but it was a distress call she whistled back. Alexa nodded towards some boot prints on the muddy ground; still supporting Nina, Alexa moved carefully through the bush, and when they got through, Alexa instinctively tossed Nina backwards while she herself balanced precariously on a small rock ledge for a second or two before falling into a large mud pit disguised with leaves, cursing quietly but with great vehemence. Nina heard no splash or anyone landing on the ground, and for a moment she feared that her friends had fallen off a cliff with the bottom very far below. Still on her back, cursing Alexa silently for her rough treatment and having lost her rifle in the fall, she moved slowly back on her stomach. She retrieved her rifle, then preceded with caution towards the ledge. The many bushes and lianas hanging from the trees obscured her view. She could hear some breathing not far ahead, though, and finally she reached the ledge; and when she looked down she couldn't help letting out a small laugh. Nina was stuck in quicksand up to her shoulders, while Alexa was mired to her waist, both with their backs turned to her.

"That's what you get—punishment from Gull for not letting me have some, you sluts!"

Tara sputtered, "Get us out of here, you horniest of all creatures in creation."

"Might wanna hurry." Alexa sounded a bit concerned, not so much for their amateur predicament but more for the noise they were making.

Nina got on her feet and noticed a rocky ledge a few feet to the side, where the ground was more solid. Before moving down to better ground, she tore off a couple of lianas from the wall of them dangling before her, and then moved slowly and carefully, inspecting the ground; she was absolutely in no hurry. After removing her boots and emptying them of water, she removed most of her clothes, not wanting to get them muddy. She looked over the funny situation again; by now, only Tara's head was above the quicksand, though both she and Alexa had managed to turn facing her. Alexa was shoulder deep; and as they had been taught to do in such a situation, she had her arms stretched out to her sides, trying to slow the sinking.

Nina tossed the first liana to Tara, who caught in her mouth on the second try. Nina then tied her end to a large root on a tree. She watched as Tara struggled carefully, and eventually got one of her arms above the mud and reached for the liana.

"Lose your bloody boots or you'll never make it," Nina advised.

"Go to hell," Tara whispered angrily and ignored the advice while Alexa used one hand removing her boots and each time she sunk deeper. Eventually Tara got her second arm up and could pull herself in. By then, only Alexa's head was showing and Nina repeated herself. After a while, all three girls were laying muddy on the small rocky cliff, very muddy and dirty except for Nina, who got dressed slowly, smirking at the damsels in distress that she had rescued. Both Alexa and Tara had also lost their pants from the strong suction in the quicksand or mud rather.

"You do realize that if you hadn't been injured, you'd be muddy too," Alexa assured Nina while trying to clean her weapon.

"Crap, I lost one of my boots," Tara complained. "Oh well." She removed the other boot and tossed it into the quicksand, watching it vanish into the mud. The girls walked around the natural trap, and headed back towards the path—but now they couldn't find it, no matter how hard they searched.

"Let's backtrack to the river," Alexa suggested.

"I wonder why the locals and the alien were in such a hurry? They could have recovered much more loot."

"Maybe they couldn't carry more, Nina."

"Not true, Tara, several of the ones who took up the rear only carried their weapons."

"Who cares?" Alexa demanded. "Let's get moving!"

They turned and went back to the river, then followed it until they found the track. In order not to lose it again, they decided to stay on the path until they passed the large quicksand region to their left. At that point, they turned to the right of the path; the ground there was much better.

Suddenly a large shadow fell from a tree toward them, and the girls let out frightened cries. Facing them was an enormous cat-like creature with a long, snapping tail. It charged Nina, sensing that she was the weakest of the three.

Alexa aimed her blaster and fired, but nothing happened; it had jammed from being submerged in the quicksand. Tara tackled Nina to the ground and fired off a series of rounds, hitting the large monster in mid-pounce. It landed on both Tara and Nina, both of whom were kicking and screaming and cursing up a storm. Alexa lunged forward towards the beast and used her knife, slicing its throat, splashing thick purplish blood all over Nina and Tara.

"You guys all right?" she asked, after the dust settled.

"Yeah, yeah, just get this bloody thing away from us, and I do mean *bloody*," Nina spat blood from her mouth while struggling to get out from under the beast.

Both Nina and Tara had been injured by the monster's claws; Nina on her forehead, and Tara on an arm. Alexa tore the sleeves off on Nina's jacket and used them to stop her friends' bleeding.

"It's really getting hot now...the temperature, I mean," Alexa noted, blowing away a sweat drop on her nose.

"Think they heard us?" Tara wondered.

"I hope not," Nina said, retying her bandage on her head.

"Listen!"

"Shit, another one!" Nina warned.

Another monstrous feline jumped to the ground; it stopped and stared at them, and then at the dead creature next to them. When it saw its mate dead, it let out a roar of anger and then charged the girls. They scattered. The monster charged Alexa, who had drawn her knife when it had first appeared. Meanwhile, both Nina and Tara fired off several rounds, killing the beast. It landed, dead, right in front of Alexa's bare feet.

"Must have been its mate, I think," Tara suggested.

"Could be. I hope that's the last one," Nina said, looking towards the treetops.

Alexa walked over to the second dead beast and pushed the knife blade into its neck, making sure it was dead. She then sat down on it and started to clean her blaster.

"You know, your history of having weapons that misfire should be recorded," Nina said, sitting next to Alexa, picking up parts of the weapon to help her with the cleaning. "You should have a new nickname, Alexa. Instead of Lex, we should call you Jam."

"Your Highness the Princess of Jamming," Tara laughed.

Alexa ignored their cheeky remarks. "Tara, keep an eye out, just in case."

"No problem, Princess Jam."

"Stop calling me that."

"Sure, Your Highness."

"Bitch!"

"Well, now it should be working," Nina said. "Mud was clogging the battery contacts." She snapped the battery back into the blaster and aimed at one of the dead animals; and just as she fired off a round, Tara tried to warn her against it.

"Great, you bonehead, someone's coming," Tara hissed as she hurried to help Alexa in supporting Nina.

"Which way?" Nina asked.

"Over there," Alexa nodded to the path ahead.

With Nina between them, they headed behind a pair of boulders rearing out of the brush, and took cover just as a small arrow hit a tree trunk next to Alexa's head. "Cover, we've been made," Alexa signaled in Grisamm battle-sign.

"By the numbers," Tara responded in the same language.

They took cover behind the rocks: Alexa to the left, Nina in the middle, and Tara to the right. Several dozen locals came down the path from deeper in the forest, either the same as those who'd captured their colleagues or so similar they could see no difference. "Remember, the alien has a magma rifle," Alexa said calmly, quietly. "Don't bother to injure them; they don't care about the fallen."

"Kill 'em all," both Tara and Nina said calmly.

"And let Gull sort 'em out," Alexa replied.

The locals rushed toward the dead felinoids, where they paused to genuflect for the animals' souls before setting to skinning and slaughtering the dead beasts, taking care to preserve the wild manes that surrounded the great skulls. They moved with great efficiency while the others charged with loud roars towards the girls.

"Check your flanks, don't forget your flanks," Nina reminded them, then shot the local leading the charge. His tooth-and-claw studded club tumbled to the ground as he pitched backwards. "That's one," Nina said, calmly aiming and firing again. Alexa shot the next one in the chest and then she aimed her blaster to another, as Tara took out a native with a three-round burst to the chest.

"Conserve ammo," Alexa shouted over the firefight.

More of the natives charged them and inevitably fell, which just maddened the survivors more. They couldn't kill every local that menaced them, so the girls made wounding shots when they could; in one case, Tara, took off the right arm of one with a "wing-shot," removing the menace of the stone axe it carried and putting it out of the fight. A split-second later, a dart smacked the rock next to Nina, who didn't realize the danger because her eye was glued to the scope of her magma rifle as she picked off one native after the other. Fortunately, Alexa saw it and turned to her right; in the brush were several more natives, trying to outflank them. She set her weapon on automatic and let it rip through the dense jungle, and was rewarded with loud screams.

"Check your flank, Tara," Alexa ordered. Tara responded by firing off several rounds that took down the rest of the flankers.

Nina stopped using the scope, because the attackers were too close; instead she aimed with sights on the end of the barrel, firing off quick shots from one target to the other as quick as she could pull the trigger, without resorting to automatic fire. The Grisamm training, in combination with her pirate past, had combined to turn her into a sleek, effective killing machine, and her sister Vixens were no different.

"Triangular formation for withdrawal," Alexa called, "And watch out for the ones with the long sticks—they fire darts, probably poisoned." Nina moved first and took up position by a tree a few paces back, and then Tara followed, taking a spot even further back; last came Alexa. All tried to stay synchronized with each other, but the horde of enemies made it difficult. One large native swung over their heads on a liana to land feet-first before them; Alexa shoot him in the face. The girls retreated toward the second river, leap-frogging their way down they trail as they covered each other, hoping they could cross it and make a stand there. Nina had problems, wobbling along limping; they were all out of breath and still weak from their previous experiences, but kept retreating one by one, firing back at the attackers. They reached the stretch near the river, and just as Nina and Tara were about to head down it, Alexa altered her direction towards the quicksand. Understanding, they followed, luring the natives toward the mire.

When they reached the dangerous area, they eased carefully around it to take up station on the small stone shelf with the river at their backs. The aliens charged after them, screaming. When they saw the girls slowing down, trying to climb the shelf, they ran straight forwards them—and half the creatures got trapped on the quicksand before the rest realized the danger. Some of them went back onto the path in an attempt to cut the girls off, while the rest followed them directly.

The girls took cover atop the ledge, changed magazines, and then fired into the mass of aliens, dropping a half-dozen in as many seconds. "Back, back to the river," Alexa shouted, providing covering fire. Tara helped Nina, and both struggled back the same way they had come for a second time. The scream and calls of the natives had scared most of the local animals away, though birds and near-birds were still shrieking in the trees overhead. All this only added to the chaos.

Alexa soon followed Tara and Nina; she stumbled out of the forest and slammed into the others, who had stopped in the water on the edge of the river, afraid to move. "Now, those guys would *definitely* eat us," Nina said.

On the opposite side were more natives. These omanoids were short and muscular, similar to the other aliens but still quite different; they had no hair at all, and had decorated themselves with paint and mud. Their weapons were similar to the those of the others, and there were hundreds of them lined up on the opposite side, screaming in unison, shaking their weapons in the air and beating them against tree trunks. Without hesitation, they surged forward and attacked the aliens that had attacked the girls, both sides clashing in the center of the river in a melee that soon stained the river maroon.

"Come quick," Alexa ordered, leading the girls back into the jungle behind them, following the riverside but leaving the battle behind them. The kept going as far as they could, and finally had to stop to catch their breath. They didn't know how far they gotten, but the battle could only be heard faintly now.

"Don't drink that, Nina," Tara warned when she saw Nina about to drink some water, "Too much of their blood's in it. You'll just have to hold up for a while."

Nina nodded in consent, and then looked around until she found a long stick. She broke it in the middle at its juncture with another branch, tossing away part of it and using the rest as a crutch. "Should have made one sooner," she growled.

"Thought Myra made you one."

"She did, Alexa, a good one. And if you make another joke about Myra being in love with me, I swear to Gull I'll tie you up in your sleep and tickle those precious feet of yours before I shove *this* crutch up your ass."

"Bitch."

"Princess Jam."

"I wouldn't do that to Princess jam, though," Tara said thoughtfully.

Nina turned her head towards Tara. "And why not?"

"She'd probably get off on it."

"Listen who's talking. I remember back in my shower room on board the *Bitch* that when Nina and I let you have it, you screamed like a little whore."

"Go to hell, both of you. Shitheads."

Nina was laughing quietly, while Alexa just nodded. All of them realized that this silly talk was a sign that they were afraid, very afraid; and only a fool wouldn't be in their situation. They might be veterans, even at their young ages, but they were still fearful of death, and had barely evaded it or capture several times in the last few hours. Their nerves were on edge and they remained hypervigilant, jumping at the slightest sound.

"So, Nina, don't you have any weaknesses?"

"Besides my fucked-up legs right now? We've been over this conversation many times, Tara. About all of us Vixens are ticklish, but you know it just makes wet and horny, and I don't have time for that right now."

"Tara," Alexa said, "did you know that Nina is the only woman in Zuzack's crew who was gang-raped only once when she reached adulthood?"

"Nope, I did *not* know that. That true, Nina?"

"Yep. I tracked down each of the bastards and cut off a finger for each time they raped me. Told 'em it would be their dicks next." Nina said nothing more; she ignored the conversation, instead working on ripping rags from her jacket to wrap around the armpiece of her crutch to make it more comfortable.

When she was satisfied, they stared picking their way into the deep jungle, heading at a wide angle towards the path, to a point that should take them well away from the fighting. Alexa trusted her own intuition that she could find the path.

"No, really, what happened after that first time?" Tara wanted to know.

"Once the captain and the other senior officers had 'initiated' Nina," Alexa smiled like an innocent rose, "this mad slut wanted more. She couldn't get enough; she kept at it until she fuckin' wore them out. Eventually Zuzack had to carry her all the way back to my quarters and tie her down, ordering her never to return to officer's country alone again. Whenever she had to go back, I had to be her chaperone."

Tara looked at Nina and then Alexa, trying to decide if she had just heard a lie, but nothing in their expressions gave it away. "Nina, you're one horny toad, you know?"

With that said, they continued their journey into the jungle. After having walked for a very long while, they stopped, realizing they were lost again.

"We need some way of getting our bearings," Alexa complained.

"The trees. One of us has to climb up and see if we can find a focus point," Nina suggested.

Tara handed her weapon to Alexa, and she started to climb a hoary forest giant. When she reached the top of the very tall tree, she could see the mountain range far behind them, and much further south, the volcanoes still sending fire and ash into the sky; but the wind was in everyone's favor for now. She saw the large crack in the mountain through which they had flown, and tried to calibrate where the path had been. In the far distance were a few more mountains, some small, others large; the jungle seemed to be a large but isolated sea among them. She climbed back down, and after a short rest, they altered their course. They soon reached another clearing dominated by large, beautiful flowers, where they stopped and listened.

"I think we're all right to go on. Can't hear anyone," Alexa whispered. "What do you think?"

"I think we can go on. There was a small mountain with a waterfall not far from here. Maybe we should get there and try to climb it so we can get a better view."

"Take the lead, Tara; and you, Nina, come over here. Let me be a second crutch to you. Not that you deserve one, but it wouldn't hurt to get out of this jungle for a while."

Three more times they had to climb a tree, looking for the mountain with the waterfall. Alexa and Tara took turns. Alexa had just climbed down and was sitting on the ground resting, when she heard Tara shouting for help. She got up and grabbed her blaster.

Nina looked confused and said, "She was just here. She was going to take a leak over there," Nina pointed to a large bush. Next to it lay Tara's weapon.

Nina picked up the weapon, then hobbled along behind Alexa, who dashed away through the brush. Tara screamed again, but the sound was muffled, as if she were gagged. Alexa reached a small clearing and found flowers similar to those they'd seen before; but there weren't many of them this time. In fact, there was only one huge plant with about a dozen large flowers, and inside one of the closed flowers was Tara, with only her feet outside, kicking up a storm.

Alexa went for her knife, when she suddenly felt something wrapping around her ankles; and before she knew it, she was hanging upside down, heading towards one of the giant flowers that was opening up to take her in. She heard several shots fired, and then saw a cursing Nina also hanging upside down, heading towards another flower. Nina was still firing her single-shot rifle at the plant, causing serious damage. Alexa struggled, but another liana wrapped around her and tightened until she could barely breathe. The more she fought, the tighter it got. She had dropped her weapon; it still hung on the end of the rope that was attached to her shoulder, but still, she couldn't reach it. She raised her knife as she was forced inside the flower. This one was smaller than Tara's, and it had her by the middle, so both Alexa's head and feet stuck out. She screamed at the top of her lungs and so did Nina; Tara had stopped kicking. Alexa felt some strange, sticky juice flow onto her, juice that made her skin itch like mad; and she struggled even more, only to realize she was suddenly getting very tired. Her vision blurred as she began to feel drowsy and ecstatic. Her focus on the knife made her search for it, but by the time she found it, she was so tired she could barely move. She tried to cut through the flower, but it was thick and hard, like leather.

Nina saw the giant flower open and prepare to engulf her, and with one round left, she aimed at the stem and blew it apart. The flower fell to the ground, wilting instantly, but she was still tied up by many lianas, and the plant just moved her toward another gaping flower. As that happened, Nina passed Alexa's flower, where she noticed that Alexa's eyes were glazed, and that she was smiling, as if she were high. There was a hole in the flower, though, and Alexa's hand stuck out of it, a large knife in her slack grip. Nina went for the knife and grabbed it just as Alexa dropped it; in the same motion, she bent her body upward (which hurt like hell), and with one wide sweep of her arm managed to slice through the half-dozen lianas pulling her toward the carnivorous flower. She fell hard on top of the plant, and as she did, she felt many lianas grabbing at her from all directions. She stabbed the plant over and over again, as fast as she could, but soon found herself tied up like a spider's silken bundle, headed for one of the flowers.

But just as she was forced inside, all the lianas fell slack and she dropped to the ground, hard. She struggled away from her bondage and crawled back towards the main plant. She found the knife stuck in it, and she started to stab it again; however, every time she did, it seemed the plant came back to life, at least briefly. Quickly she realized that the metal in the knife must work like poison, so she jammed the knife deep and hard into the plant's central mass and let it stay there.

She heard two thumps behind her as the flowers containing the other two girls collapsed. She turned around and saw Alexa and Tara's predicament. She ignored Alexa for the moment, because her face was in the clear and she could breathe, but Tara's situation was far worse. Nina really had to struggle to get Tara free; and the moment she did, Nina started to push on her chest. Soon she realized Tara was just sleeping, with the strangest smile on her face... Nina then turned to Alexa and helped her out of her bounds; she too was sleeping happily.

They were both slathered with a sticky juice where the plant had grabbed them, and beneath it, their skin was turning an angry red. Nine decided it had to come off; luckily there was a half-filled slough nearby. She peeled them out of their clothing, washed them thoroughly with the rags from her crutch cushion, then rinsed out their clothing until she was sure there was no residue remaining before hanging the rags on branches to dry.

Alexa woke up with a sigh and a splitting headache. Next to her lay a naked Tara, moaning softly as if she were making love.

"About time you woke up."

"What happened?" Alexa asked as she struggled to sit up, realize she was also nude.

"We almost got eaten by a plant, of all things."

"What? How? I don't remember anything but a wonderful sensation…"

"I'll say. You guys have been lying here moaning and groaning like you were screwing, and poor me had to listen to all that shit."

"Had I known you could have sex with a plant, I'd have grown me a garden."

"Well, hurry up and get well, because we need to find another plant. This time *I* want to get high and horny."

"Yep, Alexa, she's mad," Tara whispered softly, then smiled and yawned while stretching her arms, thrusting her ample chest out invitingly. "Man, that was so cool. I dreamed I had a hundred dudes and got to fuck every single one. If we could do it under controlled conditions, we could make a killing selling these horny plants."

"Shut UP! Gross!" Nina hissed at Tara, not wanting to hear more. She then gave Tara and Alexa a sly smile. "This is the second time I saved you sluts from getting eaten, and we *will* find another plant so I can get off."

"You don't want the headache," Tara said, rubbing her face. "And sweetie, if that's all you want, we'll do it for you," she said, staring with wanton eyes. Worse, so was Alexa.

The forest creatures kept their mouths shut later that evening, as the screams of three passionate females echoed through the trees. They used the large leathery flowers for blankets that night; and no matter how much Nina rolled around on the insides of the flowers, the sludge from them didn't work anymore. Eventually she stopped, exhausted.

Alexa woke them in the morning and they kept heading towards the small mountain that was their target. When they finally reached it, they climbed the top to find a beautiful valley spread out below them; in the center of the valley, amid a patchwork of cultivated fields, lay a village made of strange clay huts with skin roofs.

Alexa looked over the village. "Let's get to the next bluff, and we'll have a better view from there. Maybe we'll be able to see the others."

"We have to watch out for sentries."

"Doubt it," Nina said, and pointed toward the few people moving about the village. "Looks like they're still back there fighting."

"If that's the case, we'd better hurry. Might be a great opportunity to save the others," Tara said.

"Or not. By the way, did any of you see what happened to Myra?"

"Why, Nina, are you missing your love-toad?"

"May an asteroid smite thee upon thy head, Princess Jam af House Malfunction!"

When they got closer to the village, they noticed that the battle was apparently over, and had been for a while. The headhunters who either lived in the village or had conquered it had won, and now they were busy beheading many of those they'd captured. Other prisoners were held inside cages and huts, and once in a while the headhunters let some of them out so that they could chase them for fun.

The girls lay on a small bluff covered with trees and bushes, peering out through the cover, looking for their friends or the alien with the laser whip and old magma rifle who had acted as the leader of the headhunters.

"What's your ammo count?" Alexa asked.

"One magazine left, fully charged. Nothing else."

"Used my last on that damn flower," Nina grumbled.

Alexa gave Nina another clip. "And I have almost full magazine," she said, scanning the village. "You see anything, Nina?"

Nina was using her scope to scan the village, and had suddenly stopped. Her shoulders sagged, her gaze dropping to the ground below her cheek.

"What? Do you see them?"

Nina just nodded and handed Tara the rifle. "I'm sorry, Tara."

Tara stared through the scope, and then tossed the rifle aside and stood up suddenly, heading back down the bluff. Alexa was about to go after her when Nina put her hand on her arm. "It's that guy she hooked up with…well, his head."

Alexa took the rifle and peered through the scope, where she saw the gruesome scene of Private Elaan's head impaled on a pike. Many of the natives sat around fires, and had many of their victims spit roasted over hot coals, eating and passing what seemed like leather pouches around with drinks. Alexa steadied herself and kept watching; and as she did, she asked Nina to comfort Tara.

Nina and Tara were sitting and talking to each other when Alexa joined them. Tara cried, but didn't say much.

"I found the rest of them," Alexa reported. "They're still alive, three of them in one cage and the other in second, along with that alien with the whip."

"Soon it'll be dark. We could get them out then."

"You're gonna walk down there and rescue them, just like that?"

The gravelly voice behind them made them freeze for a second before they realized Myra was back.

TWENTY-ONE

MYRA tossed a large duffel bag filled with weapons on the ground. She then walked to the top of the bluff, standing tall for anyone to see.

"Uh, maybe you should take cover?" Nina suggested.

Myra smiled at her gently, then turned her eyes back towards the scene below. "Nah. You girls might want to gear up for battle." She nodded towards the bag.

Tara and Alexa poured out the contents, revealing everything from laser cutters and force-grips to grenades and several different blasters, along with belts filled spare charge clips. After having geared up, they brought Nina a few clips and the rest of the weapons they couldn't carry in the bag and lay them next to her.

"What happened, Myra, and where did you get all these weapons?" Tara asked. "We checked the ship, but could barely find anything."

"We were hit by what I *think* was a magma blast fired from a great distance—hell of a shot. The weapons were hidden below the cockpit floor…you lassies should know, once being pirates and all, that there are always many weapons hidden in any pirate ship."

"How did you escape?" Alexa asked.

"Got out right after we struck the ground."

"Leaving the rest of us behind?" Tara sneered.

Myra shrugged. "Honestly, I thought she was gonna blow. When she didn't, and I returned to the ship, the locals were there. Didn't have any weapons at the time. But I watched the Nastasturians getting captured, and after that, when you guys crawled towards safety…didn't see any of you guys helping *them*. After the locals left with the guy I think shot us down, I returned to the ship; and by the time I reached the spot where you had hidden, you were gone. I followed, and now I'm here. By the way, it was real stupid of you to be making out like a bunch of horny demons in the middle of all this mess."

"You saw that?" Nina asked, turning her head and blushing.

"No, but I heard."

"We were under the influence of a toxin," Alexa said primly.

"Whatever. You might wanna get ready, because here they come."

"That's your plan—no plan? Just attack?" Alexa demanded.

"Pretty much. Figured that the little bastard who shot us down might have a ship that works. Maybe we can get outta here." Myra locked and loaded her heavy machine blaster, and spun the four barrels. She flipped the switch that put it on semi-automatic.

"Any other survivors?" Myra asked, then looked down at Nina. "How're your wounds?"

Nina pointed out the cages with the survivors; and when she mentioned that Private Elaan was dead, Myra muttered something inaudible.

"As for my injuries, healing nicely," Nina said, "but my muscles do cramp once in a while."

"You just have our backs with that nice sniper blaster while we take care of the rest, Missy. I placed a couple of smart mines behind you by the forest edge, in case someone tries to attack you from behind, but check your six once in a while. These locals are a little clumsy, but very stealthy."

Alexa took Myra's right side, while Tara took the left, juggling two grenades in on hand. Myra grinned at her antics. "Well, lassies, let's show these turds what happens when you mess with hardcore pirate bitches."

"Hardcore *former* pirate bitches," Tara insisted.

Myra smirked and rolled her eyes.

By now, hundreds of headhunters were headed in their direction, some sounding horns and others drumming on leather hand-drums slung at their waists as they came. The girls had no doubt the drums were made of the skins of their enemies. Howling and screaming, they charged the bluff. Some of the captives that had been chased saw their opportunities, and fled into the wild in the opposite direction, ignoring their many compatriots still locked in the large wooden cages.

Nina aimed her magma blaster, sighting through the scope at a large native leading the charge. For moment the creature was out of sight because of a small dip in the terrain, but soon it reached the top of a smaller bluff beneath them, still several hundred paces away. Nina relaxed and squeezed the trigger, firing one shot that burst the native's head asunder in a mist of blood, pulverized bone, and brain matter that dusted the warriors swarming behind him. The other headhunters ignored the loss and kept charging; his body was trampled underfoot as they continued onward toward the present and *former* pirate bitches.

Nina kept aiming and firing, taking down many of the headhunters, making sure they were dead. Kill shots were the only thing that counted in this kind of situation. There were so many attackers that the hills facing them were dark with them, and more seemed to show up from the jungle to their right, from the path. They must have an outrageous reproductive rate, or most of the natives within a thousand kays had gathered here. The howling increased as the distance between the girls and the attackers decreased.

"Hold it, hold it, hold it," Myra said loudly, in a very cold, harsh voice.

Everyone on top of the bluff stopped, stern, battle-hardened expressions on their faces. "Grenades," Myra ordered, and two grenades—one from Myra's arm, one from Tara's—flew far in the air and exploded just above the heads of the tallest warriors, directing their fragments downward in a thick hail of needle-shrapnel. Dozens of warriors were scythed down by the two munitions, leaving a carpet of blood and guts that those behind them slipped and stumbled on, making them easy targets for the guns of Alexa and Nina. A second round of grenades took down twice as many of the locals. Then Myra's heavy blaster began thundering again, plowing furrows into the advance guard, and soon the sound of gunfire blended into a continuous roar as raw energy blasts and heavy metal sleeted into and chewed up their enemies.

Alexa aimed and fired short, controlled bursts, and so did Tara, while Nina kept firing single shots and taking out specific targets. Whenever they had to reload, they shouted to the others so that they could keep up the firing. It was a slaughter, pure and simple: the headhunters were like mindless beasts, dying in windrows, and none of them even got close to the top of the bluff. The few who carried spears and short bows were unable to reach the girls, no matter how hard they tried.

Suddenly a large explosion erupted from the trees behind them, and immediately Nina turned to face hundreds more headhunters intermixed with another strange clan of centaur-like beings with six legs. Dozens had been taken down by Myra's booby trap, and as she watched, another explosion ripped holes in the native ranks. It turned out the six-legged creatures could jump like grasshoppers, and one of them flew at Nina, who lay on her back, planted the blaster butt on the ground, and took out the six-legger in one center-mass shot. There came another loud explosion, and suddenly they were almost overrun. Nina rolled to her side as an enormous club slammed into the ground where she'd been, and rolled back as another club came down at her from the other side.

Suddenly the two attackers were ripped in half by blaster fire. Myra stood with her legs wide apart over Nina, firing from the hip.

Meanwhile, Alexa and Tara were kneeling and firing at the attackers coming up the bluff, knowing that this would be their last stand at the top of the hill. When Myra's heavy weapon clicked on empty she threw it at an attacker, hitting it right in the face and sending it crashing back into another two beasts. Then the massive saurian woman drew her pirate cutlass and let out a loud roar as she waded into the fray. One good thing about blades was, they never ran out of ammo or charge. Locals went down, dismembered and sliced open, as Nina struggled to her knees, now firing a smaller blaster with both hands, taking out new targets as fast as she could pull the trigger.

They were goners for sure...but suddenly there came a tremble through the ground, almost like an earthquake, followed by many more as the ground jittered and shook. The attackers stopped and listened; in the distance, they all heard the sound of a horn blatting. The sound grew in intensity, even as the ground kept trembling. A shadow fell over the landscape, and in the air they saw a flock of the enormous bird-like beasts of the kind that had attacked Myra's ship shortly after it entered the atmosphere. The girls kept firing as their attackers fled in all directions, melting into the jungle; but some suddenly reversed their direction and came dashing out to certain death at the guns of Myra and the Vixens, chased by a dinosaur five times their size. Quick glances in all directions revealed that other beasts, some larger, some mammalian rather than saurian, were exiting the jungle from the direction of the earlier volcanic eruptions. All these animals had in common was massive size and the huge, sharp fangs of apex carnivores. Some fell on the dead natives and started feeding; others charged into the clearing below, attacking anything that moved.

"Must have smelled all the blood," Myra shouted, while trying to recover her weapon. Alexa hurried to her side with a large recharger, and removed the old one on Myra's back while attaching the new one.

"Last one," Alexa shouted warningly, and when finished, she hit Myra's right shoulder to let her know she was ready to go.

There were a few attackers left who didn't seem to be especially frightened by the new threat; the girls figured they were the stupider ones. Myra tossed her sword at a nearby six-legger, piercing it through the head; she laughed as she watched it crumple. At least she knew where her sword was for now. She then reloaded her weapon and started firing in controlled bursts.

Alexa fired from her hip at several nearby six-leggers, and suddenly noticed that Tara had stopped firing. She turned her head and found that Tara was down with a spear in her shoulder. She shouted to the others, but they were far too busy killing. She sensed someone close, and turned to face a large headhunter twice her size; without thinking, she jammed her weapon into its belly and fired away, opening a huge hole. She then rammed her weapon inside and kept firing through him at his fellow attackers until he finally realized he was dead and fell on top of her. She struggled, yelling lustily, until the heavy beast was shifted away, and there stood Myra, covered in blood, guts, and ichor, smiling from ear to ear. The big woman turned away and called, "Nina! See what you can do for Tara and you Her Highness Princess Jam, then be so nice as to follow me. We need to get to the cages and free the others, then capture the little shit who shot down my *Titanette*."

For a brief moment, Alexa gave Myra's back a puzzled look before she realized that the attackers had finally fallen back. Then she shook her head, looking for a weapon; hers had been bent into uselessness as the headhunter fell on her. She crawled over to the duffel and grabbed another, attaching a couple of spare clips and one charger to her belt.

"You guys all right?" She turned towards Nina and Tara.

Nina was helping Tara with the spear; next to her lay a small medkit. Tara laid on her back and side, holding her weapon one-handed, eyes searching for new threats.

The sky went very dark, very suddenly.

"Get under the trees," Myra shouted as she rolled on her back next to the others, pulling Alexa down with her. She then directed a hail of shots into the air at the large dragon-like flier darting towards the ground, three large legs stretched towards them in an attempt to capture someone, talons sticking out like biological swords. The beast crashed into the tree line, and Alexa couldn't tell if it had been hit or just misjudged its landing. Myra grabbed both Tara and Nina and rushed towards the safety of the forest while her weapon hung on her right side, bouncing and in the way. Alexa followed as fast as she could, while maintaining cover for the rest. Myra leaped on top of the enormous bird, which Alexa now saw couldn't be much deader, and used it as a ladder to scramble to the crotch of a large tree—only to be met by one of the six-leggers, making hissing noises and waving a war club. Not bothering to grab her weapon, Myra just darted forward and bit down on the beast's neck, hard, and let her own fangs do the work. Blood, skin, and feathers with fishlike scales covered her face as the beast fell to the ground holding the ruin of its neck; it was dead by the time it hit the forest floor. Myra then placed Tara and Nina on a large branch, while Alexa tossed up Nina's weapon along with a small ammo pouch, then heaved up the weapons duffel, which she'd grabbed before she retreated.

Myra jumped down next to Alexa and nodded for her to follow. They moved swiftly towards the village, trying to maintain cover as they advanced. Most of the flying threats kept their distance now, realizing that Myra had killed one of their number. They were enormous, some larger than Myra's former ship. Once in a while, a giant lizard-bird would swoop to the ground and capture one or more stragglers among the natives, carrying him off to who-knew-where. A smaller (but still large) species of bird with a very long neck would remain hovering in place while it skewered and it devoured its pray. One of these beasts kept eating even when a giant lizard with a head the size of a small fighter and fangs the length of an Oman arm bit down on a wing; then the pain signals got to its tiny brain, and the two beasts started to fight each other. More of the birds and near-birds joined in on the melee, starting with the long-neck's mate.

Alexa stayed right next to Myra, and in time the entered the clearing, with its mutilated bodies and heads on pikes. When they finally reached the first cage, everyone inside had their arms stretched out through the bars. In one of the corner were the Nastasturian soldiers. Myra used her sword, which she'd retrieved from the six-legger before hightailing into the woods, and struck down hard on the primitive lock. The barred gate slammed to the ground, and locals swarmed out, fleeing for their lives in all directions—only to be hunted by beasts on the ground and from the air. A giant bird grabbed one of the cages, but for some reason couldn't move it. Alexa noticed then that the cages had been built around high tree-stumps that were still rooted in the ground.

Alexa beckoned the Nastasturians to leave the cage, while Myra hurried towards the cage the little alien had been in; but now she couldn't see it. She opened it up, again using her sword, letting all the captured run for cover. The locals ignored her, dashing for the jungle; after they were gone, Myra found the little bastard in the far corner of the cage. Myra walked over to him and knelt next to him.

Alexa couldn't for the life of her guess what the hell Myra was doing kneeling by the alien. She took an awful long time with it. Meanwhile, Alexa handed Major Bree her small hand blaster; he was better with it than she was, and she had a magma rifle. The others had no weapons. They were bruised and battered, but otherwise seemed okay.

"Did you bring anything to drink?" Bree asked.

Alexa handed him a small box with ten small openings. Three were empty but there were still seven left, revealing small gelatin-like squares. "All the juice concentrate that's left; take one each," Alexa ordered. "Plenty of water in the forest."

Bree gave each of his soldiers one before he ate one himself. He handed the box back to Alexa and nodded towards it. "No thanks, already had one. We need to save them." Alexa was sweating profusely from the heat and all the fighting, and so were the others except for Myra, who'd been born on a world like this one and was used to damp weather and high heat.

His expression serious, Major Bree did something to the hand blaster, and then aimed it at one of the grass-roofed clay huts before firing a few rounds into it.

"Are you crazy? Stop wasting ammo," Alexa said in protest, but the major ignored her.

A small fire begun at the edge of the roof, and the Major began firing towards another, and then another. By then, several huts had blossomed with flames, which served to keep the animals away from them. Once Alexa realized what he was doing, she joined in, and soon most of the village was burning.

Myra joined them and knelt while looking towards the air, keeping her eyes on the birds and near-birds brawling above. "What happened to your little friend?" Alexa asked.

Myra pointed at her back, and they saw that the little alien was clamped onto her back, holding on the charger pack. It was an ugly little sentient with gray skin and big eyes, and Alexa couldn't remember ever having seen a being like it before. Its clothes were torn and soiled, but obviously originated from an advanced society.

"This here is *Shithead*," Myra introduced the little alien. "He shot us down hoping to scavenge some parts from our ship so he could repair *his*. I've convinced him of the error of his ways. Anyway: to make a long story short, he'll help us get to his ship if we take him with us, but his ship needs some repairs."

A strange, loud cry echoed through the valley, followed by another from the opposite side; whatever it was, it caused the marauding animals to hurry away from the valley, avoiding the fire, to hunt for less-difficult food—or perhaps to escaping becoming food. The flying creatures made loud shrieking sounds as they flew away.

Everyone headed back to the tree were Nina and Tara were hiding; and once they got the women to the ground, Bree and the other soldiers built a stretcher using two long branches and the remains of the jackets Nina, Alexa and Tara had been wearing. Most of them, including the soldiers, were half-naked as they followed Myra, who was many paces ahead of them, listening to the little alien on her back, who kept talking and gesturing.

They soon reached the base of a rock formation on the northern side of the village, and followed a small rocky path up the mountain. The mobile members of the party kept a close watch on the surroundings, alert to any threats. Eventually, they reached a small tunnel and walked through it, emerging on a plateau with a nice view over the valley. There were several solar catchers set up on the plateau, siphoning power into a compact battery array.

There was another cave opening down the side of the slope, hidden from anyone below, and they entered it next. The cave was lit by electric light, supplemented by low-tech torches. They soon reached an opening barred by a small wooden gate, and the stench was awful. Myra, who had the best sense of smell among them, made a disgusted expression and then opened the gate. Alexa grabbed a torch and tossed it inside. Something moved, and very carefully she and Myra entered the cave as the little alien started babbling. The light from another torch held by Bree lit up the larger cave behind the gate, revealing hundreds of miniature versions of both the head-hunters and the six-leggers.

"He's a slaver," Myra said, looking around with disgust.

Some of the children were little more than flesh and bone; and she noticed well-chewed bones on the cave, which appear to have come from their brethren that had died. It took some time, but eventually they forced all the children to leave the cave, whereupon Alexa and Sergeant Roni escorted them back to the tree line. There came a strange sound from the jungle, and all of the little sentients took off into the forest. On their way back to the slaver's cave, they met Private Echlon and Corporal Dora, escorting more children toward the forest. "We found more of them working in a mine further back in the cave," Dora explained.

Back at the mine, the little gray alien sat in the center of a circle of soldiers and Vixens, looking scared, while the rest of them stood and stared at him in disgust. He had caused all the fighting, one way or another, but no matter what the others said, the alien didn't see the logic in their argument, and couldn't seem to understand that he had done something horrible wrong. He seemed to have no moral sense at all. They were all used to the wide variety of sentient species in the known universe, with their various senses of right and wrong, and knew full well that trying to convince this creature that what it had done was wrong was only a waste of time; but still, everyone *did* try, talking to him with no avail.

"Have we found his ship?" Alexa asked sharply.

Myra gestured with her thick thumb over her shoulder, "Yeah, it's further down this mountain on another plateau, on the opposite side. Nina and Tara are there looking it over."

"So do we need this creature?"

"No, Alexa, we do not," Myra said heavily, knowing full well what was coming.

The little alien, who spoke with a heavy accent, noticed the change of mood and started to talk very quickly, while gesturing and spitting on the ground. "You harm me, my hive hunt you down and sell you all as the slaves you are!"

"Been there, done that," Alexa said. "Won't do it again." She'd had enough from the little monster, so she walked over and shot it in the head. No one, not even Major Bree, said a word or complained. It was justice.

Bree took the body to the entrance plateau, and built a pyre from dead branches and brush, upon which he burned the gray slaver. It went up like dry wood, and was reduced to ash and calcined bone in half an hour. They gathered around the fire and watched as the sun set, weighed down by weariness and depression.

The ground trembled again, this time much worse than before, and they had to brace themselves. "Bloody earthquakes. Think it's from the volcanoes?" Bree asked

"Hate to break it to you, but I think it's footsteps," Myra said loudly, clutching the cliff.

"We felt them before, I think, at the end of the battle," Nina raised her voice to be heard.

"Can anyone see anything?" Tara wanted to know, laying on the ground with her back against the rock wall. She and Nina had returned from their recon of the alien's ship in time to see the alien burned to cinders, which was better than it deserved.

Alexa walked over to the side of the mountain and looked down, she then, turned facing the others. "No, nothing...what?"

Alexa was confused by the stunned expressions of the other survivors, who stood there gaping. Nina shouted something incoherent, while Myra just pointed at her and in the air. Suddenly Alexa felt something turn the twilight even darker as a large shadow fell over her. She turned around slowly, but didn't quite make it before something large and hairy grabbed her. It felt as if she were flying for a moment, but the grip was firm and gentle without the jerking of wingbeats; it fell like a giant hand was holding her. She tried to move, but couldn't.

Then she looked up.

She really was in the hand of a giant, a creature that should have been too large to exist, yet somehow did. The great beast leaned to its side while holding onto the cliff edge with one hand; its feet we also grabbing the side of the mountain. A large simian face looked back at her, seeming surprised; then its eyes became very large as something jerked its legs to the ground. The beast fell hard and rolled over to its side, hitting its head against the mountainside but holding Alexa up and away from its body to ensure she wasn't injured. It let out a roar of anger, then quieted after ensuring its new toy was all right. Meanwhile, a creature like it but twice its size roared in anger of its own, holding two dead giant birds, one in each hand. It tossed one of the dead prey on the ground, then sat down on a hut that had burned down to a bright ring of embers. For a moment nothing happened; then the enormous ape leaped high into the air, its ass on fire, tossing the other, half-eaten bird right at the cave entrance far above on the mountain. The smaller beast that held Alexa let her down gently on the ground, then it fell to the ground and rolled all over, laughing, as its older sibling jumped and screamed in a dance of pain.

Alexa, having gotten over her shock, turned to the rocky path and ran for her life. She didn't stop until she had not only passed her friends and run through the large cave, she kept running deep into the mine. She had never been so scared in her entire life, and was heading to the relative safety of the spaceship on the other side of the mountain. That was the idea, anyway. As she passed her friends, who were trying to push the half-eaten giant bird off the plateaus, she could hear all of them laughing. Bastards. Alexa ignored them and kept running for her life, hoping to find a place to hide somewhere in the alien's ship cargo hold; but she took a wrong turn, and suddenly she ran into something sticky. The more she struggled, the more she tied herself up. It was pitch dark, of course, and she couldn't see a thing. After a futile struggle, she swallowed her pride and called for help. After a while, she saw the light from a torch approaching, and soon all her friends stood there, laughing even more.

"You must like bondage, slut," Nina said loudly, and the rest joined in on poor Alexa's distress, laughing their guts out.

Alexa was getting very pissed off. She spat webbing out of her mouth, screaming at the top of her lungs, stopping only when she noticed her friends' frightening expressions. "Now what? Another bloody ape?"

A hissing sound came from behind her, and a large hairy leg settled onto the web to the right of head, which made Alexa's eye pop; and then there was the sound of several blasters firing at once, and a splashing sound as a giant spider-like thing exploded, spewing its entrails over Alexa. Lovely. She fell to the ground as the web gave way, and Bree helped her up, smiling as he peeled off the gluey web. Needless to say, Tara and Nina leaned on each other laughing. Some friends.

"May an asteroid hit the both of you, you boneheads, and the damn spider too!" Alexa screamed.

"It's not a spider," Myra said grimly, kneeling by the dead creature.

"It's a Tilter," Bree agreed, kneeling next to Myra.

"What! How could the alien live with a female Tilter?" Roni asked.

"Looks like a bloody spider to me," Alexa said, parking herself sitting on the ground and trying to get the rest of the webbing out of her hair. "Only Tilters I've seen have looked like dogs."

"Those were males; they only have four legs. Female Tilters have ten legs; and yes, it *does* belong to the spider family, kind of, but it's not a spider," Nina said educationally, while wiping her tears from her eyes. "And to answer your question, Roni, he probably fed it regularly. Look over there." Nina pointed at a pile of bones laying on the ground. "Those are baby natives. Tilters aren't indigenous to this world, so that means that the alien brought them here, violating quite a few universal laws."

"On top of the slavery, and feeding sentients to a dangerous animal," Dora pointed out.

"Great, ain't that some shit," Alexa said, still angry over the sticky crap in her hair. "Makes pirates look like jaywalkers."

Bree said, "We'll need to report this to the Universal Court, so they can send a cleaning crew to this region and cleanse it of any advanced involvement. Assuming we can get out of here." It was bad enough they were on an undeveloped world; interrupting a world's natural evolution was the most serious crime in Universal Law. Being cut off from the rest of the universe, they had no idea what Florencia had recently done to Omar.

Myra nodded. "I might be a pirate, but even I would never do something like this—and to be perfectly honest, I know of no known pirate leader that would condone and allow it. The Brakks will *really* be pissed off."

Nina joined in, sounding like a teacher, "That's because they see any world as a future investment, no matter how many thousands of years it takes before its inhabitants reach the stars. If they ever do. "

"Are we in trouble?" Tara asked, sounding very concerned.

Bree smiled at her and said, "No we're not in trouble; we had to land due to an emergency. The alien, however, did not, and introduced a non-indigenous animal species to this world. If it were still alive, it sure as hell would be in trouble."

"As the saying goes, where's there Tilters there are slavers," Alexa muttered.

Her words caught everyone's attention, and in silence, they turned towards her. She was still occupied with cleaning the webbing out of her hair, but when she noticed the silence, she looked up. "What?"

"Slavers. Where there's one, there are others. We need to get the hell off from this rock," Myra said, immediately heading towards the cave opening where the cargo ship was stored.

"What about the cocoons? Soon there will be hundreds of Tilters running around here—small, maybe, but still dangerous!"

Myra shook one of her large arms in the air and shouted back, "Ignore them! Unless they're already hatched, they'll all die without nutrients from the mother."

It took several days to fix the slaver's ship, and they were able to accomplish that only thanks to the spare parts and nano-builders the alien had taken from Myra's ship. Its cargo bays were half-full of precious gemstones, but everyone agreed that the riches would remain on the planet, so they poured it all down the side of the mountain. Then they did their best to clean up any evidence of they or the little gray alien ever having been there. The locals, meanwhile, had reunited with their children and returned to the valley, rebuilding their huts peacefully.

After four days of endless work, the little cargo ship finally took off with Alexa at the helm and Nina as the navigator. They headed back to the lake where they'd camped previously, mapping the region and establishing latitude and longitude as they went. These coordinates would eventually be turned over to the proper authorities, who would send a special crew and cleanse the entire region, ensuring that the world could evolve unmolested by outside interference. When they reached the lake and waterfall, they spent a little time hovering overhead, then headed towards the mountain in search for more survivors. They searched for a week, but found no one. In the far distance, the recently erupted volcanoes provided a deadly but beautiful backdrop to their efforts.

When they finally achieved orbit, they would scan the surface. Bree made a vow promising to return, one way or the other, and keep looking for his lost people, as did his fellow soldiers, however their mission was priority; to save the hostage.

BEHIND a waterfall not far from where they had originally camped, an elderly chieftain chipped away at the wall, creating pictographs. Next to him stood his children, with paints they would use to decorate the images. On the rock wall was the history of the proud Lake People. The paintings were represented in five sections; birth, growing up, daily life, old age, and death. But above all these old paintings and carvings were some new ones: One displayed their many-legged water god being killed by another god, a scaly one who stood on two feet, while another painting showed a circular craft hovering in the air with sunbeams stabbing out of it.

Last of all were all the bodies of the Lake People warriors, lying dead after having battled the gods and lost.

TWENTY-TWO

AN angry major Bree charged into the cockpit, cursing. "Why aren't we scanning the surface for survivors?" he demanded.

"Problems controlling the steering," Alexa shouted, struggling with the yoke beneath her hands.

Nina pushed past the major, hurrying toward a computer where she intended to try to hack to regain control of the ship. "The bloody ship is pre-set to return to specific coordinates," she spat after a long moment.

"Which means we're heading right towards trouble," Bree said, "going right to wherever the damned slavers are waiting for that crap the gray mined. Holy Gull!"

Myra leaned into the cockpit and rumbled, "I suggest we get suited up, and hope this ship contains some uniforms or clothing of some kind we might use as disguises. Oh, and let's get the few weapons we have left ready for a fight."

"Crap, I can't alter or bypass the coordinates from this station," Nina said, then warned in a louder voice, "Prepare for FTL!"

In a blink of an eye, the ship vanished into the Deep Dark. While Alexa, Nina, and Tara, with some help from Myra, tried to regain control of the ship, the rest went over it with a fine-toothed comb, looking for anything that might aid them in their predicament. All of them but Myra were dressed in little more than their underwear; their suits and battle-gear had been lost to the gray and the locals he'd strong-armed into helping him. The only thing they found was several large white blankets, and with the help of a knife, Bree turned them into simple tunics.

The journey took quite a while, so they searched and re-searched the ship for several days. Ultimately, it was just a small mining ship, nothing special about it, and Myra concluded that it was heading for its mothership. She doubted the grays were actually dealing in slaves; mining on restricted worlds before they had evolved to spacefaring was as illegal as hell, considered even worse than piracy, and that could only mean one thing: trouble. Whoever was behind this operation wouldn't want any witnesses, so they would somehow have to fight themselves out of this mess. This everyone agreed, so they prepared themselves for battle.

What they didn't understand was why no one had come to help the stranded alien. They generated several theories and discussed them as they searched, but none that would aid them.

When they finally dropped out of FTL, Myra ordered, "See if you can find any maps or charts, Alexa. I don't recognize any constellations. You?"

"No. And sorry, everything's locked down. Nina and Tara been trying to hack the comp-system for days, and there's not a scrap of paper or plastic in here."

"We're slowing down," Nina called over the intercom, and everyone not already there made their way forward to the little cockpit/bridge.

Tara was busy trying to get a fix on their location while Alexa steered the ship. They'd fallen out of FTL near a pair of planets in a mutual orbit, with several moons dancing around both; a large yellow sun was visible in the far distance, partially screened by an unusually dense asteroid field. The ship zig-zagged through it.

Nina was still struggling with the computer, but had accomplished exactly zero so far.

"There's our destination." Alexa pointed at a blip on the lidar screen.

The ship continued to slow, and after several hours they could see a ship in the distance, gradually growing in size as they approached. There was no hail over the communicator. The mother ship was enormous, more a station than a ship, and as they approached they could see cargo ships similar to theirs departing from it while others docked. Suddenly the ship trembled as a tractor beam caught it and pulled it towards a docking bay. When they'd settled on the deck inside, they found themselves surrounded by several other docked ships.

"Let's get ready for the welcome committee," Myra said, smiling coldly.

"Time to free the galaxy from scum and criminals," Sergeant Roni added, checking the charge on his blaster.

Myra rolled her eyes at his comment, and Tara laughed. They fell silent as a metallic scraping and clattering came at the lock, and the ship trembled, setting off several alarm signals. They positioned themselves by the main hatch in the back of the ship as the ship shook violently; through the hatch, Bree could see large robotic arms attaching themselves to depressions in the ship's hull. The docking bay began repressurizing, made clear by the misty vapor filling the room; hopefully, it would be breathable. As air replaced the vacuum outside, they could hear klaxons echoing outside the ship, followed flashing warning lights.

Howling alarms sounded briefly, then a hatch hissed open across the bay—double doors opening to a hallway in blatant invitation. A cold breeze hit them as the pressures inside and outside the ship equalized, and the typical metallic and plastic smell of a ship that had been in space too long flooded in. By now the vapor had almost vanished but for some small outlets along the bases of the walls, and there was a faint scent of disinfectant.

"I'd give an arm and a leg for a bloody probe right now," Major Bree whispered. "Move out."

Bree took point, followed by Echlon, Dora, and then Roni. They advanced in two-by-two formation. Behind them followed Myra, and last, in a triangular formation, came the Vixens. They passed swiftly through the bay, which was cluttered with crates and gear; it was very messy, but provided a lot of cover. They kept looking any for cameras or sensors that might be recording their advance, but none were evident. Either it was an old vessel, the owner was cheap, or the sensors were so small they weren't obvious.

They soon cleared the hangar and entered the hallway. It ended in a smaller entrance hatch; it was locked. "Roni and Nina, see if you can get through that," Bree ordered, looking around calmly. They arranged themselves in a semicircle around the hatch, most facing out, but Echlon backed up Roni and Nina in case they were surprised by something when they got the hatch open.

A quiet sound of satisfaction from Nina was followed by the sound of the hatch sliding open. Bright light spilled out from a corridor on the other side. Bree took a quick look inside, then nodded for Echlon to take point. When everyone was inside the new corridor, they took note of a small white light flashing on the low ceiling.

"Probably an alarm we set off when we hacked the lock," Roni whispered.

The corridor, which was oddly circular in cross-section, split in two directions, curving out of sight farther ahead. The bright light emanating from the walls and ceiling made everyone blink until they got used to it; whoever had designed the vessel must come from a very bright world. Bree murmured, "Sergeant, you and Dora take the left; Echlon, you're with me. Let's see where these corridors lead and then meet back here. The rest of you remain here, please."

Private Echlon and Major Bree took the right corridor at a slow hustle, while Sergeant Roni and Corporal Dora took the other; and as asked, Myra and the Vixens remained at the junction. The soldiers returned shortly after they finished scouting.

"Major, our side leads to several hangars similar to the ones we docked in, then terminates at what looks like an elevator," Roni reported.

"Thank you, Sergeant, same here. We had three more docking bays; how many did you have?"

"Six, sir."

"That makes it ten total. None of ours had any ships except for our own."

"We found one ship docked, probably one we saw during our approach, but there were no crew aboard," Roni said.

Myra leaned against the wall and looked through the entrance at the cargo ship they had arrived in. "Perhaps this *is* some type of slave ship."

"What do you mean?" Bree asked.

"Perhaps they have to reach a certain quota before they can return to the mothership?"

"Doesn't mean there are slaves here," Sergeant Roni cut in.

Myra shrugged.

"If they're slaves, they can't be punished for what they've done. Besides, we don't know what other worlds or systems they're mining on."

"True, corporal. However, the world we came from is very restricted."

"We need to find a blueprint of this ship," Alexa interrupted, getting bored by the conversation.

"True, but first, we need to find the crew and the captain and secure the entire ship."

"Good plan, Major." Myra gave him a malicious smile while fingering her blaster. It gave Bree goosebumps, and a quick glance at Alexa reminded him that she and the other former hostages had warned him about Myra being a notorious pirate. He knew all too well that she was a carnivore, a killer; then again, so were he and his soldiers.

"Should we split up?" Myra suggested.

After a quick glance at Nina and Tara, who were leaning on each other, still injured, he answered, "No, we stick together. Sergeant Roni and Private Echlon, take point; Corporal Dora, take the rear. The rest of you accompany me in the center."

They moved cautiously down the corridor, and every time they reached a hangar entrance they peered through the ports set into the hatches, making sure they hadn't missed any crew. When they finally reached the elevator, they hesitated briefly. Bree didn't want to risk everyone inside the lift at once, but at the same time, he didn't want to split up.

"Sergeant, remain here with the ladies," he decided. "Corporal and Private, follow me. Sergeant, once we're clear I'll send back Private Echlon to get you."

"Yessir."

It seemed forever for the rest while they waited, and finally the elevator opened up to reveal Private Echlon, smiling. "Follow me," he said, without telling the others anything more.

The elevator apparently went to only four levels, one below the one they'd been on and two above; however, the top level was locked. When they reached the third level and exited, Dora and Bree were waiting. Dora signaled for them to crouch and be silent. The corridor they were in was made of a silvery metal, and the ceiling lights were dim. Several large waist-high ports appeared to be closed off with shielding, and all the hatches were shut and sealed tight except for one; they could hear the sound of voices issuing from that one. Major Bree signaled to the others that there were six hostiles. The soldiers, Myra, and the Vixens positioned themselves along the walls, alongside the open hatch, covering all their flanks. A quick signal, and Bree entered the room, followed by Dora and Echlon. Myra, however, wasn't one to miss any action; she hurried after, having ignored Bree's signal for her and the others to remain in place.

They entered what seemed to be a cantina with six people of almost as many species among them, including two Omans; three of the individuals sat at one table with a port affording them a view of the Deep Dark, speaking in Nadjarish and a sprinkling of some other language. Two more sat at another table further away, and one individual stood at an autobar on the wall, ordering either food or drink. With expedient professionalism, the Nastasturian elite soldiers secured the cantina, gesturing with hands and guns for the crew to be silent.

The miners stared bewildered and baffled at the threat, and the slight, thin rat-like man by the autobar dropped a mug with some fluid in it; it clattered cross the floor. Myra grabbed him, and sentient started to struggle; but Myra laid her large hand over his mouth and squeezed, flashing him an evil smile. He froze.

The others entered the room, and Nina fashioned makeshift bonds by tearing apart one of the Omans' tunics. With the help of Alexa, she soon had their captives bound, gagged, and lined up for inspection. Myra immediately got to work on one of the female Omans she thought might be in charge, as she was the only female. The woman, a dark-skinned specimen with a pleasing pattern of pale spots tailing from her forehead down the sides of her face to her neck, seemed to have some alien blood in her; and Myra wondered out loud if the freckles went "all the way down." The woman refused to reply, eyes defiant. Her short, dark hair was plaited in a strange fashion.

Bree demanded, "Who's the captain? How many crew, and where are they?"

No answer. Myra tried the query in several languages to the same response; but finally, by squeezing the prisoner's neck hard enough for her vertebrae to creak, Myra got her to start talking. It sounded like Nadjarish, but her words were muffled.

"Yeah, might want to remove the gag there," Nina said calmly.

Myra smiled at the hostage and carefully removed the gag. Attacking the crew onboard target ships and scaring the crap out of them was standard procedure for Myra; Bree and the others knew this, and allowed Myra to do her thing. The Oman looked around desperately at everyone, and then she noticed their clothing; and if it hadn't been for all the weapons, she would have spat in Myra's face once she had worked up the courage. Myra knew this, and only squeezed harder while pulling at the woman's left breast.

"I will tear it off and eat it, cunt, if you don't start spilling your guts—preferably though your mouth using your vocal cords, but I'm fine with slicing open your belly. Trust me: I don't care either way."

Suddenly Myra let go of her breast and waved a large, sharp black knife in front of the Oman's eyes. This time the hostage nodded her head fast and stuttered, "The captain is E-e-Vongi Desai from Athorz."

Myra played with the knife in front the prisoner's frightened eyes, encouraging her to continue.

"We, there are nine onboard counting the captain. The rest are all on the top deck, either resting or on the bridge. Who *are* you?"

Myra smiled and blinked her left eye. "Why, my dear...we're pirates. And we love to acquire new booty." Myra licked the frightened Oman on her cheek with her purple-black tongue.

Bree raised his eyebrows, and couldn't help smiling. After she got the girl to tell them how to obtain access to the bridge, Myra tossed the hostage on the floor and then used her knife to rip off all the hostages' clothing, leaving them with their underwear only and making sure their bonds were tightly secured. Bree and Corporal Dora crossed the room to the other entrance, and Bree signaled for Myra and Private Echlon to follow while the others remained with the hostages.

After a while Myra returned, the barrel of her blaster red hot. "Everyone up top, including them."

Myra gestured with her thumb over her shoulder as she carefully shouldered her blaster, then grabbed two of the hostages and tossed them into an elevator. Once everyone was inside, they headed up to the top level. When the doors opened, there were treated to a miasma of smoke and the smell of burnt flesh. A dead Oman male lay roasted on the floor.

"Meet the captain, overseer of this particular operation. Bastard didn't want to give up the ship," Myra growled.

Next to the charred body sat two more crew with their hands on their heads, shaking with fright. The bridge proved to be an oval chamber with seats for fifteen technicians and watch-standers spread across the room. Between the pilot and navigator seats was the command chair, raised on a low dais so that it towered over the rest. Alexa ignored the whimpering hostages and headed for the command chair, while Nina and Tara stalked over to the computers.

"Myra, see if you can get them to give us the codes for the computer. I think I can hack this bastard, but that would take time," Nina barked.

She was immediately interrupted by a howl of anguish. Having dropped on her knees, the dark Oman woman began wailing next to the body of the dead captain. She let out a roar of fury and suddenly lunged for Myra's back; Myra spun with lightning speed and sliced off her head with her knife. The head tumbled through the air before hitting the deck, splattering crimson blood all over the bridge. Everyone was shocked into immobility, even the Nastasturus elites; they'd never harm a hostage if it were unavoidable. But Myra was in her own element and loving it. She just smiled through the blood-spatter on her face, ignoring the sounds of protests from Bree and his soldiers. The Vixens basically ignored it; they were used to far worse.

"You know, it might help if we had all of the crew alive, just in case there are some hidden codes we need for the comp-system," Alexa said calmly, staring at a holo display.

"Making yourself at home, dear?" Nina said to Myra without lifting her eyes from her computer screen.

"Nothing like a little bloodshed to liven up an afternoon, right?" Tara noted as she tore a small hatch off the wall and inspected the fluidic wiring within.

"Well, can you get it to work?"

"That remains to be seen, Major. Perhaps you and Myra can get the rest of the crew to help us?" Alexa suggested.

The Nastasturians left the bridge and secured the rest of the ship after helping themselves to several communicators from the hostages. After several hours and with no help from the crew—because, as it turned out, only the captain and his wife had the proper passwords and commands—Nina and Myra managed to hack into the system, while Alexa and Bree had to go down to the engine room right below the bridge and work from there.

"This ship is actually two ships," Nina reported finally. "The most important one can be detached from the mining barge that contains the docking bay."

"Good job, Nina," Myra said. "We need to get all the supplies we can to this ship, and then get the hell away from here."

"Should we just leave this mining operation intact?" Dora asked.

"We must," Myra said. "The main reason is that it can't really be defended, since there are no major weapons except for a couple of asteroid turrets. Aside from that, all it's got are shields. Barges like this attract dangerous hostiles because it's easy prey."

"What about the hostages?" Tara wondered.

Myra chuckled and shrugged. "The fewer witnesses, the better."

Major Bree entered the bridge. "We'll leave them here, and once we've reported this highly illegal and dangerous operation, the proper authorities will send someone to arrest them. Alexa has destroyed their main engine, and when we leave only their life support will remain intact. Alexa has also programmed the system to order the other barges to return; once they're docked, Nina's new program will disable their engines."

"Almost done with that," Nina said.

A massive disk-shaped spacecraft detached itself from the mining barge slowly, then moved away into the Big Dark, where it streaked into near-FTL. The seven surviving crew stood half-naked on the bridge, staring at the vanishing ship and wondering what to do next. One of them, a gray like the alien on the planet the *Titan*'s crew had been marooned on, spat angrily on the deck. "Stupid pirates forgot one thing."

"What?" asked a large, purplish hairy creature that may or may not have been female.

"Emergency beacon."

"I thought it was on the ship they left with."

"One, yes. Another on *this* ship."

"**LET** me know when you have the coordinates programmed," Alexa said over the intercom to Nina, who was still hacking the mining ship's computer. Myra and Tara stood with Bree around a circular table further back in the bridge, reviewing holos of several different stellar constellations and systems. The rest were going through a series of crates, dividing clothes in different piles. They looked up as a proximity alert went off.

"Shit! Incoming!" Alexa yelled.

Everyone froze.

"Crap, we forgot to check for an emergency beacon on the mining facility! There she goes!"

Alexa tapped a button to show the beacon missile exiting the ship at a high rate of speed before arcing into a wide orbit around the ship, and blaring its presence on all channels, both real-space and subspace. Shaking her head, she poured extra velocity into their escape.

"Only a fool would do that," Myra said, nodding at the screen showing the launched beacon.

"Why do you say that?" Bree asked.

"Think about it. What they're doing is so highly illegal it actually makes piracy look lame—and that's a wide-spectrum beacon. It'll attract all types of ships, including LEOs."

"There may be no law enforcement officers around if we're in some remote corner in the universe," Alexa chimed in. "Gull only knows how far we traveled with that new program, Myra." She began plotting a new course Nina had just sent her from her own station. "Screw this. Get ready for FTL. Buckle up, everyone," Alexa called over the intercom. She tapped the initiator key, and the ship vanished from the real universe.

They kept their detectors on the beacon back at the mining ship. "Think it's going to work?" Bree asked Myra.

"Oh, it'll work. Someone will show; it just may not be who they want."

"Quiet, everyone," Alexa barked. "Someone is responding already. Check the screen."

The screen blinked and a poor-quality transmission came on, accompanied by a scratchy voice.

"State the nature of your emergency."

"We have been attacked by pirates, and there has been a..."

Static burred the audio channel; suddenly the screen flickered as another signal overrode the initial offer of assistance. The image was clear, and the person in it said just one word: "Report."

Back on the mining mothership, the eyes of the surviving crew members grew wide when they saw the person on the screen. They had heard about him, of course, but never in their lives had they expected to *meet* him, much less discover that they *worked* for him. Now they realized why the captain and his woman had behaved so secretly.

Gazing at them calmly from the monitor was the most feared pirate in the known universe: Horsa of Clan Wulsatures.

TWENTY-THREE

THE disk-shaped ship altered its shape to oval as it passed into FTL. Alexa sat in the cockpit, in a compartment a bit fore and below the bridge, with five steps and a ladder separating them. The opening could be shut with a hatch. The cockpit also functioned as a lifeboat, and could hold up to four people. Next to her sat Tara, acting as co-pilot; behind her sat Nina, her eyes fixed on the main computer. Standing next to Nina was Sergeant Roni, who also something of a computer wizard; they worked together on the system, exchanging terse words and steams of jargon occasionally. Next to them sat Myra, taking up space for three normals in an adjustable seat, working navigation. From time to time she sent coordinates to Nina, who tried to reprogram their destination into the ship's computer; but every time, Nina let out a curse as she failed.

"Whenever we're on impulse power we can control the ship," Alexa said curtly to everyone in earshot, "but the moment I leave this seat, it reverts back to its pre-set course. It's completely under control of the computer in FTL, so there's no use even trying to control it; we'll end up wherever Horsa wants."

Major Bree's voice issued from an intercom near her seat. "As soon as we reach neutral or friendly space we can signal for help." He sat at the command seat on the bridge, trying to follow what they were doing down in the cockpit on several screens. Myra climbed up from the cockpit and walked over to the port looking out into space.

"The problem, Major, is that we don't have control of the ship, and we can't change the preset coordinates. We simply don't know where we'll end up."

The ship abruptly dropped out of FTL and slowed. They appeared to be in the middle of nowhere. "Myra, what's going on?" Bree demanded.

"Don't know."

"Myra, Bree, I think I know," Alexa interrupted, having listened in on the conversation. "We're almost out of *Anti-Materia*, and without it we're limited to sublight."

Nina broke in with, "Hello, looks like we're heading towards an asteroid."

"On screen," Bree and Myra ordered in unison, then smiled at each other sheepishly. No one had taken any real command, but everyone except Myra felt that command should be on Bree's shoulders. Myra had more experience with spacecraft than anyone aboard, but after all, she *was* a pirate, and Bree still considered this his mission.

The asteroid grew from a barely discernable speck to fill the forward screen as they approached. An automated voice warned the crew to prepare for docking.

"Gear up and get prepare for battle," Bree ordered; before he finished the sentence, everyone but Alexa had hurried to their battle gear, such as it was, in the hold behind the bridge. Everything wearable lay neatly organized on the floor; Corporal Dora and Private Echlon handed out the various weapons from a rack on the wall.

"I'll take Alexa's stuff," Nina said.

Myra looked on, already geared up; unlike the others, she had never removed her spacesuit. "Now that we have pressure suits for all of us, you should always wear them," she advised again, while the rest passed her.

Nina threw her a kiss while struggling with Alexa's gear. "Will do, dear, will do."

"This shit gets hot after a while," Tara complained.

"Yeah, but this same shit will keep you alive," Myra countered.

As the ship approached the surface of the asteroid, they could see a small station nestled between several craters. It was a mobile station, and its camouflage made it difficult to make out. The holoscreen outlined it in blue to make emphasize its configuration. Alexa had no difficulties landing on the pad provided; after the dust had settled, a long robotic arm extended from the base toward the main hatch, docking with the ship. It adjusted itself and clamped onto the entrance.

As soon as the hatches opened to equalize pressure, a thick smog poured inside the ship. By then, they were all locked up tight in their pressure suits, so no one was affected by anything in the smog. Bree and Myra took the lead, heading inside docking arm to enter the base. When they called clear, Corporal Dora and Private Echlon followed, while the Vixens remained behind. After what seemed forever, Bree's voice came on the intercom.

"All clear, ladies, no one's home."

After a few minutes of poking around on the computer system, they discovered that the station was a supply and fuel depo; that sent them searching for better clothing, EVA suits, and more and better weapons.

"Lot of stuff here about their mining operation, along with a list of gems mined and some apparently very rare crystals I've never heard of." Nina whistled when she saw the worth of the cargo collected so far.

"That's why they only used small ships. Cargo like that doesn't need large freighters. Small, relatively lightweight, high value."

"True, Myra, but wouldn't you at least include some weapons on your ships for protection?"

"Hell no. If the authorities caught them, they could claim to be doing research or some such. No weapons, no problems."

"Maybe that's why the ship is so fast," Alexa said from behind them. "To avoid capture."

Myra turned and looked at Alexa, "Probably so, but the little tin can does drink a lot of fuel. Any chance we can override the steering and navigation?"

"Perhaps if we can find the main codes for the program, but I'll leave that to Nina and the Sergeant."

Ultimately, they remained at the space station for months, trying to solve the navigation problem. They never found a workable solution, and there came a time when they had to leave because their supplies were running low. The imminent threat being visited by whoever was behind the mining operation was a constant reminder that they had to hurry; so in the end, they decided to take their chances and go to wherever the preset coordinates delivered them, and then see if they could escape on impulse power when the ship dropped out of FTL.

All of them were eager to return home, except for Myra, who had nothing left to return to. She'd lost her ship, and the pirate clan she had once been part of no longer existed. They all thought they were far out on the unexplored edged of the known universe when they piled inside the craft for the next leg of their journey, so they were surprised when, an hour after jumping into FTL, the ship suddenly dropped out and altered direction before blinking into FTL again.

"I don't like this," Major Bree said. "Prepare for battle. The minute we slow to impulse, be ready to fight on a moment's notice."

Alexa cursed. "Again, no bloody controls. Nina, want to see if you can do something?"

"As soon as I distribute the EVA suits to everyone."

Myra and Bree were already in their suits; they just shook their heads at the others.

A few minutes later Alexa warned, "Everyone, we're slowing down!"

The ship dropped out of FTL and rapidly decelerated until it was at a standstill, altering its shape to its circular resting form. A navigation holotank came to life, displaying thousands of stars and other celestial objects, a number of which started to pulse in red as the computer identified the star systems. The ship's main thrusters rumbled to life, sending them toward the center of the system they lay currently at the outskirts of, aimed toward the orangish sun in the far distance.

Major Bree leaned on a railing, looking out of one of the ports on the bridge. "Where are we?"

"No idea," Alexa answered.

Nina peered at a holographic map. "We are…I think we're in the system of…"

There was a moment of silence on the bridge as Nina rechecked her monitor, but then someone interrupted her before she could answer Bree's question: "Gala. We're at Gala," Myra said, sounding concerned. "I recognize the ringed planet we just passed."

"We're heading towards *that* planet," Alexa told them, putting a small world on the forward screen. It rapidly increased in size as she increased the magnification, until they were looking at a typical blue-green water world, frosted with white clouds.

"Torq," Myra announced, now sounding anxious and even a bit frightened.

"Never heard of it," Bree said, checking his people's weapons and equipment.

Nina finally had some information on the system and planet: "It's a small colonial world in a neutral polity."

"Good, then we can make contact with home," Bree said.

Myra shook her head and leaned forward on a console, with her eyes closed. "Of all places in the universe…" she began. She opened her eyes and looked at Bree. "My dear Major, Torq is not somewhere *you* want to be. It's a safe haven for warlords, criminals, and pirates, one of about a dozen such places that I know of, and this happens to be one of the worst. You'll find no relief in this Gull-forsaken system."

"Explains the illegal mining," Bree snorted.

"Ah, the controls are back," Alexa said happily. "I think."

Myra turned, facing Alexa, "Then get us out of this trap before we get company. This little tin can has no weapons."

"True, but it's very fast little tin can." Alexa let out an excited howl as she turned the ship and accelerated away from Torq.

"Don't jump to faster-than-light or we might lose controls again," Tara advised from the co-pilot's seat.

"Nina, plot another course, one that will take us to friendly space," Alexa said.

"Already ahead of you," Nina shouted back.

A klaxon echoed through the cockpit, and warning lights suddenly started to flash all over the ship.

"Incoming; we have incoming," Bree said, calmly looking dead ahead as a ship appeared in the far distance on an intercept course.

"And we're being hailed," Tara said calmly.

"On screen," Bree ordered.

"No, wait!" Myra shouted to deaf ears.

"Welcome..." The voice trailed off as the person on the forward screen stared in disbelief. He was a hideous omanoid, whose surprised expression suddenly morphed into a frightening smile.

"Why, it's my pretties! Aren't we all a happy little family today." Zuzack smiled one of his evil smiles at Myra, Alexa, and the rest.

"Oh, crap," Tara said.

"Out of all systems in the universe, you had to take us to this one?" Alexa shouted, hitting the console in front of her. She poured power to the ship's engines in an effort to evade Zuzack and escape the system before they were captured.

"Sir, I'm Major Bree of the armed forces of the Nastasturus Federation," the Major announced to Zuzack. "You should know that you will be handsomely awarded by our government if you escort us back to Nastasturian space."

Zuzack looked to the side with his index finger under his chin, as if he were thinking, and he then turned his scarred face towards the Major on the screen. "Normally I would have taken you up on the offer, as the honest poor trader I am, Major. However, one must think of one's crew. Should I spoil their potential entertainment? I think not. Besides...just finding you was a handsome reward." His face went purple as he shouted, "Run my pretties, run for all you are worth! For here comes *hell*!"

The screen went blank, and Myra turned away from it in a thoughtful mood. Then her face broke into an evil smile to rival Zuzack's. She moved down to the cockpit and asked, "Alexa, did you say you have the steering back?"

Alexa, focused on her flight recorder and steering, replied irritably, "Yes, why?"

Myra ignored the question. "Nina, are we heading away from the system?"

"Of course we are."

Myra closed her eyes and shook her head. "Don't."

"Don't what?" Alexa and Nina asked in unison.

"Don't head back into open space; that's what the ugly bastard wants."

"Why would he want that?" Nina asked, sounding hesitant.

"Trust me on this one." Sounding more concerned and worried than ever, Myra continued, "He wants us to be in open space so he can attack and capture us. Most likely he has a hidden beacon on this ship, and the pre-programmed course will take us to Zuzack's ship."

"So, what will make him *not* do that within the Gala system?"

"Because, Nina, no one can attack anyone within the system. It's a safe haven; the local administrators would kill whoever broke that treaty. That's the point with a safe haven: no weapons, no war. Just trust me."

"Makes sense," Nina agreed.

Alexa nodded her head and made a fast turn towards the center of the system, heading for Torq; and when she did, Zuzack's flagship, the *Bitch*, accelerated in an attempt to intercept them. The *Bitch* was looking awful these days: it appeared barely spaceworthy, with large metal patches scabbed all over the enormous hull. It was classified as a destroyer, but some would argue that it was a small cruiser instead.

"Tara, see if you can send a mayday towards Torq," Myra ordered. Then she sneered under her breath, "Think you can outsmart Myra, you bastard?"

"They're firing on us," Alexa warned. "Missiles."

Two large explosions alongside the mining ship forced Alexa to make evasive maneuvers. A few more missiles followed, but Alexa's piloting skill and the oversized engines on the ship outran the oncoming threat. The missiles detonated far behind them as they ran out of fuel.

"The firing has ceased," Bree's voice came over the speakers.

"Because we just entered the inner system!" Nina shouted. "And look, there are more ships heading this way!"

The *Bitch* powered down its weapons and closed all its missile ports, then accelerated until it flew alongside the mining ship—as though it were escorting them in, as if nothing had happened.

"Let's just hope that the new ships are friendlies," Alexa cautioned, her eyes fixed on the two cruisers approaching.

"Probably not friendlies, but ships belonging to the world's administrators," Myra noted. "Here to make sure everyone lives up to the rules."

"Yeah, well, this is a stolen ship. What if they arrest us?" Bree demanded.

The women looked around at each other and then laughed almost hysterically. As she wiped away tears of mirth, Myra explained, "My dear Major, if we arrive in a stolen ship, that will seem normal—even if we *have* stolen it from the Wulsatures. This is a pirate haven; stolen ships are part of its nature."

"Be that as it may, Myra, we both know that Zuzack will be back," Nina pointed out.

"True, but we've bought some time, and chances are, we can contact someone to help us."

"Let's hope she's right," Alexa, said glancing over her shoulder at Nina before she turned and looked at Tara.

Myra stood leaning between Alexa, eyeing the approaching ships, looking very concerned. "Something's wrong here."

"What is it?"

"First and foremost, those cruisers out there are Florencian, and there should be much more traffic inside the system."

"But there are thousands of ships in sensor range," Nina protested.

"There should be ten times that number. Traders love systems like these, where the tariffs are low and everything's safe, and they flood in here from all over the known universe. No war, no piracy. So where is everyone?"

Nina leaned over her shoulder to get a glimpse of the cruisers. "Think the system is in Florencian hands?"

"I don't know, but I think we'd better get ready for more trouble."

"Well, then, everything is normal, in other words," Alexa said ironically. "Look here—I'm picking up a lot of space debris in those sectors." Alexa pointed at her screen and relayed the information to the others.

"There's definitely been some sort of battle here," Myra said. "There's even more debris in planetary orbit. They've taken out the orbitals and defense platforms!" Myra said, sounding alarmed.

"I'm not detecting any Florencian battle stations, though; but they could be hidden behind the planet. By the way, the cruisers are on course to bypass us. They haven't altered course much; seems like they're just patrolling. Okay, now they've split to go in opposite directions."After they passed the Florencian cruisers, which the computer logged as being of an older model, the *Bitch* altered its own course towards a cluster of stations orbiting Torq in its L-5 point. There seemed to be no planetary control organizing the ships in orbit; Alexa had to use her superlative piloting skills to avoid the thousands of ships darting about, either approaching or leaving Torq. It turned into a bit of rollercoaster ride, despite the ship's inertial dampeners. There were so many stations of various sizes in orbit that, along with the recent debris of many of their fellows, they formed a near-solid ring.

"Where to now?" Major Bree asked, once Alexa had inserted them in a high orbit.

"We can't go to any of the Trader stations, because the girls and probably I have bounties on us. I definitely know that your primary target on this mission, Alexa here, has one or more," Myra said calmly. "Any messages sent from this ship will take too long to reach Nastasturian space to be of any use for us; the computer onboard is very old."

"Well, my troopers and I can get onboard one of the larger stations and send for help, while you and the girls remain on the ship," Bree suggested.

Silence fell across the group on the bridge, where everyone had gathered except for Alexa, who remained at the helm in the cockpit.

"You could let off one or two of us," Sergeant Roni suggested after a long moment, "and we can send for help."

"I rather not split what little force we have left, but we'll probably have to do that." Bree answered.

"Does Ogstafa's clan have a post here?" asked Tara.

"No idea," Myra replied, "but even if they do, I wouldn't venture there for all the money in the universe. Not after what I did. Flight recorders are easily recovered, even from a large explosion, and if there's evidence that I helped you guys...well, you know what will happen."

"Who's flying the bloody ship?" Bree demanded angrily as Alexa joined them.

"Calm down, Major, we're in a stable orbit. The autopilot will keep us safe for now."

"And what's to keep the ship from altering its course to head for Zuzack's ship, like before?"

"No worries, Major. Listen, and you'll notice that I've powered down the engines. We may get some occasional retro bursts to stabilize our position, but that's it."

"Very well, then," Bree replied, looking a bit chagrined.

"Any suggestions, Your Highness?" Myra asked.

"I think the surface is our best bet. If we can find a Federate Merchants post there, we can send a secured message."

"What about the Traders?" Bree asked.

"They're slavers, and as Myra pointed out, we all have bounties on our heads."

"Well, can't they find us on the ground? Clearly this ship has a tracking device on it."

Alexa looked tiredly at Bree. "Perhaps, but if we enter pretty much any space station here that trades with slaves, we'll be scanned and all types of alarms will go off."

"Would that old captain of yours rat on you guys?" Private Echlon wondered aloud.

"Zuzack? No, I don't think so. He wants us for himself."

"Yeah, well, he can forget about that," Bree said. "I still suggest we dock on one of the stations that seems busier, while two of my troopers are dropped off. The rest of us remain onboard the ship while they send for help, and when they return, we head for the surface if we have to."

After a long uncomfortable silence, they all agreed. Sergeant Roni and Corporal Dora would try to make contact. The rest would remain onboard the ship, ready to pick them up when they had succeeded. Alexa returned to her seat in the cockpit, followed by Tara and Nina, and then they took the ship towards a nest of casino stations; and as she zigzagged through the maze of ships and stations, Alexa decided to dock at a casino/hotel station that reminded them of Tota's place, the *Star Dice*.

They received docking instructions quickly, and guided the ship towards one of the smaller bays. There was a line of ships waiting to enter ahead of them, so while waiting, Nina turned to an open channel. From the space station came a steady stream of music, films, and advertisements about their wisdom in choosing *The Lucky Scavenger*. There was the standard information about rules and regulations; one of the last was that weapons and scanning equipment were absolutely prohibited. Eventually, they entered the station and docked, following the directions of a holographic saurian woman who appeared in the cockpit. Myra looked her up and down appreciatively; their species were very similar.

"Now, why would anyone want to dock inside when they have such big, beautiful private yacht?" Corporal Dora's voice came over the speaker.

Corporal Dora's words made Alexa glance to her left. Her eyes widened in horror when she saw the yacht entering the bay via a larger entrance. "Oh no," she whimpered in despair.

"What now?" Nina said, while reading about the different entertainment options the casino space station had to offer.

"The...the dark lady, Zoris af Sun—that's *her* ship. And look who's docked to it."

Alexa tapped a button and the cruiser-sized yacht was displayed on the forward screen. Attached to the starboard side of the yacht was *The Bitch*. Zuzack had docked with Zoris's ship.

Alexa started to alter her course, against the vehement warnings of the holographic woman. "Screw this. Let's get to the surface and take our chances."

There were a few objections from Bree and the other Nastasturians, until Myra explained that if Zuzack had informed Zoris about them, especially Alexa, then they had to hide. But Bree wouldn't have it, not this near to getting them home. He insisted on dropping off his noncommissioned officers.

"Anyone leaving this ship might get captured and tortured. Is that what you want, Major?" Myra asked.

"No, but this is one of our specialties." He then turned to Sergeant Roni and Corporal Dora. "In the event of capture. you're both ordered and allowed to perform TT. Hold out your wrists. Remember: it's of outmost importance that you make contact with the authorities back home."

Bree did something to his left wrist, and what appeared to be a dim light glowed under his skin. Both Roni and Dora did the same. He then placed his wrist over the others' one by one, transferring the order.

"You both have your mission and know what to do. Buy time for us and do your best to survive. I'll return for you—or someone else will, if I can't."

Bree then marched into the cockpit and, sounding very officious, ordered Alexa to complete the docking procedures. "Before you object, know this: I've lost almost two hundred people in rescuing you, and I will *not* lose you now. My troops are experts at their jobs and they will succeed, so please, just dock and let them go and do what they're trained to do."

Alexa glared at the Major as Nina transferred to the soldiers' wrist-comps a series of mapped locations where there ought to be public communicators. Myra leaned toward Bree and asked in a low voice, "What is TT?"

"Terror Tactics," Bree said coldly. "In the event of capture, my troopers will have a nasty surprise for our enemy."

With that, Bree left Myra on the bridge while following his soldiers to the hatch. Sergeant Roni and Corporal Dora left the ship unarmed. They were met by an android that informed them of the most significant rules and regulations of the casino station; they then passed through several scanners before entering a long corridor. At that point, the android turned to the Major and asked if their ship needed repair or fuels. Bree ignored the tin can and was about to close the entrance when the android handed him a computer memory stick.

"This is what we have detected is wrong with your ship, good sir. Our maintenance service recommends that you have these issues repaired. Should you need any further assistance, please let us know."

Major Bree was about to shut the hatch when Nina popped up behind him. "Major, wait. Please ask the andy if they've detected any after-market software not belonging to the original ship, or if there are any alien objects attached to the standard ship build."

Bree gave Nina a puzzled look, but did what she asked. The andy was given permission to jack one of its arms into the ship's computer console by the entrance and begin a diagnostic before they departed. It reported crisply less than a minute later, and bid them a good journey.

The pressure doors closed, Major Bree and Nina smiled at each other, and then hurried back to the bridge, where the rest had gathered. Everyone was checking their weapons and equipment.

"Listen up! Nina here might have saved the day. Tell them, Nina."

Nina blushed a bit as she began her presentation. "I asked the welcome andy for some help with the software and technical configuration, and look at *this*." She plugged the memory stick into the map table on the bridge, and instantly a 3D blueprint of the ship appeared over it. A list of programs ran down the right side, and on the left side appeared an image with three objects highlighted in red on various parts of the ship.

"What are we looking at?" Tara wondered.

Myra turned towards Nina and swooped her off her feet, landing a sloppy wet kiss on Nina's face. She then put Nina gently back on the deck and slapped her ass hard, sending her into the wall, cursing. Myra sometimes didn't realized her own strength; when she saw what she had done to Nina, she charged the room and lifted "poor" Nina up gently and refused to let her down. Nina looked like a little child in Myra's huge arms. Nina crossed her arms and looked grumpy.

"My little princess just found the problem with our navigation software, along with all the trackers attached to the ship!" Myra crowed. "I suggest we remove them and then get the hell out of here."

Nina protested, wanting back on the floor, but Myra would have none of it; she enjoyed being close to Nina. Instead, she tossed Nina over her shoulders and smacked her ass hard gain. Nina cried out and started to kick and scream.

"Wonderful, Nina," Alexa said. "Myra, slap her ass for me, too!"

"Me too!" Tara shouted.

Later, Nina stood working at the computer station, rubbing her bruised behind while occasionally cursing her so-called best friends between gritted teeth.

"Here they are," Alexa said proudly. She tossed several complicated-looking devices onto the map table. "That should be all of them—all the trackers, control modules, and whatever else our friendly neighborhood Wulsatures grafted onto this ship. Now we need to move the ship and re-dock, just in case Zuzack got our location. I hope our friends get back soon."

"Alexa, we can still move the ship," Major Bree reminded her. "The soldiers have subdermal locator chips so we can find them and they can find us. Plus, they have mil-spec wrist-comps. And before you ask, Myra, only my troops know how to work them."

Meanwhile, on *The Lucky Scavenger,* Sergeant Roni and Corporal Dora had to take a turbo-lift and a pair of monorails before the blueprints in their wrist-comps led them to one of the station's many "town squares," which was lined with all the businesses a traveling sentient might need, from clothing shops and brothels to food stores and cash kiosks. Undercover as a loving mining couple, dressed in faded but clean coveralls, they headed into a Federated Traders bank and investment office to wire for some funds. The wire itself was actually a code that would eventually be received by Nastasturus Military Intelligence with highest priority; the amount of money wired was a code that spelled out a message. The coding was complex, by necessity, but their wrist-comps kept it all straight. Once the money had been deposited—which could take time, as they had to wait before the amount had been confirmed—they would wait for notice of receipt, which would confirm that the message had in fact been received and understood.

Once the transaction had been completed, the clerk gave them a small computer tab letting them know he would send a confirmation once the transaction had been deposited into their temporary account. They headed away from the office toward a Marengan restaurant across the atrium.

Just as they exited the office, there was a blip from Sergeant Roni's breast pocket. "That's weird," he said quietly as he removed the chip. The chip blinked green, confirming that the amount of credits they'd sent for had now been deposited, and there were two messages on the transaction queue. One was from the Federated Traders, informing him that he now could use the computer chip for any transaction and that they had automatically given him a line of credit for the casinos; for that he had to activate a computer card that waited in the nearest office. Once the advertisement message had been read, he deleted it and a message from his "aunt" popped up, informing him that he should call his parents and that he owed a certain amount of money that his beloved aunt wanted back upon his return.

Corporal Dora leaned over his shoulder lovingly and she whispered, "It's impossible for the confirmation to have arrived so quickly. Are you sure you did it right?"

Sergeant Roni shot her an irritated glace. "Of course I'm sure. I don't know what's going on; I'm guessing we have spies aboard, and if we do, they'll never reveal themselves. We need to get back ASAP and tell the others that our message has been sent and received."

"Wait, my love. We should buy something so it doesn't look suspicious. Maybe go ahead and eat."

"You're right; let's find something quick, and then return to the ship."

They wandered into a few stores and shops, acting like a normal couple, buying clothes and some souvenirs. Roni also purchased two tickets to a game of astroball for later that day, along with some overpriced crap representing one of the ten teams that was about to play. After that, they headed back to the ship, taking the nearest monorail. The train was crowded, most of the passengers standing and clutching straps hanging from the ceiling, talking into communicators or to each other; it was very loud, as an astroball game was being played on several monitors, and apparently many on board had made bets on it. There were screams of anger and encouraging shouts occasionally, and there were also a couple of guard droids patrolling the train.

"We're being followed," Sergeant Roni whispered into the ear of Corporal Dora, as he embraced her in a loving hug, and gently kissed her on the tip of her ear, looking over her shoulder. A rough-looking rat-like omanoid wearing a beat-up ship's officer's uniform was staring at them, accompanied by several large saurian and omanoids of various species. They weren't subtle in their perusal of the couple. Dora, who stood with her back towards them, glanced at her wrist. Moving her mouth toward Roni's ear, she whispered, "Bree moved the ship to another level."

"Do you have the location locked?"

She nodded her head and gave him a kiss, a peck on the lips. "Transferred to you."

They got off at the next station and headed towards another business square, in hopes that they would lose their followers. They didn't; in fact, things quickly got worse. "Looks like Florencian regulars heading our way, and they have weapons," Roni warned in a low voice.

"Station security trying to intercept us from another direction," Dora replied just as quietly.

Trying to look casual, they entered a large cantina, intermingling with the many different species inside. It was smoky and dark inside; the music was loud and the many monitors displayed scenarios from various sports and news channels. They bellied up to one of the circular bars in the back and ordered drinks, while looking around for their pursuers. They quickly identified the rat-man, who surprisingly seemed to be in charge. Along with them, filtering into the bar a few at a time, were about twenty station guards, Florencian soldiers, and others they suspected were pirates.

"So, are you ready for this, dear?" Roni asked, brushing his hand over his wrist-comp.

"Any time, honey. Let's give 'em hell."

He winked at her. "If we make it out of here, Dora, I wouldn't mind a little real-life fraternizing."

She smiled briefly, murmuring, "Let's keep our minds on the mission, sir."

"They're splitting up, securing the other exits, and some of the Florencians are heading this way with the station guards. Let's go for the soldiers; they have blasters, while the station security only have stunners, and I don't see any weapons among the pirates."

"Probably hidden blades, knowing the girls and Myra."

They stood with their backs turned, apparently enjoying their drinks at the bar, until a young Florencian officer placed his hand on Sergeant Roni's shoulder. Big mistake. Roni spun and chopped his open hand very hard into the throat of the young man, who immediately hit the floor as Roni snatched the hand blaster from his opened holster. Dora, meanwhile, dropped to her knees and punched another Florencian between his legs, snatching his own blaster. Both fired almost simultaneously at the other Florencians, pulping their heads into a fine red mist. Before anyone realized what had happened, six Fish Fuckers lay dead on the floor, and they were firing on the pirates.

By then the entire cantina was in a panic, and they couldn't easily fire without risking the other patrons. They fired anyway; as professional soldiers, they understood the concept of collateral damage, as much as they might not like it. When it was clear they weren't going to be able to take down Rat Face and his crew, they tucked their weapons away and became part of the milling crowd fighting to reach one of the exits.

Corporal Dora suddenly found herself face-to-face with Rat Face, whose head kept wobbling all over as he stared confused at the people rushing the exit. Suddenly they made eye contact; the man smiled unpleasantly and was just about to say something when Dora kicked him between his legs and then spun around, hitting him in the bridge of the nose with her elbow. Rat Face hit the floor hard.

In the ensuring confusion, they managed to get outside, whereupon they made a quick circular sweep of the area and headed for another monorail, only to find that all long-distance transportation had been locked down. They rushed down a street perpendicular to the spreading riot, hiding the hand blasters under coats they'd purchased earlier. That's when Sergeant Roni noticed that Corporal Dora still carried one of the store bags with some of the souvenirs inside. "Are you *kidding* me?" he demanded with a friendly smile, as they slowed to a normal pace so they wouldn't stand out. Occasionally, he made a sweep for any pursuers, doing it in a non-obvious way that used glass reflection and the cam on his wrist-comp to track what was behind him.

"Good camouflage," she replied. "And we *did* pay for it, after all."

They hurried down several blocks and made many different turns. After a time, Roni said, "We should split up. It's only a matter of time before they deploy centurion andies, and they'll soon have a lock on us. Those Fish Fuckers aren't playing around."

When they reach a junction where the monorails still worked, they split up. Sergeant Roni gave Corporal Dora a peek on her cheek and whispered into her ear, "Probably my last order, but stay safe. Get back to the ship, warn the others, and let them know we succeeded in sending the message."

Corporal Dora pushed him back and stared at him. "What about you?"

He only smiled and whispered, "TT Time."

She looked at him for a long moment, and then gave him the closest thing to a salute she could under the circumstances: a sharp nod. She then said evenly, "I regret that we'll never be able to fraternize, sir."

"Me too, Dora."

Without a word, she turned and hurried into the monorail car. As it left the station, she watched as her Sergeant walked calmly towards a cluster of security personnel and Florencian soldiers, with andies, who had just entered the square. In the background, she could see Rat Face and his followers shouldering their way through the crowd; but now they seemed to be led by the ugly man who had hailed them earlier on the ship's com, a huge fellow who looked like his face had been flayed off him. Roni held up his hands in a pose of surrender, and he was quickly surrounded.

That was the last Corporal Dora ever saw of him as the train moved swiftly away.

A few minutes later, when she was many kilometers closer to their ship, and stepping out of the door of the monorail car to hurry toward the nearest lift, the deck trembled underfoot and there was a distant rumble; and far in the distance, along the curve of the station, Dora saw a fountain of fire shoot into the artificial sky. It seemed so small, but she knew it was large enough to threaten the integrity of the station, and she knew she had to hurry before they put the entire structure in lockdown. As gasps and screams rang out around her, she stayed focused, her face sad but her mind locked on the mission.

For the first time in a long time, Alexa noted, everyone seemed relaxed, almost happy; perhaps there was some light at the end of the tunnel after all. That didn't last very long, though; a sudden concerned expression on Major Bree's face and a startled glance at his wrist computer caused him to curse.

"We just lost Sergeant Roni. They're on to us."

Now there was fear in everyone's expressions.

"Alexa, undock this ship immediately."

"What about Corporal Dora? We can't just leave her behind!"

Major Bree turned and looked at Alexa with a stern expression. "You, my lady, are this mission's highest priority—and we must leave *now*. I'll make sure someone comes back for her when I can, but for now, we need to go."

Major Bree was just about to say something more when another bleep on his computer snagged his attention.

"Wait, listen up. It's from Dora; she's sent an emergency message, but she…nothing, nothing more…wait, here's the last message."

Major Bree looked sadly at his wrist computer, which was lit with a single written word:

Run!

ABOUT THE AUTHOR

Photo Credit: Marit Lasson

ERIK Martin Willén loves creating worlds of epic proportion and exploring those worlds in the stories he creates. He is the author of the science fiction series Nastragull (*Pirates*, *Hunted*, *Dawn Sets in Hell*, *Section Twenty-one*, and *The Beast*) and the suspense thriller *The Lumberjack*. He lives in a small village in south Sweden where he is currently working on his next novel.